Praise for Terry Grosz's books:

"His tales have the momentum of a burning wagon rolling downhill toward a cabin full of bad guys. Above all, they are driven by Grosz's love of wildlife and hatred of the incredible illegal slaughter that is happening in this country."
— Ed Dentry, *Rocky Mountain News*

"Environmentalism meets Indiana Jones in these rip-snorting tales of a former wildlife conservation officer. ... A bear of a man—six-foot-four, over 300 pounds—Grosz relates his exploits in adventures full of slam-bang action and bravado tempered by a coolheaded sense of humor."—*Publishers Weekly*

"Out thin cadre of wildlife agents scattered across the American landscape are some of our finest law enforcement professionals. Often away from family and home, placed in lonely and dangerous situations, they confront devious characters and unpredictable events in their continuing fight to protect our irreplaceable wild resources. Agent Terry Grosz, one of the nation's best, gives us well written, hearty tales packed with high stakes, drama, tears and laughter."
— John F. Turner, former director, U.S. Fish & Wildlife Service

"This is a book locked and loaded with larger than life, heroic stories—written by Terry Grosz, a larger than life, heroic man to match. These page-turning morality tales remind us, in harrowing and frightful detail, that often the only thing standing between the public's wildlife heritage and the bad guys who want to despoil it are the brave men and women carrying the game warden's badge. *Wildlife Wars* is the new sportsman's thriller."
— Todd Wilkinson, author of *Science Under Siege: The Politicians' War on Nature and Truth*

"From the first chapter till the last, the reader will find no dull moments. This is one of those books that are hard to put down once you start. ... After you finish Terry's book, you will be looking forward to the next in the series."   —*International Game Warden*

"As our urbanized society continues to lose its connection to the land, along with our precious fish and wildlife resources, we need more agents like Terry whose inspirational tales show how he dedicated and risked his life to protect that which he loved. Be prepared to simultaneously feel joy and anger as he details his hair-raising efforts, and those of others, to prevent the destruction of our natural heritage."   —Len Ugarenko, North American Waterfowl Management Plan Coordinator, International Association of Fish and Wildlife Agencies

"After reading *Wildlife Wars*, I wondered if Terry Grosz could keep up the pace with a new set of memories and fascinating law enforcement experiences. Not to worry. *For Love of Wildness* takes you into a world almost never visited by even those of us who love the outdoors. Seldom does one who possesses a depth of knowledge in one field of endeavor rise to be able to chronicle that knowledge and experience in an entertaining and compelling manner. Grosz has risen above all but a very few professional authors. Don't miss this one!"   —Larry Jay Martin, author of *The Last Stand*

"His collection of tales needs to be told, for it helps combat an enormous problem concerning our country's natural wildlife. Grosz is obviously a very committed individual—and also a natural storyteller. This collection consists of stories about his early years as a warden in California. They relate many close calls with mother nature: wild creatures and savage lawbreakers. ... Those who cherish the outdoors for hunting and fishing as well as those involved in environmental studies will benefit from this work."
—*Booklist*

"The book is a page-turner, a remarkable if not heroic glimpse inside the cat-and-mouse competition between wildlife enforcement and wildlife poachers."   —*The Reel News*

A Sword for Mother Nature

A Sword for Mother Nature

The Further Adventures of a Fish and Game Warden

Terry Grosz

Johnson Books
BOULDER

Published by Johnson Books, a division of Johnson Publishing Company, 1880 South 57th Court, Boulder, Colorado 80301. E-mail: books@jpcolorado.com.

9 8 7 6 5 4 3 2 1

Cover design by Debra B. Topping
Cover photo of a great horned owl © Jeffrey Rich Nature Photography
Author photo © James Bludworth

Library of Congress Cataloging-in-Publication Data
Grosz, Terry.
    A sword for mother nature: the further adventures of a Fish and Game warden / Terry Grosz.
        p. cm.
    ISBN 1-55566-281-1
    1. Grosz, Terry. 2. Game wardens—California—Biography. I. Title.
    SK354.G76 A3 2002
    363.28—dc21   2002013941

Printed in the United States by
Johnson Printing
1880 South 57th Court
Boulder, Colorado 80301

*Special Agent
Joseph Oliveros*
(photo by William "Bill" Ferguson)

WHEN I MET my waterfowl identification class years ago at the National Academy, one individual stood out. He was a small, pink-faced individual who looked as if he must have been brought to class by his father. I soon discovered that he was none other than Special Agent Joseph Oliveros, one of the most tenacious students I ever had. Learning wasn't enough for him; he wanted *everything* I had to give. It was as if he was riding a whirlwind—and he was. He went on to several duty stations and became the very best migratory bird enforcement officer in the nation! When it came to catching outlaws, especially those taking migratory birds, many in the business in the Southeast came to know Joe on a first-name basis. It was almost as if the migratory birds talked to Joe, telling him who was doing what to whom, and where. As if wildlife protection wasn't burden enough, Joe took time to teach, passing on his talents. He was a hard taskmaster, but so is extinction, and Joe had no intention of letting the latter win on his watch. Joe was also a loving husband and family man, and how he packed all that into such a small carcass was beyond me. I now know that God puts truly unique people on earth for us mortals to learn from, though most of us never realize when such a person has touched our souls. Joe was one of those people from another time, who graced not only my life but many others as well. It wasn't until he contracted terminal cancer that I realized the blessings I had had in knowing and working with such a fine human being. Cancer is a dread that hovers over all of us, and when touched by it many go no further in their lives. However, I never saw a case of cancer dragged so hard by one who had a mission he was going to complete, come hell or high water. And he did! Joe is with us no more except in the memory of good that came from being touched by an exceptional human being and his teaching that there is nothing we can't do with a little elbow grease and a lot of dedication. Joe, I don't know where you are right now, but if you are chasing a bunch of chaps killing too many canvasbacks, go slow. Save a few for the rest of us so we can help chase the killing sons of bitches into oblivion when our time comes. Rest in peace, my friend, for those of us and your family left behind have truly lost a dear friend, as has our country and the critters. Make way, Lord; here comes a *real* "catch dog" and a one-of-a-kind human being. ... It is to "Little" Joe that I dedicate this book.

Contents

Preface

IN THE FIRST OF MY SERIES of wildlife law enforcement books, titled *Wildlife Wars: The Life and Times of a Fish and Game Warden*, the reader met a twenty-five-year-old kid fresh out of college, recently hired as a Fish and Game warden in northern California. His first assignment after attending the academy was in Eureka in Humboldt County. Humboldt County during the 1960s was still a rough-and-tumble extension of the Old West, and it didn't take long for the author to immerse himself in the same spirit, only as "the long arm of the law." Commercial fishermen taking short salmon, short crabs, and over-limits or fishing in closed zones; deer and elk spotlighters; hounds and men running bear and lion during the closed seasons; falconers illegally "scooping" nests of protected birds of prey; sheep ranchers shooting bald and golden eagles to reduce lamb predation (mostly a lame excuse for their poor animal husbandry practices); so-called sportsmen taking too many ducks, brant, salmon, razor clams, and snipe; snagging of salmon and sturgeon on the north coast rivers by out-of-work lumbermen; Indians gill-netting salmon under their treaty rights and then selling them illegally to the fish houses in Eureka; logging operations polluting the waterways and salmon-spawning streams with their slash; pulp mills polluting the ocean; and a dash of everything else imaginable described this lawless West Coast spirit of northern California. In short, it was a game warden's "stew." Being young and full of piss and vinegar (and sometimes devilment), feeling immortal, and protected by two hardworking guardian angels, the author didn't take long to bury himself in all the illegality that played out as far as the eye could see! *Wildlife Wars* reflects that time of life when a young officer was trying to be everything possible to the world of wildlife. Alternately funny, sad, deadly serious, and unique, *Wildlife Wars* keeps the reader in suspense until the last chapter is devoured. It also begins to introduce the reader to the very real world of wildlife law enforcement and the dangers inherent therein for the critters as well as those sworn to protect them. The book fast-forwards through four years in northern California, ending up ultimately in the Sacramento Valley of north-central California as the wildlife law enforcement profession grows on and begins to change the author *and the reader.* ... It also leads into the next adventure!

In my second book, titled *For Love of Wildness: The Journal of a U.S. Game Management Agent,* the reader finds the author still engulfed in the wild and woolly world of wildlife law enforcement. However, the officer is four years older, ninety years wiser, and carrying the gold badge of a U.S. game management agent instead of the silver of a California state Fish and Game warden. This change from state to federal service is the fulfillment of a lifelong dream, and it turned out to be everything expected. Although the new fieldwork is similar to that of a Fish and Game warden, there are several major twists. With national authority, the author finds himself teaming up with his state and federal counterparts to swing a bigger bat, and harder, at the "big boys" breaking the laws in the world of wildlife. The reader will also discover that the wildlife outlaws described in this book are even more dedicated, pernicious, and very good at their "trade." The author dis .overs that many of this new breed of violator have a bite and more than once finds himself walking down the road of life without a seat in his pants, if you get my drift. ... The author still stumbles into the soup; gets involved in the illegal interstate transport of sport-shot wildlife; has a few brushes with death; discovers examples of greedy so-called sportsmen placing massive amounts of bait in the field to attract large numbers of dove to the gun; gets involved in outright conspiracies by landed and wealthy interests to manipulate the land, laws, or politicians in order to take more than their fair share; crosses paths with commercial-market hunters shooting waterfowl; and just for the pure joy of it still sometimes rides with the devil. Of special note is the quiet maturation that is slowly taking place. The reading is starting to get more serious and reflective because Terry is beginning to realize the real size of the "monster" facing him. With that realization, he doubts whether he will accomplish what needs doing in order to save much of the land's resources for those folks yet to come. The courts are tougher and demand more evidence of wrongdoing. Defense attorneys are better and more aggressive in protecting their affluent and politically sensitive clients. Politics from within and without begins rearing its ugly head more frequently, depending on the nature of the crime and the name of the individual involved. Fiscal, staffing, and equipment limitations are beginning to slow enforcement-directed field operations. Terry also begins to realize that those carrying the badge must run the edge of life in order to apprehend the very worst wildlife criminals, and he takes some risks greater than imagined. However, being young in spirit, guarded by two guardian angels, and cared for by one of the world's greatest wives, the author finds the energy to keep pushing the envelope and finding those needing finding.

Book number three, titled *Defending Our Wildlife Heritage: The Life and Times of a Special Agent*, is a study of the author's progress in wildlife law enforcement, this time as a special agent for the U.S. Fish and Wildlife Service. Whereas the U.S. game management agent was a position split between wildlife management and wildlife law enforcement duties, the special agent position is that of a wildlife criminal investigator—sort of like the FBI but of the wildlife world. It is basically a step up into the soft underbelly of those involved with the smuggling of wildlife, illegal commercialization of wildlife, gross illegal take of wildlife, and illegal commercialization of the parts and products of wildlife. He continues to conduct other wildlife law enforcement work because it is like broken glass under bare feet, but emphasis is now placed on the serious drains on the world of wildlife and law enforcement's limited resources. In *Defending Our Wildlife Heritage* the reader finds the author moving up through the ranks of the agency in different parts of the country and, by the very nature of these new positions, taking on ever different windmills, politics, special interest groups, outlaws, gutless and thoughtless members of his own agency, weak-kneed solicitors (the government's attorneys), and every kind of standing invertebrate in between. The level of seriousness is even higher than in the previous books, and the complexity of his actions makes many a mysterious wind before the blow is over. The stories run from the simple to the ethereal. Also, for the first time the reader gets to travel abroad into international intrigue and experience secondhand just how cheap life, wildlife or human, *really* is. Of special note is the chapter dealing with the formation of the world's only wildlife forensic laboratory and all the behind-the-scenes articulations, politics, and intrigue. Today that lab is one of the Service's crown jewels, made all the more special when one realizes its incredible value to the world of wildlife law enforcement! Yes, at the time of this writing it is meeting requests from all over the world. Nationally, it is like having an extra hundred agents in the field. It is just too bad it took the better part of ten years to convince the shortsighted Service leadership of its value. In the meantime, that ten-year period without forensic service was illegally strewn with the lives of thousands of critters and their parts and products. ... As is evident, there is enough activity to go around, and frequently the reader finds the author, now a senior supervisor, getting called into action at the lowest levels because of staffing shortages, with surprising results. The reader also gets to experience those greedy landowners illegally draining this nation's wetlands and witness the extremes of people left out in the prairie wind too long. ... That "war" is still ongoing and is vital to 65 percent of the *total number of ducks produced in the continental United States!* Lose our wetlands in the Dakotas, Minnesota, and adjacent prairie provinces, and you lose your waterfowl. Throughout the rest of the book are stories showing just how small the world is getting and the length some folks will go to meet their personal needs of greed and ego. More importantly, in the wildlife tapestries woven throughout this book, the reader sees the damage done by corrupt politicians; nonexistent federal budgets designed to keep Service law enforcement under operational control; poor senior agency leadership, from the director on down; officers limited by their own weaknesses and emotions; death angels in their many forms, regardless of the best efforts of those who serve; and the not uncommon sheer joy of our successes in the face of tremendous odds. The reader also experiences the lengths to which those wearing the federal gold will go to stop the carnage by using every legal tool known to humankind, and a few known only to God.

In the book you are holding, titled *A Sword for Mother Nature: The Further Adventures of a Fish and Game Warden*, the fourth in the series, the reader is treated to a surprising change of pace. It is the sequel to the first in the series, *Wildlife Wars*. In it are contained the last of the stories of Terry's experiences as a California state Fish and Game warden. Again there are stories of apparently simple cases turned deadly; stories involving an overeager game warden who runs out of his shoes in a manner of speaking; and stories involving the usual serving of those hell-bent on destruction of the resource. Woven in among those stories are several of a surprising nature, including one that will make you laugh as you cringe and one that will make you cry. A book of this nature wouldn't be complete without a chapter titled "Screwups" and another involving "A Game Warden's 'Stew.'" ...

There are approximately ten thousand conservation officers in North America at the federal, state, tribal, provincial, military, and county levels who could weave similar stories. Consider that and the fact that there are more than three hundred million people scattered throughout North America, and then consider the odds the "thin green line" faces on a daily basis as it tries to protect our fragile environment! Many times I think Custer had better odds.

However, on the balance side, the reader needs to keep in mind that for every outlaw chased and run to ground in this series of books, there are many good sportsmen and sportswomen out there doing things right. Thoughts of an old friend named Marvin Clary from Vallejo, California, a true man of the soil, well intentioned, and a crack rifle shot, reminded me of the ethical sports-loving folks. Years ago I used to hunt with him at the family deer camp in eastern Plumas County, and he was as fine a gentleman and caretaker of the land as I ever knew. He wasn't a total angel, but he did keep a sharp eye on the health of "his" natural resources and loves them dearly to this day. He even once gave me a hand in catching some of his kin hunting deer without the required licenses and deer tags. If you are reading these lines, Marv, remember? Then I got to thinking I had met many like him over the years and travels represented in this series of books. So the readers, with Marv and the millions like him, need to be recognized for the good they do for the resources of the land in proportion to the bad guys rounded up in these stories.

This book is the fourth in a series of what I hope will be at least five, dealing in part with my life's experiences as a conservation officer. The events you experience through the books are true, with alterations so no one will be able to identify many of the real-life characters who have paid their debt to society. You will also find I have incorporated some blind alleys into the text to throw off the really astute students of wildlife law enforcement, be they pursuers or pursued. The locations are real as well and are altered only occasionally to prevent the discovery of the actual characters committing the crimes. You will find many of these tales sad, disgusting, moralistic, evil, funny, or just plain gross. However, they have come from my life's fabric, and sadly, many similar situations continue to this day all over North America in spite of the efforts of the "thin green line." Imagine what it is like south of the Mexican border, through Mexico and into Central and South America.

Enjoy the natural resources we have in this great land of ours with your family and friends. Hunting, fishing, outdoor photography, hiking, birdwatching, exploring, and many more outdoor activities await you as part of the heritage of this land of ours. Enjoy them to your heart's content, but don't become one of those who illegally take and destroy until they are slipping in the rivers of blood. Leave those fools to the hunters of men, and pray that those hunters are successful in their endeavors. When you ask what you can do as an *individual*, that is easy! Don't do the evil things represented in the stories. Don't mix with those who do, and for God's sake, teach your children the meaning of conservation, especially as they grow older and move away from home.

Pray that they will carry away the wisdom of your early conservation teachings. Get involved with your Fish and Game organization, especially if you are in a conservation organization, and see that they have enough officers, fiscal support, and equipment to do their jobs. There is a lot one person can do to stop these black-hearted activities so that those yet to come can experience the beauty we still have today. I suggest that America get off its dead hind end and give a hand. If you don't, then you are part of the problem and just as bad as the poachers.

Acknowledgments

MY FIRST IMPRESSION of Mira Perrizo, publisher for Johnson Books, was that she was no bigger than a small duck. How else was I to think with two degrees in wildlife management and twenty-seven years of teaching waterfowl identification at the national academy, standing at six foot four and she just a little over five feet? However, during that first meeting I noticed she always had a genuine smile and a quietness about her that foretold a larger-than-life person. Having been a law enforcement type for over thirty-two years and having interacted with many thousands of unique personalities, I undertook to closely examine my "small duck" for the hidden qualities my instincts said were there. Over the next several years of my association with the Johnson Books publishing family—and it is a family—I began to unravel the mysteries of this person, and what a pleasant surprise they held. Aside from the ever-ready smile and quiet presence, I discovered a focus and direction that were truly unique. Regardless of her senior management status in the company, she always had quality time for "her" authors—time that equated to a soft yet understanding counsel and guidance directed at furthering the author's skills. Time that in just moments of interaction would bring out the very best of the story and the author's ability to tell it. Time to encourage the author and what, in this instance, he had to tell without imposing another hand on the color or soul of the tale to be told. Ultimately for me, this gentle hand of Mother Nature and her skills wove into the thread of my stories a strength, joy, and character that many readers would come to laugh at, identify with, love, and deeply appreciate.

I am indebted to this woman's quiet guiding hand for ultimately translating into print the stories of one man's thirty-two-year struggle as a wildlife conservation officer protecting the nation's natural and inspiring wildlife resources.

A Sword for Mother Nature

1

A Game Warden's "Stew"

ARRIVING HOME IN EUREKA after twelve weeks at the basic law enforcement academy in Riverside, California, I spent the next few months as a rookie game warden learning what was expected of me. There were occasional complex and dangerous details in which I had the opportunity to assist different senior officers, but basically I spent my time learning the ropes, being a "gofer," and gradually spreading my wings. In the North Coast Fish and Game Squad in those days, the captain would let new game wardens undertake the simple assignments, and as you began to prove yourself, the details got more and more difficult until you were no longer judged a potential liability and were let out on your own.

The captain intentionally did not assign me to a geographic land unit or district like my fellow game wardens because he had come up with a unique patrol concept, and I was to implement that idea. The captain had decided that from the next game warden class (mine), he would select one officer (me) to act as a roving warden throughout the busier or more troublesome districts. As it turned out, I would work in other wardens' districts on their days off, "showing the flag," so to speak. I also filled in for the marine boarding officer on his days off if the patrol boat went to sea. In theory the idea was a good one. However, in reality it was a pain. At first the other wardens were happy to have the additional coverage. But when I started really knocking the bad guys dead in another officer's district because the outlaws were unused to the new enforcement regimen, the resident officer would often get a little jealous. Soon my presence in other districts, regardless of the captain's orders, was not truly welcomed except by John Finnigan of Arcata and Hank Marak of Willow Creek. They were always pleased to have help, and it didn't stop there. Both took the time to teach me many of the tricks of the trade. As a result of this personalized training, I managed to come out of the chute as a pretty effective working game warden quite a bit earlier than the ordinary rookie. The number of my arrests (the highest in the squad) and convictions (100 percent) my first complete year showed the wisdom of their teachings.

Looking back on the wildlife law enforcement profession and its people after thirty-two years in the trade as a state and federal conservation officer, I am convinced that it takes three to five years for a hardworking conservation officer to really learn the trade, understand a district, and earn his or her paycheck. That period may be accelerated for officers in busy districts with numerous learning opportunities, lots of moxie, and someone like Hank or John to show them the ropes so they don't make the same damn mistakes their predecessors made. It also takes a solid work ethic along with a pile of good luck—and a damn good mate. But generally, it is some time before you are *really* effective as a conservation officer. It is a unique profession, and there is so much to learn about criminal justice, animal behavior and life histories, animal science, animal identification (including parts and products—how many people can identify a duck by just its wing?), and the human subculture utilizing those resources that one cannot absorb all there is to know without first spending a fair amount of time in the traces.

The north coast area of California was a real jewel of a place to practice my newfound trade. There were abundant resources of every kind, from clams to the noble Roosevelt elk. The people living in the area were often out of work or struggling to make ends meet. A large human subculture dependent on seasonal work in the lumber, fishing, and tourist industries, along with several colleges with their thousands of poor, always-hungry-for-food-or-adventure students, made a real devil's mix. Anytime you have such a mix of wildlife and people (including many of the poaching persuasion), you end up with substantial death and destruction in the animal world.

During those first months spent learning the ropes, I hit a run of cases of such scope and degree that they provided a level of excitement and learning that really sparked my interest and love for my chosen field. My adaptation to this arena was even more profound because my academic training and background had been in wildlife management as a biologist, not a law enforcement officer. But my interest in law soon developed into such a love and intensity, a dedication to those without a voice, that it never left me throughout my years of service. It continued to sustain my heart and soul and made it a pleasure to come to work every day of my career. Not many people can say that about their professions, and I now realize that I was blessed by the ability to do so. At the beginning of my career, it seemed that everywhere I turned there was some new case of such complexity that it only whetted my appetite for more of the same. These early events were so varied and rich that I came to call those days, and the many that followed throughout my long career, a game warden's "stew." The following stories are "meaty lumps" from that stew. ...

The Gill Net and the Douglas Fir

THE MAD RIVER, located just north of the town of Arcata in Humboldt County, at one time was a great salmon stream. Today, because of past logging practices and subsequent siltation; overgrazing; pollution; overfishing, sport and commercial; and the constant illegal removal of spawning fish, it is a mere shadow of its former self. Like most north coast rivers and streams it was full of twists and turns, dotted with numerous deep pools and long, graveled riffles. Its point of origin was at Ruth Reservoir, far inland, and it contained many miles of prime silver salmon, king salmon, and steelhead trout habitat. The river was fed by numerous smaller streams or creeks, many of which carried lesser numbers of steelhead and salmon during the spawning season. One small creek feeding into the Mad River particularly caught my attention. I believe it was called Deer Creek, and it fed in from the north, passing under state Highway 299 through a thirty-six-inch culvert. During the annual steelhead and salmon migrations, the fish would swim up Deer Creek from the Mad River and rest in the pool below the culvert until they had gathered the necessary energy to continue. Then, with a run through the pool to gain speed, they would splash noisily through the shallow water in the culvert to the deeper water on the other side and then continue upstream to spawn.

Years before, while attending college at Humboldt State, near Arcata, I had heard rumors of people occasionally running a small gill net for salmon in the pool below the culvert on Deer Creek. With this setup during the season, they could effectively catch every migrating salmon in that evening's run. Those rumors persisted around the game warden grapevine during my tenure as an officer in the area, and I made a point of keeping an eye on the small pool below the culvert every time I went by on the highway during salmon season. Gill net cases were a serious wildlife crime, right up there with fish snagging, as far as I was concerned. Anyone who did such a thing obviously knew what they were doing, had only evil intentions, and cared little for the resource because such activity was always fatal to a part of the fishery. A good gill net case was a real feather in one's cap, not to mention the fact that catching these people was invaluable to the survival of the fish.

One evening, coming home from Willow Creek after a stint helping Hank Marak, I passed over Deer Creek on an almost deserted highway. Stopping, I took a quick look over the embankment with my flashlight, expecting nothing to be there, as in all my past examinations. I couldn't believe my eyes! Floating across the center of the small pool below the culvert were the telltale floats of a short gill net. I had stopped there a hundred times before and had never seen anything out of the ordinary. Suddenly I saw several of the floats dip under the water as a fish slammed into the net in the dark. I could hear the splashing as the fish struggled to free itself and then nothing as it suffocated to death moments later. Coming back to reality, I scrambled back to my patrol car and hauled my hind end out of the area before I was seen by the culprit, hoping I hadn't already been spotted.

Parking my patrol car about a quarter of a mile down Highway 299 on a brushy old abandoned logging spur, I grabbed my gear and trotted back to the culvert. Taking my time as I got closer, I crept down to the stream, finding no one there, though there was at least one twenty-pound female king salmon hanging lifeless in the gill net. I ran my diffused flashlight beam over the set and saw that it was anchored on both sides of the bank so that the entire migration of salmon that evening would have to swim into the net. The net was anchored to heavy steel fence posts driven almost out of sight on each bank of the stream, and it reached from the top of the water to the bottom of the streambed. There were no two ways about it: whoever was running this net knew exactly what he was doing, probably had done it before in this stream, and definitely needed catching. Needless to say, I was excited. I had worked gill net cases with Hank Marak in the Willow Creek area, but this would be the first one I had initiated all by myself.

After taking another careful look around from my place of concealment, I crawled on my hands and knees to the edge of the net on my side of the bank, lifted the float line, and followed it out with my hands to the closest salmon hanging lifeless in the deadly mesh. Taking my Buck knife, I sliced off the adipose fin (between the tail and dorsal fin) to mark the fish for identification later on in court if the case went that far and then carefully lowered the fish back into the water, avoiding making any splashing sounds. That would be all I needed, I thought—alerting someone coming back to check his net by stupidly making a lot of noise. Crawling upstream about five yards, I lay down on my stomach behind the remnants of an old redwood stump and began my wait. Soon the fatigue from working many long hours and days with Hank and the soft duff of the forest took their toll, and I fell fast asleep.

The damp ground and cold air woke me up about two in the morning, and I quietly looked around my redwood stump. The gill net was still there, and the floats were busy bouncing up and down, showing that another salmon had fallen victim to its insidious meshes. Damn, I thought; when is this lad coming to tend his net? Then the thought hit me that maybe the net tender had seen me looking down from the road with my flashlight earlier and had been spooked. God, I hope not, I thought as I resettled myself with my back against the far side of the stump, hoping the less comfortable position would prevent me from going back to sleep. But the minutes turned into several hours, and I closed my eyes for a moment. ...

Suddenly I came fully awake to the sound of something splashing in the water by the net. Thinking it might be a black bear robbing the gill net, since there were a jillion of them living in the area, I slowly reached for the gun on my hip as I peeked around the stump. Kneeling on the bank on my side of the stream was the diminutive shape of a man not so quietly removing a dead salmon from the gill net. After laying that fish on the bank, he waded out into the shallows of Deer Creek and removed a second and a third lifeless salmon from the net. He quietly tossed their still forms onto the bank by his first fish, then crossed the creek more than halfway and pulled out his fourth and final fish, a large female weighing about thirty-five pounds. Walking back across the stream to the bank on my side, he laid it next to the rest. Then he crossed the creek once more and, since dawn wasn't far away, began to untie his gill net from the steel stake on the far bank. (Daylight not only might lead to discovery; it would also make the mesh visible to the migrating fish, who then would not swim into it.) Once it was untied, he began to wrap up his net in arm-length folds as he crossed back to my side of the creek. He then untied the net from the second metal stake and stuffed it into a gunnysack. After the net was put away, he knelt on the stream bank and began to gut the salmon he had caught, tossing the entrails into the brush where they would be out of sight. He knew such goodies would disappear before the next night into the hungry maws of skunks, raccoons, mink, feral cats, or the ever-present black bear, so there need be little fear of discovery. How damn clever, I thought. By eliminating the entrails, he lightened up the load of fish and net he had to carry; plus it is always better for the quality of the meat if one draws an animal fairly quickly after its death. It was readily apparent that this fellow had "been there, done that" before. ...

Picking up another gunnysack in the semidark, my culprit began loading the smaller salmon into it. I figured I would see what he did with the net and then spring my trap. Once the salmon were loaded into the gunnysack (except the large female, which he was going to hand carry), my lad picked up the sack containing the gill net and walked right to the stump that I was using for cover! Damn, I thought; it's now or never! The moment he reached the stump, I quickly stood but promptly slipped on a foot-long banana slug that sent me head over hind end into the damp earth.

"Ho-ho-ho," came the startled voice of my gill net fisherman as he saw this unexpected assailant slamming into the ground very near where he stood. His survival instincts kicked in, and he tossed the heavy net bag on top of me as I thrashed around on the ground trying to get up. Then he turned and fled. Up in a flash and tossing the net bag off my back, I hotly pursued the chap, who was still fearfully yelling. Down the bank, across Deer Creek, and into the surrounding brush we went like two crazy bulls. Crashing and thrashing, we broke through the rank Humboldt County brush, hurdling downed and rotting logs like two college track stars as we flew along. I tried to keep the man in view by using my flashlight beam to partially illuminate him and the ground between us so I could see where to go and what to avoid. We stayed pretty even, but I was taking one hell of a beating from the branches and limbs flying back into my face as he roared through them just in front of me. It is really amazing just how fast a person can run when he has done something wrong and the law is hot on his trail—especially if the law is making one hell of a racket in the pursuit!

We ran over a small, heavily wooded ridge without my gaining much ground and down into a steep-sided, rocky, moss-covered gully. My chap jumped the small feeder creek at the bottom and lunged for the far bank, only to slip back down when he hit the rocky, mossy face. Lunging for his midsection, I just missed as he took off again, and in the process I bellowed, "State Fish and Game

warden; hold it right there!" I grabbed him by the right foot, but
his tennis shoe came off in my hand as he kicked hard and escaped
once more. Up the bank he went on all fours, with me right behind him, but this time I was a little farther back than before. I
just wasn't built to scramble on all fours like a lizard on those slick
surfaces! Damn it, I thought, he is beginning to outrun me! Re-
doubling my efforts after clearing the gully, I promptly ran into a
large overhanging limb from a Douglas fir that spun me around,
ripping my uniform shirt almost clear off in the process. Whirling
away from the limb and hoping my badge was still attached to the
shirt, I could see that we weren't far from the Mad River. Once
there, I thought, if he chose to run along the river bank, I might
have a better chance of catching him with less brush tearing at my
body—which was slightly larger than his.

Then I realized that my flashlight beam was probably helping
him even more than me! That little bonehead was using the light
to aid him as he picked his way through the brush, logs, and other
obstructions in the dark. I thought, that old game is rapidly coming to an end. When he hit the bank of the Mad River, my chap
turned west, and I could see him really turn the speed on, even
with one shoe missing. Well, I thought, now's the time to "turn it
off"—the flashlight, that is—and quickly scanning the next thirty
feet so I wouldn't have a wreck myself, I shut off the light. Moments later, I heard a soft *whump* followed by a bloodcurdling
scream. The sound scared me so badly that I turned on my flashlight immediately and stopped dead in my tracks amidst a shower
of flying rock and river sand. I listened with all my hair standing
straight up, but all I could hear was the water running over the
rocks in the Mad River. I waited a few more moments, listening all
the while, but I could no longer see or hear my man fleeing along
the rocky river bank. I frantically swung my flashlight beam back
and forth in the direction I had last seen him, but nothing met my
eyes in the form of the man I had been chasing, and still no sounds
of fleeing greeted my ears. Damn, I thought; I lost him!

Then, not twenty feet down the edge of the stream, I saw an old
Douglas fir that had been uprooted in years past from its home up-

stream, probably during a winter flood, and had floated down-stream until its roots had lodged in the boulders of the river, with the tip still facing upstream. Over the years during many winter and spring floods, the water, moving rocks and soil in the river, had polished that tree into the form of a massive wooden lance. Its tip, polished a gleaming white, was sticking up parallel with the ground and maybe two feet above it. Hanging on the polished tip of this natural spear was an obvious large flap of blue-jean material! Slowly walking toward that old tree, I continued swinging my flashlight beam all around. When I reached the tip, I saw a bright red splash of still-wet blood under the flap of jean material and all down one side of the tree. I quickly realized that my chap, running full tilt, had not seen the tree when the light went out and had run full force into the polished point, impaling himself.

Expecting the worst, I began to track the man by the large splotches of bright red blood on the river gravel until I found him lying by a pile of driftwood. He was holding his left knee with both hands, rocking back and forth and groaning softly. I knelt by him, identified myself again, and asked what had happened. All he could do was groan and rock back and forth on his back as he held the bloody damaged knee in both hands. I pulled one of his hands away to see if I needed to put a compress on to stop the bleeding and saw what was the matter. The tree tip had skidded up his shin, opening it up to the white, glistening bone until it hooked under the kneecap and then, owing to the lad's velocity, had ripped the kneecap and a slab of meat from the lower femur with its group of tendons almost completely off. Damn, what a mess. If I hadn't been trained as a biologist in college and worked on so many bloody animal bodies, I might have lost my dinner right there!

Removing my uniform shirt, I took one of the long sleeves off at the armpit with my knife and wrapped the knee as best I could to stop the bleeding. Then, picking up the lad in a cradle carry, I walked back to my patrol car with my softly moaning cargo, who occasionally shrieked when the free-swinging knee hooked on some brush as I carried him along. Carefully loading him into the backseat, I drove to the hospital in Eureka and left him in the capable hands of the emergency staff. It was only a few hours later that they got a surgical team together and operated on the lad in an attempt to save the knee and reconnect the damaged tendons. In the meantime, knowing he wasn't going anywhere, I returned to the gill net and loaded it and all the salmon (minus one, which had been carried off by some critter) into my car as evidence for any court action that was sure to follow.

The next day, I returned to the hospital to visit my new acquaintance. His name was Robert Davidson, and he resided in the small town of Blue Lake. He worked in the local mills when he could find work, but the local police reports and discussions would show that he had been unable to keep a steady job because of an ongoing drug problem. I issued the fellow a citation for the illegal use of a gill net and gave him an evidence tag for his net and salmon. I wasn't anyone he really wanted to see right then, so I left as soon as I finished. Several weeks later he hobbled on crutches into the Arcata Justice Court and pleaded guilty. The judge fined him $250 but because of the injury sustained in the escape attempt suspended all but $50. The net was forfeited, and he was placed on a year's probation and would pay the full fine if he was apprehended during that period for another Fish and Game violation.

I saw Robert several times over the next year, but I never saw him running a gill net again, or even sport-fishing. Maybe it was because his left knee was so badly mangled that he was never able to walk normally again. A cane filled his hand at age twenty-six instead of a gill net or an illegally slaughtered salmon. ... Mother Nature is a fairly gentle lady and tends to be forgiving of intrusions into her "pantry" caused by ego and greed. However, when you really piss her off, *be careful.* ... She can sometimes wield her own "sword" of justice.

Clam Beach

JUST NORTH OF THE MCKINLEYVILLE AIRPORT, where Strawberry Creek runs into the ocean, lies Clam Beach. In the late 1960s it was known for its great razor clam fishery, and every year during the clam season it was home to hundreds of people pursuing that culinary delight. These clams are well described by their name. They are very long and narrow, with a shell edge that if grabbed incorrectly will produce a cut like a very sharp knife or razor. They are found in beds just below the breaking surf line, with many more close at hand in the slightly deeper water. When the waves wash up on the beach, a person standing back in the shallow water can see a siphon hole open up in the sand so the clam can suck in the water and nutrients that just washed over. The trick is to take your shovel, sticking it seaward of the siphon hole, and dig like a banshee in the hope that you will get the clam before it digs its narrow body deeper into the sand and out of harm's way. You will dig many an empty hole before you are rewarded with a razor clam that didn't escape. The pursuit is a lot of fun, and the culinary reward is beyond belief.

In those days the daily bag and possession limits were both twenty. However, it took a number of clams to make a real meal, and therein lay the rub. People simply found it very difficult to stop at twenty. They knew twenty clams would make only a small eating portion, so they tended to take matters into their own hands. Those gifted enough to be good at digging up the critters would far exceed the daily limit by bringing their families along and filling the limits for everyone in the group. Sometimes I would even see little children out at the water's edge with little backyard play shovels and buckets and a dozen or so razor clams. Of course, when I talked to any kid's father, I would hear in short order that the little child had "dug them all by himself." Let me tell you, I spent many an hour chasing razor clams during my off-duty time, and I don't think I ever dug up more than a dozen or so on my best day! So a five-year-old boy with a pile of razor clams in his bucket always made me a bit suspicious. Maybe I was just a klutz and didn't know how to dig them. However, when the clam tides were just right, it was not unusual to find five hundred to a thousand people on the beach going after this delicacy, little boys with their buckets and all.

Sitting back at a distance and watching the folks on the beach was one way to count how many clams certain suspicious indi-

viduals took. If I spotted someone breaking the law, I would head
out to the culprit from my hiding place and attempt to catch them
before they ditched the goods or got lost in the mass of humanity.
Another way was to dress like the rest of the people on the beach
and get right in among them. That way I could get a more accurate count of what was taken and get to the rascals before they
tossed the evidence, gave it to other willing hands, or buried the
broken clams in the sand, thereby wasting some of the resource.
Now, not everyone used shovels in their attempts to catch the
clams before they dug themselves out of sight. Many folks used
what were then called "clam guns." A clam gun was nothing more
than a three-foot-long piece of pipe about six to eight inches in
diameter (size depending on the digger's arm strength). The bottom of the pipe was open, and the top had a plate welded over it to
form a seal. In the center of the top plate was a thumb-sized hole,
and there were smaller pipe handles welded at the top of the pipe
to form a T. The user of this device would stand in the water as it
ran up on the beach, and when a clam's siphon hole was spotted,
he would quickly place the open end of the tube over the hole and
shove the clam gun down in the sand to the handles. The opera-
tor would quickly place his thumb over the hole in the top plate,
forming a vacuum, and then pull the device up out of the water
and sand. Walking over to the shore, he would take his thumb off
the hole, and the column of sand and water held by the vacuum
would be released and fall out of the cylinder. With a little luck,
the clam would be in that column of sand, and the fisher would be
off toward a quick limit of clams and some damn good eating.

One day I had hurried into the Fish and Game office to finish
up some paperwork before heading out to Clam Beach to see
what I could stir up. Many reports had come in to the office about
the good clamming as well as several complaints about people
taking over-limits. After finishing my paperwork, I changed into
some grubby clothes and a sloppy hat and headed downstairs,
where we kept our extra equipment. I threw a shovel and the rest of
my law enforcement gear into our undercover truck, cranked it,
and headed north on Highway 101 to the beach. Just as reported,

the parking was limited and there were about six hundred people already out on the beach, waiting for the clam tide. Sitting there, I watched the area for about an hour to get a feel for the folks clamming on the beach, attempting to spot someone doing what they shouldn't.

At the north end of the beach among the horde of fishermen clamming, I saw two men with clam guns. They appeared to know what they were doing and were catching razor clams one right after another. Each man had half of an old inner tube with a rope tied at both ends slung over his shoulders. Small slits had been cut in the top ends of the inner tubes, and when one of the lads got a clam, he would hurriedly pop it into the inner tube through the slit. The more I watched these lads, the keener grew my interest in just how well they were *really* doing. They were a good half mile from where I was sitting among a bunch of parked cars, so, knowing they would be none the wiser, I replaced my binoculars with my thirty-power spotting scope and took a really good look. It was always nice to work with a spotting scope in Humboldt County because it was a temperate rain forest and was cool most of the time. Lower temperatures always helped keep the heat distortion in check, and today, with the cool offshore breezes, my view was commanding. I watched this duo for about an hour, and in that period they kept everything they caught, large or small, and had, to my count, taken at least one hundred razor clams between them, or sixty over the limit. Anyone that greedy, to take everything no matter what size and an over-limit as well, clearly deserved my attention.

Figuring enough was enough in this instance and that I had reached my patience threshold, I got into my hip boots, grabbed my shovel, and set out to ruin their day as they had ruined the day for the poor damn razor clams. I paused for one last look and was glad I had taken the time because the lads had stopped clamming and were looking down the beach toward the main body of clam fishers as if they had seen something they didn't like. I knew I was supposed to be the only game warden out there that day, so I didn't think it could be a game warden problem. But I checked the beach anyway and was surprised to see Warren Duke, another squad game warden, checking fishing licenses along the beach out in front of God and everybody. Damn! I thought. Warren, you are not even supposed to be here! Anyway, what a time to check fishing licenses when there are over-limit cases, which are one hell of a lot more important to the resource, to be made.

Getting back into the truck, I mounted the spotting scope on the window once again and took another look at my lads. They were still watching Warren and appeared to be considering what to do next. Damn, I thought, what a bad break and poor timing. At that point I thought I'd better hold tight and see what the two fellows were going to do. It wasn't long in coming. They headed over to the sand dunes, took off their inner-tube clam carriers, and buried them in the sand near an old driftwood stump. Then they took two empty inner-tube carriers from a gunnysack, tossed them over their shoulders, walked back into the water, and began clamming down the beach toward Duke as if nothing out of the ordinary had happened. They took about a dozen clams between them as they walked right up to Duke. Duke obliged them by checking their fishing licenses, and the three of them talked for a moment or two. Then the two lads began working their way back up the beach as Duke continued checking licenses on other nearby fishermen. Eventually my two lads were again on the northern fringe of those taking clams, and when Duke got to their area he just waved, having already checked them.

Brother, I thought, those lads are sure cagey. They deliberately had the warden check them to get him off their backs and then continued to violate, knowing he would not check them again. And sure as hell, Duke walked right by them, not knowing they both had over-limits of razor clams in their possession once again! Boy, you talk about a couple of smart outlaws. It also told me they had probably been doing this for a long time because they were damn good at it.

Soon Duke tired of the routine of checking fishing licenses, not having written a single citation, and left the beach for better fields. The two chaps under my eye continued to take more razor clams than the law allowed, especially now that the law was leaving. Well, not quite, lads …

For the second time I put away my spotting scope, grabbed my shovel, and headed across the dunes toward the beach. Looking like all the other fishermen, I slowly worked my way up to the two lads with their inner tubes again partially filled with clams. I hadn't gone halfway toward them when I noticed they were heading for the driftwood stump again. This time I couldn't see what they were doing, but when they came back their inner tubes appeared to be empty. That's it! I thought. Your days of taking too many clams have just come to a close. Walking even faster now, I continued moving through the crowds, using them as cover, especially when my two turned their backs on me and could not see my hurried pace. When I was about forty yards away I stopped pretending and headed straight for them. They continued to clam until I was about ten yards away and then, realizing something was out of the ordinary by my rapid, direct approach, stopped to watch me close the last few yards.

"Morning, lads; how are you doing?"

"Fine," came the somewhat guarded reply.

Striding up to them, I took out my badge and identified myself. "Gentlemen," I said, "I won't waste any of my time or yours. I have been watching the both of you for some time and during that period have observed both of you take a large over-limit of razor clams. I also watched the two of you hide two inner tubes of razor clams over by that redwood stump and know what you are carrying in your current inner-tube clam carriers far exceeds the limit as well. So let's dig out your fishing licenses and driver's licenses as we head over to the stump for the rest of what you have taken."

After a lost look between the two of them, we walked over to the stump and, digging in the darker wet sand next to it, pulled out two very full inner-tube clam carriers. It took a while, but when it was all done the lads had exactly 600 razor clams, or 560 over the limit! That had to be the champion over-limit, I thought as I took a look at their driver's and fishing licenses. Both were from Brookings, Oregon, which created another problem. In those days, if you were from a state other than California and were caught breaking a Fish and Game law, you were hauled off to the slammer. Once there you could post bail, and then the state of California didn't really care if you left the state or not because the bond you posted usually more than covered the offense. Most states wouldn't allow extradition over something as minor as a Fish and Game violation, so once back in your home state, if you had only been issued a citation, you could usually thumb your nose at the state in which you had committed your offense.

Gathering up the clams and holding on to their driver's licenses, I placed the lads under arrest and told them I was taking them to the Arcata Justice Court so they could post bail. Both nodded that they understood, and down the beach we went toward my vehicle, two walking with long faces and a whipped attitude and one straining under the weight of several heavy rubber inner tubes containing six hundred evidence razor clams. Arriving back at my undercover truck, I searched the lads and placed them in handcuffs for the trip to Arcata. Boy, talk about causing a bad case of the big-eye among those clam fishermen coming off the beach and seeing my two lads in irons for taking too many clams! I could just imagine what kind of talk swept through the beach crowd once that became common knowledge.

Loading up my two fishermen, I got on the radio and called the Fish and Game office to explain that I was taking two nonresidents to the Arcata Justice Court for exceeding the limit of razor clams, to wit, 560 over. Man, talk about creating a stir. ... The next thing I heard was Captain Gray's voice on the radio, instructing me to call him immediately once I was finished in court. Damn, I thought, what the hell did I do wrong now? In my first book, *Wildlife Wars*, I spelled out what kind of chap the captain was in the story "Ishi-Pishi Falls." Suffice it to say that the captain and I did not get along because of his drinking problem and his dislike for anyone with a college degree.

When I arrived at the Arcata Justice Court, I seated my two rather forlorn-looking culprits in the courtroom and told the clerk of the court that I needed the judge to hear these two men's pleas regarding their over-limits of razor clams because they wanted to settle up with the court and be done with it and the state of California. I filled out their citations and gave them to the clerk, and she gave them to the judge, who promptly held court. Both men pleaded guilty, and the judge set the fines at $500 each, which in those days was a pile of money. The men forked over the fine in cash and then asked if I would take them back to their vehicle so they could get the hell out of California. I agreed, and as I was leaving the court the judge stopped me and asked what I had done with the razor clams.

"They are still in my truck, Your Honor," I replied.

He looked at me for a second and then said, in a voice smelling strongly of whiskey, "Just leave them here if you would, please. The court will personally dispose of them." With that, he turned and went back into his chambers.

"Yes, sir," I replied to a closing door ... and did as ordered by the court. That judge also had a drinking problem, and several times during my career in that courtroom, he "disposed" of the evidence.

Taking the downcast fellows from Oregon back to their Cadillac, I searched the car for any other contraband. It was clean, so I let them head on down the road. As I got back into my patrol truck, I remembered the good captain's order to call him once I was through with the court proceedings. I radioed in, and the captain immediately asked me, "Where are the razor clams?"

"I left them with the judge at his specific request," I responded.

"You did what?" sputtered the captain. "When you get your tail end in here, you see me immediately!"

"Yes, sir," I responded to a quiet radio on the other end.

Arriving at the Eureka office pissed, to say the least, I prepared to meet the good captain. I walked into his office through an open door and stood at attention until he found the time to talk to me.

"Who told you to leave the razor clams with the judge?" he bellowed.

"The judge, sir," I replied.

"You can't do that," he shouted. He was bellowing so loudly that the secretary got up and closed his door.

"Yes, sir, I can," I replied.

"By whose orders?" he yelled as the smell of whiskey pervaded the air.

"We were taught at the academy that the judge, at his discretion, can dispose of or order disposed any evidence he or she sees fit," I replied. "Also, Inspector Les Lahr told a bunch of us that a judge can order disposal of evidence if he sees fit."

"That is a bunch of crap, mister," Gray continued to yell. "Now, get the hell out of my office, and don't ever do that again."

"Yes, sir," I replied, whirled around, and left his office with a big smile. ... As I said, Gray and I didn't get along too well. And the judge can legally do as he or she pleases with any evidence once a case is closed!

I later found out from the office secretary that when I had reported over the radio that I had seized a mess of razor clams, the captain had gotten on the phone and invited a mess of folks over for dinner that night. The secretary overheard the captain mention to one of the party that the menu would center around fresh, deep-fried razor clams—and for once all they could eat. I guess there must have been some embarrassment that evening at Walt's when his guests had to eat something else and he had to eat crow. ... That made the uncalled-for ass-chewing worthwhile!

The Old Man and the Sea

NORTH OF THE CITY OF EUREKA is a small, sleepy fishing village called Trinidad. First as a college student and later as a Fish and Game warden, I came to know it as a great place to launch a boat and fish offshore for the mighty silver and king salmon during the season. I remember that many times when the salmon were running, it was not uncommon to count five hundred to a thousand small boats fishing off Trinidad in a huge flotilla. I can also remember when the salmon were running seeing over a hundred boats and trailers lined up any time of the day along Trinidad's roads, waiting their turn to be launched so they could go to sea and catch salmon. I clearly remember one day as a warden in which I checked 198 fishermen in a row with full limits of fish before I came across anyone who did not have a legal limit of three—and that was only because the chap was seasick and wanted to get the heck off the ocean. It was truly unreal, and I doubt that anyone will ever see such days again because of humankind's stupidity in caring for the salmon resources. You know, when God extended to us the privilege of enjoying what he had created, I doubt His intent was that we should utterly destroy it as we have done and continue to do in many instances.

Anytime you have lots of people attempting to harvest abundant resources, you will have problems. That was always the case with the fishermen sport-angling for salmon off the coast of Trinidad. It was not uncommon for people to take large over-limits when the fishing was as excellent as I described earlier. Another problem was party fishing, a situation in which one soul in the boat catches other people's fish for them, thereby exceeding his personal limit. Then we had even trickier anglers who would bring a legal limit ashore and place the fish in ice chests in the trunks of their cars. If not checked by game wardens, they would go back out and catch another limit of fish, with none the wiser. This illegal strategy was called "double tripping" and was terribly destructive to the salmon resource. And so it went. People don't seem to realize that when wildlife biologists suggest a season or bag limit for a particular species, it is with the understanding that some folks will be successful and others won't. Knowing that not everyone will take a full limit of a species allows the biologists to set season and bag limits in line with the health and wise use of an animal population. So when people party fish or party hunt, they are taking more than planned for, and it is just a matter of time with that kind of overharvest until it is all gone or extinct. Such abuses are part of the reason why California no longer has much of a salmon fishery compared to just a few years ago. That, plus other problems such as overfishing by commercial interests; loggers wrecking spawning streams with silt and slash; Native Americans gill netting the hell out of everything; poachers snagging salmon on the spawning grounds; illegal markets for the meat; pollution;

obstructions in the spawning rivers and streams, such as dams, that preclude the salmon from reaching their ancestral spawning grounds; and on it goes. It is a miracle that the salmon in the lower forty-eight states lasted as long as they did.

My awareness of the limitations of the salmon resource, even in those heady days, and my great respect for them and their life history meant I always found time to spend with them when humans were present. One warm day in June I waited in line to launch my patrol boat at five in the morning. Soon I was in the water and out to sea, looking for all intents and purposes like all the other eager fishermen. Now, those of you who have read my book *Wildlife Wars* will remember that I get seasick. And I don't just get seasick—I get violently seasick! But here I was, gently rocking and bobbing in the Pacific Ocean swells a few miles off Trinidad, pretending I was fishing so I would not arouse any suspicion among those wanting to do the devil's work. Many people think all a game warden does is hunt and fish. Nothing could be farther from the truth! When the best hunting and fishing are going on, that is when we are working the hardest because that is when the violations are occurring. That is also when a warden earns his money, so to speak. Officers who aren't out there doing their thing during wildlife's time of need are part of the problem and just as bad as the poachers, to my way of thinking! Don't get me wrong. There are the good, the bad, and the ugly in the conservation officer corps, just as in every other walk of life. But generally conservation officers have good hearts, know what odds the wildlife are facing, and know what they are tasked with professionally. You reduce those odds by being there for the critters and in so doing will cross paths and eventually swords with those who need your attention.

Well, here I was—already starting to sweat, have a dry mouth, and wish I hadn't eaten anything for the past three days! Soon I was chumming, if you get my drift, as I set up my fishing rig. That is, I had a fishing rig, but, in between bouts of puking over the side, I was rigging a six-ounce lead at the end of my line so it would keep the line taut to make it look as if I were trolling. With that setup, I could look like a fisherman and yet have the opportunity to watch and see who needed the services of one damn sick (and getting sicker) game warden.

That morning was unreal. Everywhere I looked, the sea was covered with small fishing boats, and at almost any time I could see anywhere from one to six boats all landing fish at the same time. That catch level made it difficult to watch everyone, and, being a rookie, I was falling prey to that error. Finally I took about five boats under my eye and began to concentrate on them. I had a small notebook that I laid on the seat beside me. I took one page for each boat and listed the fishermen in that boat, identifying them by numbers, letters, Roman numerals, and such. Then when someone in a particular boat caught a fish, I would go to that page, list a mark for a fish, and record the time. Within an hour all five of my chosen boats had reached their limits of three fish per person and left without violating any of the state's laws. After their departure, I moved near another clump of boats and did the same thing. Within an hour they too had reached their limits out and headed for home.

Not feeling so sick now, mainly because I had puked everything inside me up and over the side, including my heart, liver, hind end, and gizzard, I headed for another larger clump of just-arriving boats and followed the same procedure. Thirty-three minutes later all of them had reached their limits and left. Damn, I thought; someone out here has got to break the law with the fishing like this. Moving to a clump of boats a little closer to shore, I set up housekeeping once more. All the boats had two occupants or more except one, which had only one man fishing from it. I reordered my notebook and was ready to go. In eleven minutes, eleven salmon were pulled into the boats I was watching. Here we go again, I thought as I began to look for another clump of boats. Then I got a break. The lad fishing alone in an eighteen-foot Chrysler inboard-outboard caught what appeared to be his third fish. Stowing the fish in an ice chest, with two trailing alongside the boat on a stringer, he continued to fish. Bingo! I thought. He was in deep brown, viscous stuff if he caught another salmon. He could continue to fish because there were other species of fish in the ocean, but he couldn't catch any more salmon. Within minutes he had another fish on, and this time it was about a thirty-five-pound king salmon. Finally landing the fish, he knocked it on the head with a resounding *whack* and put that one in the ice chest as well. I guess he figured that if a game warden came by, the officer would see the two salmon on the stringer, figure the fellow was legal, and go right on by. Well, not this time, I thought, grinning. I continued to act like I was fishing and losing fish from my position about ninety yards off his stern. Soon my lad had another fish on the line and in a few minutes had another nice silver salmon on board and in his ice chest. That's enough, I said to myself as I reeled in my line with the sinker on it. He had two fish on the stringer and at least three in the ice chest, so that would be more than enough to convict him with a limit of three.

Starting up my boat, I pulled even with his while I was still about forty yards off to one side. Then I turned and headed slowly toward him, practicing good boat safety, all the while watching his actions. For a few moments he was so engrossed in his fishing that he didn't pay any attention to my approaching vessel. Then it dawned on him that I was moving toward him. Standing up in the boat, he yelled, "Hey, you son of a bitch, you have the whole ocean to fish in. Go find another place."

My response was another dry heave over the side of my boat. He looked at me and said, "Hey, candy ass, didn't you hear ✓hat I said? Go puke somewhere else."

Slowing my forward speed at ten yards out, I said, "State Fish and Game warden. I will be coming alongside."

"The hell you say," he said as he grabbed his ice chest.

"Don't mess with that ice chest, mister," I yelled as he struggled to lift it and headed for the far side of his boat. "As a state Fish and Game warden, I demand to check your fish in that ice chest!" But the man dumped the contents of the ice chest overboard, and those fish were gone forever. However, he was a tall fellow, and as the fish fell out, I could count them in the space between the bottom of the ice chest and the gunwale of his boat. Five salmon went overboard from that ice chest. Boy, seasick or not, I was pissed! Talk about waste!

As I pulled alongside and tied our boats together, I was amazed to find myself looking into an ancient face, twisted by contempt. This guy appeared to be older than glacial soil! I identified myself with the badge, and he said, "I heard you the first time. What the hell do you think, that I'm deaf or something?"

Brother, I thought, this old man sure got up on the wrong side of the bed. Well, he's going to wish he had stayed in bed before I get through with him. "May I see your fishing license and driver's license, please?" I asked.

"What the hell for? I am not driving a car, as you can plainly see, and I only have two salmon, which places me well within the limit. So what's your problem?"

Having had a gutful of this chap, even though I had puked most of my guts overboard earlier, I said, "Listen to me, old man, and listen well. I am about one micron away from clapping your ass in irons and hauling you off to jail for possessing an over-limit of salmon and for failure to show upon demand those very fish you tossed overboard! Do you understand?"

"I didn't dump any fish overboard," he growled.

"Well, you can tell that to the judge if you would like," I retorted.

"I most certainly will," he replied.

We stared at each other for a few moments, and then he reached into his pants pocket, dug out a wallet, and handed me his fishing and driver's licenses. I about crapped a brick when I looked at the guy's date of birth! It was June 18, 1868, and the current date was June 12, 1966! The man I had just apprehended was ninety-eight years old and feisty enough to go another twenty years! His fishing license also indicated that he was ninety-eight.

Getting out my citation book between bouts of dry heaving over the side of my boat, I issued him a ticket for possessing an over-limit of four salmon (with the fish dumped overboard), another for taking an over-limit of two salmon (I had observed him taking only two over), and failure to show because he would not show me the fish in the cooler upon demand. The old man was wise in not saying anything as I had him sign the citation and seized the two salmon he had on the stringer. He needed a trip to the bucket, but I didn't have anything other than attitude to haul him in for, so he didn't make that particular trip. In those days we didn't jail someone unless they were a nonresident, had committed a very bad act, were an escape risk, had committed a felony offense, or had insufficient identification. Unfortunately, this fellow did not meet any of the above criteria, so he walked and I fumed.

I met my razor-clam-eating Arcata judge later that week and took the time to sit down and explain what had happened on the ocean (minus the puking incidents). He listened closely. Finally he said, "I think I need to teach that chap a lesson, Terry. How many fish did he dump overboard again?"

"Five, Your Honor," I said.

"Well, I will set the bail at two hundred for taking the over-limit, four hundred for the possession over-limit, and one hundred for the failure-to-show violation," he said. Seeing that I was only making $516 per month as a game warden, I felt that was more than adequate! As we started to part company, the judge asked, "Terry, where are the remaining evidence salmon?"

"In the evidence freezer, Your Honor," I replied.

"You might bring them by tomorrow. I know a needy family that would love to have them," he said.

"Yes, sir," I answered, grinning as I remembered the misplaced hind-end chewing I had received from my captain over the six hundred razor clams. ...

A mature female king salmon will lay about two thousand eggs on her redd (spawning) site. By the time they go from those eggs to the number of salmon returning to spawn, that number has been reduced to two! Dumping those five fish overboard that day in and of itself didn't create the salmon population problems we are facing today, but it certainly helped.

That fellow was the oldest person I ever arrested or cited in my entire career, and he did pay his fine. Given his attitude, I wonder how many more illegal salmon he had taken over the many years of that long life of his ... and I wonder what kind of a spawning loss that represented over time. I would bet it added up to the tens of thousands. I don't think I would want to be with him when he arrived at the Gate of Saint Peter because I hear Mother Nature is related to God, and after all, those were her fish. …

The Wrong Sex, the Wrong Time, the Wrong Place, the Wrong Person

WARREN DUKE, a fellow game warden and rookie like me, came busting into the game warden's room in the office one day and said, "Terry, you've got to help me."

Looking up from my paperwork, I said, "Now what?"

Warren and I had gone to college together, but he had been a fisheries major and I had been in the wildlife program. He had always been a little excitable, and today was no different. "I've got more deer hunters in my backcountry than I can shake a stick at," he grumbled. "There is no way I can cover all that backcountry and keep an eye out for the cattle rustling that really rears its head this time of the year as well. All the other guys have a slug of backcountry problems themselves, not to mention their own ongoing deer seasons, and I could really use some help if you have the time."

Well, I had the time but was at a bit of a disadvantage when it came to the geography of his enforcement district. Warren was one of those officers, at least back then, who usually felt he could cover his district himself without much assistance. As a result, I hadn't worked his area much at all and didn't know the roads, the ranches, or the names of the ranchers. Oh well, I thought, not knowing the country is a small problem. You know how to catch the lads straying over the line, and that's all that matters. … You know, it's truly amazing how often a rookie enforcement officer can trivialize the obvious. The key to good law enforcement is knowing the playing field, and that includes the geographic details. One can always catch the dummies, but a thorough knowledge of the arena in which I would operate always led to the apprehension of those who really needed it. I was soon to find out just how important it was to know and understand those limitations.

Agreeing to give Warren a hand, I said I would work in his area from Friday through Sunday. That period would cover the sportsmen's heaviest-use time and would allow him to patrol the areas that needed more informed attention. In short, I would go after the dummies, and he would attend to his more pressing backcountry problems. Warren and I sat down with a map of the area, and he lined out the areas where he wanted me to work. They were all the back roads and backcountry in the Iagua Buttes area of Humboldt County. This was prime deer country, everything from pasture lands to pristine forests. In other words, it was an area where a lot of different microenvironments came together, forming many edge effects for the deer, which translated into almost perfect habitat. The area was also riddled with hundreds of logging and ranch roads leading every which way, which was exactly what the lazy, road-hunting deer hunters wanted. With road grids across both public and private lands, those not wanting to climb up and down the steep hillsides or lacking permission to hunt on the private lands could drive around and see many feeding deer on private lands or other areas closed to hunting. Then it was short work to shoot a critter, quickly haul it across the fence to your waiting vehicle, and be gone, usually with no one the wiser. The country also had a fair number of feral hogs running around, and the outlaw shooters would seldom pass one of these up. Because of their diets of mushrooms, roots, acorns, and other plant life, the hogs were lean and excellent eating.

Early Friday morning I found myself in the assigned area checking deer hunters in a light, misting rain. Rain is common in Humboldt County, and every time it drizzles, it seems the deer are on the move, day or night. This day was no different, and I saw many deer feeding and moving in the open areas, avoiding the wet, brushy hillsides. Taking a spot on some high ground, I parked the patrol car, opened the windows, and quietly sat and listened. I hadn't been there more than an hour when I heard a single shot down in the Mad River bottoms. Not having anything more pressing to do because the hunting pressure was still so light, I started working out the muddy roads, heading that way for a look-see.

About an hour later I came upon two men in a pickup driving toward me on an abandoned logging road. Both men were looking over the side of the road and down the banks, apparently looking for deer. Since deer season was on and these lads were on public ground, it was no big deal. The driver took a quick look down the road and then quickly looked back over the bank as he proceeded slowly toward me. Then, realizing there was a game warden's patrol car sitting in the middle of the road thirty yards away, he snapped his eyes back for another unbelieving look. His expression was one of utter shock, and he said something to his passenger, who was still looking over the bank, unaware of my presence. The passenger took one quick look at me and then bolted out the door. He wasn't carrying a rifle or anything—he just leaped out of the vehicle in his shirt sleeves and disappeared into the dank underbrush alongside the road. At the same time the driver put his truck into reverse and hastily drove backward down the road as if by doing so he could shake my unwanted presence. In a few moments, the reality of my patrol car in his face and the howl of the siren told him that his actions were futile, and he stopped. Getting out of my car, I crossed over between the vehicles and approached the truck driver, whose eyes were riveted on mine.

"Turn the engine off," I commanded, and he did. Walking up to his door but not standing right in front of it in case he tried to quickly open it and knock me down, I said, "Good morning, state Fish and Game warden. Anything the matter?"

He just stared at me in disbelief as I quickly scanned the inside of his vehicle. A hunting rifle was propped up on his seat for quick retrieval, but nothing else of interest met my eyes. He still hadn't said a word, and a quick look into the bed of his pickup said why. Lying in the back of the pickup was a dead forked-horn buck (two points per side, Western count) with nary a deer tag affixed to the antlers, as the state law required. Quickly bringing my eyes back to the cab and still watching out of the corner of my eye the brushy area into which his partner had fled, I asked him to hand me his rifle. It was loaded with a live round of ammunition, another violation of state law, which prohibited the possession of a loaded rifle in a motor vehicle on a way open to the public. Unloading the rifle and dropping the live round into my pocket to log later as evidence, I laid his rifle over the hood of the truck and told him to get out of the vehicle. When the man had climbed out of the truck and was standing in front of me I asked, "What's with your partner?"

"What partner?" he responded.

"The lad who vaulted out of the truck and ran off into the brush. In fact, there's his coat on the seat."

"I didn't see no one," came his not-so-believable reply especially in light of my having seen the fellow run from the truck in front of God and everyone. I asked for the lad's hunting and driver's licenses, which he quickly produced. Still not knowing what the hell was going on, I removed his hunting rifle from the hood of the pickup, walked back to my patrol car with his licenses, and called the Humboldt County sheriff's office, still keeping a wary eye on the brush where the passenger had disappeared. Once the dispatcher was on the line, I quickly briefed her regarding the events up to that moment, my rough location, and the name of the man with the illegal deer. Asking her to record the information in case I didn't return home that evening, I got back out of my vehicle and hailed the driver over to my patrol car, telling him to bring his keys. The rain was beginning to fall in earnest now, and he was only too happy to get out of it. Grabbing his keys, he trotted over to my patrol car and got in on the passenger's side. With that, I backed up onto some high ground where I could watch not only all around me and his truck but the brush patch where his partner had vanished as well.

"Who shot the deer, and why is it not tagged in accordance with state law?" I asked.

"I did, and I don't know why I didn't tag it," he replied. He looked scared to death. I could tell this was probably his first real brush with the law, and although it was not a very serious one, it surely had his attention.

"Who was your partner?" I asked as my eyes again traversed the area into which he had disappeared.

"I can't say, mister. I can only tell you he is AWOL and just didn't want to go back to the army." I thought the way the lad spoke sounded truthful. Still keeping an eye on the brush patch and now mindful of the heavy rain that was falling, I felt it would be only moments before the drowned-rat passenger would return to his dry pickup and warm raincoat. But it was not to be. I wrote the lad a citation for possession of a loaded firearm in a motor vehicle and an untagged deer. Then I made him punch out his deer tags, and we both walked back to his truck, where he affixed them to the antler after I had photographed the untagged buck for evidence. I could have seized the deer, but I felt that the lesson learned was enough punishment, and I could see no reason to rub the lad's face in it by taking his deer. Besides, he looked like he had missed more than his share of meals already and could really use the meat.

With that, having no further business with the fellow, I carefully pulled my car off the road to avoid getting stuck and made the man leave the area without his partner. I figured my runner would come out of the wet brush and now driving rainstorm looking for cover, and I would then solve the mystery, but I figured wrong. I hung around for the rest of the day, checking other deer hunters mostly out of sight of that area, expecting to see him come walking down the road any moment. But it hadn't happened by the time night fell to the sound of heavy rain drumming on the top of my patrol car. Several times I saw his partner coming back down the road looking for him, and each time I sent him packing back in the direction from which he came. Finally, at about ten in the evening, I tired of the game and pulled up stakes only to meet the ever-faithful pickup driver coming back into the area. Once again I turned him around and told him that if I caught him doing the same thing once more, I would arrest him for interfering with an investigation. That did it! Off the mountain he went just a-fogging, and that was the last I saw of him. After one last look for my AWOL fellow, I headed out and let him walk home. The nearest town was at least fifteen miles away, and I would bet a month's pay that that fellow was one wet son of a gun when he finally got to cover since he had jumped out of his vehicle without a coat of any kind. In fact, I would bet another month's pay that about halfway through that ordeal, he was wishing he was back on the army base. ...

For the next two days I had a rainy environment to rattle around in and ended up writing about a dozen more citations for illegal deer, loaded guns, taking band-tailed pigeons during the closed season, and the like. All in all, it turned out to be pretty uneventful until Sunday afternoon, when I caught a couple of kids trespassing on a private ranch trailing a wounded feral hog they had shot. By the time we found and dispatched the wounded hog, gutted it, and hauled it back to my patrol car, it was getting dark. Two citations later for the trespassing violations, the lads were on their way, and it was now getting quite dark. I hadn't really been watching which dirt roads I was traveling, and in the heavy rains that came with the dark, I soon was unable to backtrack and found myself good and lost! Warren had since long ago gone home, so asking for assistance on the radio was useless, and I was deep in unfamiliar territory with dwindling gas supplies. By ten o'clock I was so far lost in the backcountry that every chicken I came across had a square face! My gas gauge advised that I had better find my way out soon or I would be walking just like the AWOL lad.

Dense fog was now slowly moving into the area as well as even heavier rain, and finding my way was becoming even more difficult. Taking one road that headed up the mountain, I figured I would try to climb out of the fog and see if I could spot a light from a campfire or ranch house. Then I could at least get some directions, gasoline, or both. In about fifteen minutes I climbed out of the fog, and off in the distance, just as if it had been planned, was a light! Working my way toward it on a series of muddy roads, I finally broke out into several small, grassy openings surrounded with timber. At the end of one of the meadows merrily blazed a large campfire. Hot dog, I thought. Now I will find out how to get the hell out of Warren's damn district and head for home at last. As I pulled into the hunting camp with just my parking lights on, I could see that it was a big one. There were four pickups and a trailer parked around the bonfire, and I could see several men moving around in the dancing firelight, oblivious of my approach. The rain had slacked off, and for once I was glad. I always liked working in weather, the worse the better, but after the many hours of hard rain the quiet was nice.

Pulling up behind a pickup, I got out of my patrol car and headed for the fire, hoping for some information on how to get off this damn mountain and back onto a main road that would lead me back to civilization. If nothing else, many hunters in those days carried extra gasoline in jerricans (named after German-designed gas cans carried in the desert wars), and if these lads had extra, maybe I could purchase some. As I walked toward the huge, welcoming fire, I could hear a lot of laughter. In fact, it sounded like the kind of laughter that came from a lot of heavy drinking. ... That was OK with me; just as long as the lads were sober enough to point the way home, they could have all the John Barleycorn they wanted.

Stepping into the light of the fire, I saw six men sitting in lawn chairs, drinking and having a good time. As I had guessed, there were several bottles of whiskey on the ground by their feet, and every man had a full glass in his hand. "Evening, gentlemen; how are you chaps this evening?"

The laughter stopped in an instant as every eye around that campfire whirled around and fastened onto my carcass, especially the badge clearly in evidence on my jacket. Damn, I thought, that was some greeting. No one spoke or moved, and I again said, "Evening, gentlemen; how you doing?"

"Fine," came a rather frosty reply from a man taller than I and with a pot gut far exceeding mine.

Walking closer to the fire, I said, "Lads, I'm new to the area and lost as all get-out. I don't suppose one of you could give me directions on how to get out of here and back to the Kneeland area, would you?"

There wasn't a single response, just silence as they continued to look at me as if I were a ghost. Goddamn, I thought; this is the goofiest bunch of hunters I ever ran into. It was like being a

Revenuer surprising a group of men sitting around an illegal whiskey still (yes, there are still some illegal whiskey stills in the outback)!

"Get lost, asshole," finally came a cold reply from the man mountain sitting across the fire from me.

What the hell? I thought. They can plainly see from my uniform that I am a state Fish and Game warden, not someone here to rob them. "I *am* lost, sir; that is why I am trying to find directions out of here and off this mountain," I replied in similar glacial tones.

Man mountain stood up, tossed his whiskey into the fire, and said, "Get your butt out of my deer camp, and don't let me see your putrid mug here ever again, or I will do what needs doing to change it!"

My Mr. Nice Guy attitude went right out the window as I realized that either the whiskey or a bad conscience was turning this into a confrontation, and I had better be on my toes or when I came off this mountain, it might be in a pine box instead of my patrol car! I turned to talk to one of the other fellows next to me, hoping to defuse the situation, get my directions, and get the hell out of there, when I suddenly spotted the reason for their animosity. Hanging in the trees on a long meat pole (a metal pole strung between two trees six to eight feet off the ground, commonly used in organized deer camps to hang gutted deer to cool out and drain) next to the house trailer were six deer. Deer season was in full swing, so a properly licensed hunter could actually kill two deer in those days. However, every deer hanging from that meat pole was a female, or doe, a *totally* protected animal!

Now I was not only faced with a bunch of sullen, half-drunk men but staring at a major game violation as well. It was pretty plain that they had the wrong sex of critter, hanging in the wrong place in front of God and everybody—and the wrong person, namely me! I quickly looked around for any close-at-hand hunting rifles, figuring that if trouble was to start that would be the direction some of these folks might head, and found none. Good, I thought. Maybe they had put them away so they would not get wet from the rain.

The mountain man with the pus gut, seeing my eyes run to the meat pole and realizing that the cat was out of the bag, said, "Mister, you have about ten seconds to leave before I come across this fire and kick the living stuffing out of your miserable hind end!"

By now I had had a gutful of this chap, and I'm sure my next words must have spelled out that feeling, at least in tone. "Mister, I don't know what your problem is, but I am an officer of the law and have a legal right to be here, especially in light of all the illegal deer hanging in camp. Also, you need to be aware that I am not leaving this deer camp until I find out who killed the deer, issue the appropriate citations, and seize the deer. Is that clear?"

With those brave words (I am not sure where they came from), all the lads instantly stood up and faced me. It was obvious none of them were going to ask me for the next dance. ...

"I figure you got about eight seconds left of that ten I gave you earlier, mister," uttered man mountain through clenched teeth.

Having been in a few "hoorahs" in my life previously, I knew one was coming—like a freight train! Ignoring him for the moment, I took the offensive. "Gentlemen, as you can see, I am a state Fish and Game warden, and I would like to know who shot those deer hanging over there on that meat pole."

"Why, you son of a bitch," said man mountain as he started toward me, and it wasn't to shake my hand. "Let's get him, boys. We six can whip his butt before he knows it, and I don't care how large he is!"

All the men turned as if that thought were on their minds as well, setting down their whiskey glasses as if on cue as the pus-gutted one started around the campfire toward me at a fast gait. Knowing I couldn't keep all those lads from kicking the hell out of me, I stepped back two quick steps, unsnapped my pistol, and dropped my hand to its comforting grip. "You'd best listen to me, lads, and back this kind of talk and thought off to the place from whence it came," I stated in a tone spelling out nothing but business—deadly business if necessary!

"John, go get your rifle out of the trailer and we'll take care of this bastard," bellowed pus gut as he stopped in his tracks.

"John, you make one move toward that trailer and your rifle and it will be your last," I said quietly. I wasn't scared because

there was no time for that, but my eyes were sure watching everyone and everything! I could feel my training and limited practical
experience starting to take over even though everything seemed
to be moving fast but in slow motion.

"Why, you big blubber-gutted asshole, I will take you apart with
my bare hands by myself," said man mountain as he again started
toward me.

"Want to die?" I quietly asked.

"What did you say?" he barked.

"Want to die?" I repeated, this time even more coldly. Now all
the other men were not only silent but their body language said,
Maybe I don't need or want to be here. Good, I thought. I have
only the tub of guts to contend with. "Mister, you continue to
come at me with the menace you are showing and I will shoot you
right in that big pus gut you call a stomach. I am carrying a .44
magnum, and that is where the first shot is going. When that .250-
grain bullet hits you, you are going to blow up like a watermelon
and throw guts all over your buddies. Then if the rest of you decide to rush me, and five of you could kill me if you were lucky, I'll
shoot the first three who get close. Then I will lay the side of this
twenty-nine-ounce all-steel pistol alongside the next closest fellow coming at me, crushing his skull and killing him in an instant.
That leaves only one of you, and by that time I will be so damn
mad that I will be able to kill that unlucky person with one punch.
Do I make myself clear, gentlemen?"

Even through the whiskey-soaked mind of the large one, I saw
that I had finally rung his bell. All of a sudden, realizing he was
going to be the first to die, he put his arms out like the statue of
Christ in Rio on Sugarloaf Mountain and held his buddies back.
That wasn't a real big problem at that point. Every one of them
had had time to think over what I had just said and how I had said
it, and their collective feet had turned to stone. ... Overhead in
the damp cool of the evening, I could hear the soft whirring of
wings from my two guardian angels.

With that break in the ice, if you will, and the realization that I
wasn't going away, I took the initiative. "John, you and one other

lad go and cut those illegal deer down and drag them to my patrol car. Keep in mind, any one of you two who makes a move for that trailer will die on the steps. The rest of you can sit back down and remain seated until I need to talk to you."

With that, the lads sat down, and not a word was spoken. John and a fellow named David went to the meat pole, and in a few moments all the illegal deer had been carried to the rear of my patrol car. Then they came back to their chairs around the campfire and sat down.

"Now," I said, "who shot the deer?"

There was a pause, and then one by one four of them admitted that they had killed the six deer that morning for camp meat and some extra meat to take home. Asking for and receiving four sets of hunting and driver's licenses, I wrote citations, one at a time, for the illegal possession of a protected game animal, using the hood of my patrol car as a barrier so I could watch all the rest. All four of the lads receiving tickets were staying in the house trailer, so when I finished the citations I had John lead me to where they all kept their hunting rifles. Confiscating the guns, I locked them in the front seat of my patrol car. Then I took the information for the last two lads, hoping that the county attorney would allow me to charge them for aiding and abetting. One of these last two was the bigmouth with the pus gut. I kept him on the other side of the automobile hood, and as I wrote out the information he quietly said, "Would you have done it?"

"Done what?" I asked.

"Shot me," he replied.

"Art, in my mind I was only two and a half pounds out of three of trigger pull away from making a mess of what your blessed mother had such high hopes for."

His eyes never left mine, nor mine his. ...

After I finished the information-gathering process, I loaded three of the deer in my trunk along with the feral hog I had seized earlier and jammed the other three into my backseat and floorboard. Since my trunk would not close, I tied it down to the bumper with some nylon parachute cord I always carried. Handing the men evidence tags for their illegal deer and rifles, I said, "Now, gentlemen, would someone tell me how to get out of here and back to the Kneeland area?"

I ran out of gas in the small town of Bayview but was close enough to Eureka that I called the sheriff's office and had a deputy bring me several gallons. It seemed that gas station attendants didn't work as late as did game wardens.

Several weeks later the four lads who had received citations for illegal possession of a game animal paid $250 for single deer violations, and the two who had killed two animals paid $500 apiece. The county district attorney was not interested in sweeping the remaining two men into the illegal possession net. As for taking on the pus-gutted one who had threatened me, the county attorney, himself a drinking man of note, refused. "I would have liked to have been there to see who would have won in that one," he said with a twisted grin. That was the extent of his legal help. There may have been some doubt in his mind, but there was none in mine about who would have come home that night. ...

The Snagging Hole

BETWEEN THE SMALL north-coast towns of Weitchpec and Orleans on the Klamath River in northeastern Humboldt County lies a one-hundred-yard-long deep pool at the head of a quarter-mile-long, boulder-strewn riffle. Migrating salmon and sturgeon, after navigating with difficulty the long, swift riffle, lie in that pool to gather their strength for the next difficult stretch of the river. Humans, being the type of critters they are, have discovered such natural resting locations and in short order attempted to add another dimension to the life history and survival of those highly sought-after fish species. The technique is called snagging and involves the illegal use of large sets of treble hooks, strong lines, and heavy weights cast over the backs of the resting fish to drag them foul-hooked to the shore for the personal freezer or illegal market. Snagging activity was especially heavy when the surgeon were in the river and running.

Many times I would drive by the parking lot on the south side of the Klamath and see anywhere from ten to thirty vehicles parked as their fishermen owners plied their trade in the long, slow-moving pool. Most of the fishermen would fish from the south side, but there were always some who brought small boats to cross to the other side of the river. Those folks on the other side had a little better access to the pool and generally caught more fish. In addition, it often seemed that those folks on the other side, feeling a little more secure from the game wardens with fifty yards of river between them, would get a little carried away and snag the hell out of the fish as they passed upstream. This illegal activity seemed to be a constant problem, and many a complaint came into the office in Eureka.

Not only was the area a long distance away, but the wardens were limited by lack of covert transportation. You couldn't just drive up in a marked patrol car because the word would be out in a second. If you wanted to make it stick in court, you had to catch the person snagging red-handed, and that meant getting close enough to seize their illegal gear before they tossed it into the river or let it hang up on the bottom where it could not be retrieved. Because of the lay of the land, there really wasn't any way to stay at a distance and make any kind of case, so the wardens had to be in among the fishermen or forget it. Therein lay our problem. We had only two undercover vehicles in the Coast Squad, and almost everyone in the country, especially the outlaws, knew every inch of those vehicles' tired frames, bolts, rust, and bug spots. So driving up to that area in one of those cars and parking like any other fisherman would draw instant stares from all the knowing outlaws and in-laws. And, as expected, any violations would disappear into thin air.

One day I got the bright idea of using my personal Jeep pickup and my own Super Eight movie camera with the telephoto lens. No one knew the rig, which allowed me to park close and capture all the illegal action with the camera's zoom lens. Even if the snaggers tossed their illegal gear before I got to them, I would have it on film, and as far as I was concerned, that was good enough for any court of law. Meeting Captain Gray in the office one morning, I asked him if the state would pay the mileage if I used my personal vehicle on the Klamath in an attempt to slow down some of the sturgeon snagging. He looked at me through bloodshot eyes, mumbled an approval, then walked into his office and closed the door to the world. Must've had a hard night, I thought as I cleared out of the office building before he changed his mind and gave me a fish-tagging detail in the stinking hold of some ship at the docks in Eureka.

Early the next afternoon I was on the Klamath River in the parking lot overlooking the snagging hole. There were about twenty vehicles already parked, so I moved my truck into the middle of them to a spot that had a commanding view of thirteen people fishing on the far side. Parking with the driver's side of the Jeep facing those fishermen, I walked to the passenger side and began to fiddle with my gear in preparation for fishing, or so (I hoped) all the lads thought. I got out a heavy fishing pole and stood it up alongside the Jeep where everyone could see it, then got out my tackle box and began to pretend I was gearing up. I had the tackle box on the seat on the passenger side of the truck and was working inside the cab as many fishermen would do in a similar situation. When no one was looking at me in the parking lot, I quickly took a look with a pair of binoculars at the fishermen on the far side of the river. Hot damn! After a long look at the newest arrival in the parking lot, all of the far-side fishermen had gone back to their fishing. *Every one of them was going through the snagging motions and attempting to snag a sturgeon!* I couldn't believe it!

Quickly putting down my binoculars, I fumbled around, got out my Super Eight camera, and, with a quick look around to make sure no one was watching me, began filming the first fishermen in the long line of thirteen. I would first film each person going through the snagging motions, then zoom up on him, filling his face in the lens, then back the telephoto lens off to normal, then put the camera down. Using a notebook (hidden on the seat where no one could see what I was doing), I would write down the events I had just filmed for courtroom testimony. Then I would step outside my truck again, fiddle with my fishing gear as if I was still getting ready, and then, when no one was looking, repeat the filming process for the next fisherman. The last two fishermen in the line of thirteen turned out to be two Indian women. They were just as good at snagging as the men and were recorded for posterity with the camera.

Having filmed every person and recorded the same in my notebook as they happily snagged away, I took the camera and on fast speed (slow motion) panned the entire crew from left to right, getting some great snagging activity on film. I ran out of film, changed the roll, and was starting to film some more when it dawned on me: How the hell was I going to get across the river without a boat? Damn, for want of a horseshoe nail I was going to lose the war, or at least part of it. Then one of the lads snagged a sturgeon, and I filmed him as he fought it, using the zoom lens to show him removing the set of snag hooks from the back of the sturgeon near the dorsal fin before he tied it up along the bank. Running out of film again, I hurriedly changed canisters and prepared to film some more. As I closed the body of the camera, I heard a kid's uneasy voice behind me say, "You're a game warden, aren't you?"

Whirling around, I saw an Indian boy about fifteen years old standing not ten feet away. Damn, I thought. I had been so interested in capturing the violators that I hadn't paid attention to my immediate surroundings. Looking at him for a moment, I said, "Yes, I am, and I expect you to say nothing to anyone about that fact."

He studied me for a moment and then said, "Why should I say something about you to some stinking white man? They snag all our fish and leave nothing for me or my little brothers. I don't care if you catch them all, but how are you going to do it, white man? You don't have a boat, and to catch them you'll have to cross the river."

He was right. I hadn't thought past the first part, being a damn thickheaded rookie, but I was bound and determined to find a way now that I was confronted with the problem.

Without waiting for me to answer, he said, "I have a boat, but you can't use it. I know two of those people over there, and they would kick my butt if they knew I helped a game warden."

"Where is your boat?" I asked.

"There," he said as he pointed to a twelve-foot aluminum boat anchored at the river's edge.

"Good," I said. "As a state officer and being empowered to commandeer any kind of equipment to assist me in an investigation, I am taking your boat!"

The kid just looked at me like I was nuts and said, "You can't do that."

"Yes, I can," I responded. "And if you refuse, I can take you forthwith to the nearest jail and have you incarcerated for impeding an official investigation." I didn't know if I could do all those things, but it sure sounded good. The Indian lad looked at me for some kind of sign that this was a joke and, finding none, began to look worried. "Don't worry," I said. "I'll get you off the hook if you play along."

He looked at me for a long, hard moment, then said, "OK, mister, but if you don't there are people here who would kill me or tear my boat up if they thought I was helping you catch them, especially my own kind."

"You just agree to what I tell you on the river and everything will be all right," I said. I grabbed my fishing pole and camera in its disguised carrying case, and the two of us headed for his boat.

A few minutes later my boatman landed me across the river and just below the thirteen fishermen attempting to snag the sturgeon lying in the pool before them. They hardly paid any attention to me because I had a fishing pole, was dressed in grubbies, and was being transported by a kid they knew. Stepping out of the boat, I whispered to the boy to stay right there so he could transport me back across when I was done. The look in his eyes told me he would do as I asked. I turned, took out my camera, and began to film at close range as the fishermen continued their illegal activity. It was several moments before one of the snaggers noticed what I was doing. He hollered, "Game warden!" and in an instant everyone looked in my direction in disbelief, only to discover that they were being filmed.

I yelled, "State Fish and Game warden. Everyone reel in your lines and take five steps back from the river with all their fishing gear and sit down. Anyone who does not bring in their terminal gear will receive an additional citation for failure to show upon demand."

No one moved! I don't think they believed their eyes. I repeated my instructions, only this time I told them I was filming their actions, and anyone who violated my orders would be reviewing this film right along with the judge. With that, everyone began to reel in their terminal gear. Once done, they stepped back from the river and sat down. That is, everyone except the two Indian women. They tossed their gear up on the bank after reeling it in, obviously madder than hell, and began to call me every name in the book, including a few I didn't know. I thought I could speak "sailor," but those two ladies sure knew what to say, and in a tone that reached the very soul. Man, I never heard such language from a woman.

After I had everyone under control, I commenced to issue citations to every one of them for snagging and for using illegal terminal gear. Once a particular citation was issued, I asked that person to go back and sit down minus his fishing gear, which I seized and stacked beside me for safekeeping. When I got to the man with the still-alive sturgeon tied to a rope and anchored to a stake on the bank of the river, I filmed it and let it go. Man, was that fellow pissed. I guess I would be too if someone released a 150-pound fish of mine. But I knew there was no use in killing the animal for evidence when I had the camera to record it.

Finally finishing with all the men, I called the first woman over for her citation, a lady named Julie, and man, did I get an earful. When I finished with her, I called the last woman over for her citation and got the same earful of profanity. She also glowered at the lad who had brought me across the river and said, "I will get your little ass for this, Tony."

"No, you won't," I said in a tone that captured her immediate attention. "He had no choice but to assist me," I continued. "Tony and his boat were commandeered by the State of California, and if he had refused I would have booked him in jail for interfering in an official investigation and taken his boat away."

She just looked at me with hate spewing from those black eyes, then looked over at Tony and said, "Is that true, Tony?"

"Yes," he replied, whereupon she launched into my carcass again with such profanity as I never did hear. She made it understandable that it was criminal to take a young boy like that and use his boat and so on. Looking over at Tony, I winked so that she could not see it and then returned to the business at hand. I told everyone the court dates and that they were to appear in person before the Justice Court judge in Willow Creek. This set up a lot of growling, but everyone seemed to understand, and amidst continued profanity from the two Indian women, I took all the seized fishing gear, boarded Tony's boat, and headed across the river. Just as we landed, Tony hit a rock with his prop and broke it. I helped him drag his boat ashore and told him I would replace the prop (I purchased and mailed him one after I returned to Eureka). With that, amidst the stares and some smiles of satisfaction from the fishermen on my side of the bank, I tagged all the fishing gear with evidence tags, loaded up my truck, and left with a swirl like a shark would make after a hit. ... Before I left, however, I quietly paid Tony $20 for his assistance in getting me across the river to pinch those "stinking" fishermen, to quote a certain lad of the river. ...

Going through Willow Creek, I stopped at the Justice Court to drop off my citations and had a chance to meet the judge as she entered the courthouse. She observed all the poles sticking out of my vehicle and asked, "Snaggers?"

"Yes," I answered.

As I walked with her into the court, she said, "Coming to my court, I suppose?"

"Yes, Your Honor," I responded.

"If we still have that many people snagging after all the work you and Hank Marak have done, I guess I am going to have to get their attention again," she calmly stated.

"That would sure help, Your Honor," I said.

"Any problems with that bunch?" she asked.

"Only the two ladies," I responded.

"Don't tell me about it now," she said. "You know my rules. Just make sure you spell out in detail in your case reports what the ladies did to get your attention." With that, she went into her office and closed the door.

Two weeks later I sat in the Willow Creek Justice Court while all my fishermen trooped by the judge with long faces and pleas of guilty. In each case the judge fined them $350 for snagging ($100 more than usual) and $250 for the illegal terminal gear (normal fine). Then every one of those folks lost all their fishing gear and their fishing privileges for one year, and they all received six months' probation. Oddly, the judge saved the two Indian ladies for last. Now, as instructed by the judge, I had spelled out in pretty well-defined terms the reams of profanity the two ladies had used on me throughout the proceedings on the river. I had just partially spelled out the most explicit terms, but their meaning was clear to the reader. The judge had both ladies come forward as she read their case reports and asked them how they pleaded. Without profanity this time, they pleaded guilty. The judge assessed them the same fines as the men. Then she asked the ladies if they had used any profanity against the officer on the river. That question caught the women off guard, and they stammered a little.

"Well, did you or didn't you?" the judge asked.

"Well," said one, "I may have swore at him a little."

The other lady nodded.

"What kind of words did the two of you use?" the judge innocently asked.

The two women kind of hemmed and hawed, and finally the judge showed them my case reports and asked them to read them. This they silently did for a few moments and then looked back up at the judge when they had finished. "Are some of the words or type of language you two used on the river against the officer in those reports?" she asked.

"Yes, Your Honor," came the sheepish tandem reply.

"Why?" the judge asked.

"We don't know," came the now worried-sounding reply.

"Well, I don't know either," the judge said curtly. "Here you have a state officer trying to do his job in light of serious fishing offenses, and you two ladies take it upon yourselves to belittle and call him what appeared to me to be every name in the book and a few new ones." There was no response from my two ladies, who just hung their heads. "Instead of probation, I command that the two of you each spend three days in jail for your fishing violations, and while there you will write a five-hundred-word essay on why we have fishing laws in this state."

With those shocking words, she rose, since there were no others to appear before her, and strode out of the courtroom into her office. The sheriff's deputy attending court handcuffed the two stunned ladies and led them to his waiting patrol car. All the rest of my snaggers just sat there with a case of the big-eye, wondering just how close they had come to going to jail. That was the first time I ever had two people go to jail just for cussing me out. That was not the way it went down in the court records, but sure as shooting, it was why they went. There was no doubt in my mind because the judge was a good Mormon woman who hated cursing. The two flying mouths of those young women landed both of them in the lockup, sure as shootin'. And it couldn't have happened to two nicer young ladies.

When the word of the court trials got out and about, it knocked the illegal snagging in the head so much that it dropped to about half of what it had been. As a result, some of the fish got a breather and made it upstream to spawn and carry out their genetic messages. As a result of those cases and the many others of different colors of the cloth during and after my rookie period, I grew to love my profession. There truly is something to be said for the rush that comes from hunting your fellow humans, especially when they are really in need of your attention and authority. History is replete with instances when a sane and controlling human hand was absent. In every case, then as today, others will take advantage of that fact to line their pockets or inflate their egos with the destruction of the environment and our wildlife, lands, waters, or air. Mother Nature, like any other mother, has to occasionally take her children aside and provide a little discipline to keep them in line. Game wardens help her provide some of that discipline in the world of wildlife by acting as her "sword." I discovered during those rookie days and over my thirty-two-year career that Mother Nature's sword is an excellent tool to maintain some of this nation's great natural resources for those folks yet to come. I also discovered that her sword can cut both ways if not judiciously used. … I hope that none of my readers are among those on the point of Mother Nature's sword. … If so, prepare for the whirlwind. …

2

"I Want My Net Back"

H ERB CHRISTIE, the Fish and Game warden from Fortuna, California, wearily walked into the main office in Eureka and deposited his tired frame in an old easy chair set aside for the wardens. He was a big man, at least six foot four, but carried his 250 pounds of muscle lightly on his rawboned frame. He had tousled brown hair and dark eyes that could look through you if necessary. Despite his size, he walked with the purpose and practiced grace of a stalking cat. When Herb walked in I was quietly writing out several case reports on two deer spotlighters I had arrested the night before in the Snow Camp area in the mountains above Eureka. I had not worked with Herb yet but had heard a lot of good things about him from the other veteran officers and was quietly looking forward to the day when I might be asked to give him a hand. Bear in mind that in those days a rookie like me didn't just walk up to a seasoned senior officer and ask to work with him. The really dyed-in-the-wool members of the old guard took their time observing and listening regarding the merits of a rookie before asking a junior officer to join them in a detail. The reason was just good common sense. A rookie could get into a lot of trouble, being new to the business, and hence could easily get his partner, the senior officer, into a lot of unnecessary hot water. Also, it took a lot of effort to train a rookie, and not all of the older officers wanted to be bothered with such a chore.

I had gathered from personal observations and the words of other officers that Herb was a very good game warden and a joy to work with or for. He was not only a hard worker but very gentle and considerate of others, no matter what walk of life they represented. He had a profound love for the natural resources he was protecting, and his long days in the field quietly spoke to that dedication. He was also known for his practical law enforcement savvy, especially in the survival arena (sometimes necessary when working around mean-tempered, out-of-work loggers or other lumbermen), and for the time being was the best pistol shot in the North Coast Squad (I was to replace him in that category in 1967).

Without any warning, Herb said, "Tiny, what do you have planned for this weekend?"

Realizing that this might be my chance to work with this man who had such a fine reputation, I lied. "Nothing," I calmly said. "I am free for whatever. What do you need?" Actually, I was supposed to paint the house that weekend, but I was not going to pass up my first opportunity to work with Herb and the potential it held for me to learn more about my chosen profession. Besides, Herb had a reputation for sometimes going through the gates of hell to root out wildlife crime, and I wanted to see how he did it and survived. Philosophically, that was the way I felt I wanted to pattern my career, and what better person to learn from than one who was on a first-name basis with the devil! Not that Herb was in cahoots with the devil, mind you, but that he had a reputation for going into places where only the devil would tread to root out the bad guys. I wanted to learn those techniques so I could eventually do the same and come away without the smell of brimstone in my hair or singeing all the feathers on my two guardian angels so they'd have to walk to the dry cleaners instead of flying.

Herb continued to look me over for any smooth edges (there were not many), all the while mentally calculating whether I was up to the challenge he had in mind. The bottom line was that Herb needed help, *good help of size,* and needed it now. The look in his tired eyes told me he had a major wildlife problem and was faced with using a rookie even though he had no knowledge how I would react in the field in the heat of the moment. However, Herb was on a quest and needed a strong heartbeat to assist him

in carrying it out. "Tiny," he said, "I need a partner to float down
the Klamath River with me in an attempt to stop some of the
illegal gill netting of salmon by the Indians on the Yurok Reservation. Captain Gray wants some enforcement action in putting
these guys out of business and wants it now. Are you game?"

I became aware that I was under the locally famous Herb
Christie dark-eyed intense gaze again. Herb, unbeknownst to me,
was looking for cracks in the facade of the fellow sitting in front of
him, and all the while I was misreading the look, thinking I must
be such a magnificent specimen that Herb was happy to select me.
Rookies! Hidden in that almost innocent request for assistance
was the fact that we would be floating the mighty, rugged Klamath
River at night without outboard motor or lights, guided only by
oars. He also neglected to tell me that we would more than likely
be outnumbered ten to one if we really got into the bad guys; that
if we were seriously injured, our chances of getting out alive were
nil owing to the remoteness of the area and the lack of medical
help for miles in any direction; that because of the Native American rights issue before the courts, we could only seize the gill nets
and fish and could not issue citations or make arrests until the
courts had decided we could legally do so; that we would be going
against Yurok Indians, who though small in size were large in heart
and had a reputation for fighting for what they felt was guaranteed
under their treaties. Finally, he didn't tell me that there were no
life preservers in the town of Eureka or anywhere else close at
hand that would fit either of us (we both had fifty-six-inch chests),
so we would be going without.

Without hesitation, I said, "You got your man, Herb. When do
we go?" Somehow I don't think I would have reacted any differently had I known about the dangers. You can be that reckless
when you are young and unaware, or dumb, some people would
say. As I said earlier, Herb was the best pistol shot in the squad,
and now he asked me what type of weapon I would be carrying
and whether I could shoot. I thought it was a strange question,
and when the best shot in the squad asks if you can shoot, that
alone should raise a red flag. But I missed the point and simply

said, "I will be carrying a .44 magnum Smith and Wesson revolver, and yes, I can shoot."

He said, "Good. Meet me here tomorrow with some clothing for a night detail, sleeping bag, food for an overnight, your weapon, several changes of clothes in a plastic bag in case we overturn the boat going over a waterfall and end up swimming in the Klamath, and plenty of ammunition. Not reloads, mind you, but commercial-grade ammunition." That statement was followed by another keen-eyed gaze.

"Yes, sir," I responded, wondering where I was going to get the money to buy a box of commercial-grade .44 magnum ammunition. I was just a poor game warden making $516 per month before taxes, and my bride was working as a schoolteacher for the golden sum of less than $4,000 per year. As such and in order to keep costs down, I cast my own bullets and reloaded my own ammunition for about fifty cents per box in those days. Now I was being asked to fork out $7 for a box of commercial-grade ammunition. Brother, that was going to make my bride, who really watched our meager budget, somewhat unhappy. Now, don't get me wrong. My wife could always get at least a dollar out of every nickel, but this box of ammunition at the end of the month was going to be a stretch even for her. Then it dawned on me! If I had to shoot someone, it had better be with commercial-grade ammunition (in those days you could use just about any weapon and any kind of ammunition in our agency—not anymore, however). If not, I could be in a world of civil-law hurt if I had to shoot someone and something went wrong with my reloads. Not that I expected that to happen. I had been reloading my own rifle and pistol ammunition for about four years and understood what the hell I was doing. But *if* something happened to a bad guy, my partner, or me because something didn't work, well, that would be unacceptable. Lesson number one in my rookie existence, I thought. I bought the box of commercial-grade ammunition, and my bride didn't even blink. For some reason, she had already realized the value of having me come home each night at the end of a detail.

"By the way, what kind of swimmer are you?" Herb asked, breaking through my thoughts.

I said, "I figure I can swim enough to survive the current in the Klamath River."

"After being thrown through a boulder-strewn waterfall?" came Herb's quick response.

"Hopefully good enough to get back to the boat," came my equally quick response, though I really didn't know.

Herb quietly measured my statement and its strength of tone, then slowly said, "Good. Meet you here tomorrow at nine o'clock in front of the building." He took one more intense look at one of the newest members of the Coast Squad, and I never let my eyes leave his. I was bound and determined to show the man he had made a good choice.

We parted company, Herb with a slow, measured step and I with the wild, racy feeling that comes from a dangerous assignment soon to be undertaken happily whirling around in my inexperienced carcass like there was no tomorrow! There almost wasn't. ...

Leaving the office, I raced to the nearest sporting-goods store and plunked down $7 and tax for a box of .44 magnum, .240-grain soft-point bullets. Hefting that box of shells in my hand brought home the seriousness of the detail to come. When I got into the quiet of my patrol car, I emptied my pistol of reloads and refilled the pistol cylinder with six shiny new cartridges. Then I placed the rest of the box of ammunition in a small army surplus carry bag that was to accompany me on this trip because Herb had said to bring extra ammunition along just in case. I sped home and, with a little white lie so Donna, my bride of just a few years, wouldn't worry, quickly put together my gear for the next several days. I had never floated the Klamath before at night, and I probably packed more than enough gear for the detail Herb had in mind.

The next morning found me at the Fish and Game office bright and early. I really did not want to be late for my first detail with this officer because I didn't want it to be my last. I got the rest of my administrative work done in time to visit with Warden John Finnigan, another old-timer now rapidly becoming a close friend.

John and Herb went back a long way, and my time in the office with John that morning allowed me to pick his brain on the man known as Herb Christie. John had good things to say about Herb and rated him as one of the best, especially under pressure. As we talked, I heard a car horn honking on the street and looked out the window to see Herb pulling up in front of the Fish and Game office, towing a twelve-foot aluminum boat with a twenty-horse-power motor attached. He was driving the state undercover Jeep and, seeing me looking out the ground-floor window, motioned for me to throw my gear in the boat and get in. Hustling down to my patrol car, I grabbed my gear and did as Herb indicated. Sliding in alongside Herb, I said, "Good morning." Without any fanfare, he continued looking dead ahead as he pulled out into the street, grunting a greeting like a man who was lost in thought many hours and miles away. Having been raised to keep my mouth shut until spoken to, I just sat there and ten miles later, outside Arcata, watched the unique redwood ecosystem slip by us as we sped down the highway into an area where the Klamath River split the Yurok Indian Reservation just north and west of the Hoopa Valley Indian Reservation. Plain and simply, as Herb had earlier stated, the outback we were going to was *way* out back. It was as dangerous an area as there was in those days, especially when dealing with conservation law enforcement, and best not entered unless sage heads led the expedition and one's guardian angels were at the top of their game.

Herb, as I came to find out, was indeed one of the best. Though he was very soft-spoken, he was survival smart, was a good teacher, and possessed a rare sense of the history of the land and her peoples. I soaked up every bit of knowledge he shared with me as we drove into the area that day and came to feel honored to be working in his shadow. Little did I then realize that his quiet confidence and innate survival ability would flat-out save my life in less than twenty-four hours.

Arriving at a spot on the Klamath River deep in the Yurok Indian Reservation, Herb and I looked for a place to launch our boat, all the while trying to look just like any other salmon fishermen in our undercover getup. Once the boat was offloaded with our gear, Herb parked the Jeep among all the other fishermen's vehicles on the gravel bar. With my tennis shoes on, I pulled the boat out into the cool but swift current to enable our outboard motor shaft to clear the gravel on the river bottom while Herb busied himself with last-minute duties on the boat. He primed the motor and pulled out the choke. On the second pull of the starter rope, the engine coughed to life and then ran like a Swiss watch. Outboards can be as cantankerous as a cross between a Republican-owned mule, a thirsty camel, and a teaching Catholic nun with a ruler who has had a long day. The starting ease of Herb's outboard told me he was smart enough to realize that the motor had to get us there and home, so therefore, he should take good care of it. That lesson wasn't lost on me, though I did forget it once over the next thirty-two years of law enforcement.

As Herb idled the boat out into deeper water he once again checked his equipment, spare engine parts, and tools. He then asked me about the gear I had brought for the detail to be sure that we were ready before heading the bow upstream. Seated in the bow, I was able to enjoy the cool majesty of evening in the river canyon. I had never been in that area before or done anything like this, but I was sure willing to learn. God, it was magnificent! The Klamath was a large, primitive, clear-flowing river with dangerous rapids needing to be executed with care at every turn. There were high canyon walls streaming upward several hundred feet with hardly a handhold, and I got a crick in my neck trying to look up at them in wonder. Several times in the next hour, black bear, deer, and other wildlife raced away from us and into the brush of the deep-sided canyons as we passed. Damn, was I ever in my element! Herb didn't say a thing, just watched what was happening around him, "read" the water, and enjoyed watching me act as he must have while learning on some of his first details many years before with his mentor. One thing I didn't miss about my teacher was the roving eyes. As he proceeded slowly up the river, he committed every swirl, eddy, riffle, and boulder in the water to memory. It was plain that he was coming back in the night and didn't want any surprises. I certainly didn't want him to miss anything either. Being in the front of the boat during our planned return in the dark, I realized that if he missed a spot in his memory bank, I would be the first one pitched into the dark, rapidly flowing river. ...

As we slowly worked our way upriver, I noticed Herb's eyes also constantly roaming the riverbanks and sandy spits on both sides. Finally I couldn't stand it any longer and asked, "What are 'we' looking for?"

Looking at me with a grin of appreciation that I had realized his scrutiny was an important part of the detail, he shook his head and commenced training an officer who someday might just be worthy. He said, "Terry, when people use gill nets, they put them in the eddies, not the swift-moving water, and anchor one end of the net somewhere along the edge of the bank or sandbar at the head of that eddy. Usually that anchor is a heavy limb or stick driven deep into the ground along the sandy spit or sandbar in such a manner that it won't arouse much suspicion. They don't want to attract the attention of passing fisherman because of the passions relative to the continuing legal question about using gill nets in this part of the river. Plus, if passersby see a gill net in operation, they may rob the net of its catch or cut it to pieces with their knives.

"The rope along the top of the net holding the floats, or float rope, as it's called, is attached to the partially submerged anchor stick buried in the sandbar or gravel bar above the eddy. A boat is then used to take the other end of the float rope out into the eddy, and they anchor it with a large, heavy rock attached to the bottom rope of the net, or lead line, to prevent the net from being moved out of place by the weak eddy current or numbers of fighting salmon trapped in the invisible meshes. This weight keeps the net stretched out its full ten-to-twelve-foot depth so it will fish more efficiently. Now, as the current flows through the net, it brings leaves and twigs that will soon clog the meshes. So I am looking for a good salmon-fishing eddy, a spot where a salmon would pull up out of the current to rest on his way upstream. And a place where a pile of river debris might show that a net has been dragged up on a sandbar out of that eddy and cleaned.

"The first reason the net is continuously cleaned is that if a fish sees the junk in the net, it'll sense the danger and feel a change in the current flowing through the net and swim away from it. If the mesh is clean and the fish doesn't see it, it'll swim into the net and upon contact, thinking something has it, try to quickly and powerfully propel itself through the feeling of the net on its face. This effort only jams the fish's head and gills through the net, and once hung up in the net, with the mesh over the gill plates, it quickly suffocates to death. Secondly, if the net is not cleaned periodically, it'll fill to such a degree and provide so much resistance to the current in the eddy that it might pull free from its anchor stick on the bank and be lost.

"I'm also looking for a small boat out in the middle of nowhere anchored near this eddy, or a place where a small boat has been dragged over a sandbar and hidden in the brush along the shoreline. Don't plan on seeing any nets out as long as it's daylight, however. Gill nets are only run at night because the fish can see the mesh during the day, no matter how clean they are, and will just swim around them. So watch for a likely-looking eddy, a stick driven into the ground at the water's edge, and debris piled up on the shore. If we discover such a site, we will go in and look t see if it is a fresh netting site—that is, as long as no one's around. If the site has been recently occupied and it looks like the occupant might return tonight, we will go far upstream so we won't be detected, set up camp, and when it gets good and dark float back down and catch our culprit. Keep in mind that at night we'll be able to clearly see the net if it is out because the floats keeping the net stretched open will be in evidence in the eddy. We'll then have our work cut out for us, Tiny." Herb gave me a huge grin.

Damn, that sounded easy, I thought. I remembered an earlier gill net case in Deer Creek and the all-too-clear net floats strung out across the water. However, my inexperience left out the human factor that Indians didn't tend to let one take their nets, fish, and the like without a bit of a "hoorah." Man, this trip was taking on a role of a living dictionary of law enforcement history, I thought with a very large grin on my starting-to-sunburn face.

We motored upstream about five miles, and then there it was, now that I knew what I was looking for! A small sandy spit jutted out about twenty-five yards into the Klamath River above a fairly large eddy below a long riffle, and a wooden stake was driven into the ground at the water's edge with just an inch or two exposed. On the lee side of the spit was a streak of leaves, twigs, and other river flotsam, maybe an inch deep and twenty feet long. Herb looked around to see if anyone was watching and, seeing the area clear, moved our boat over to the sandbar. We got out our fishing poles and pretended to fish, all the while trying to determine whether the flotsam was fresh. It was! Many of the leaves and twigs were still wet from the cleaning of the net the night before. Damn, we had a clearly suspicious area to work right from the get-go. We fished for salmon with lures for about thirty minutes just to make it look good in case we were being watched by unseen eyes and then, having failed to catch any fish, prepared to move on like any other fishermen.

We loaded our fishing gear and moved several more miles upstream, continuing to enjoy those surroundings God had laid out for our appreciation that day. Finding a large sandy area on the river's edge with a good place to camp, Herb maneuvered the boat out of the mainstream current and up onto the beach. I jumped out and pulled the boat up even further so it wouldn't drift away while Herb tilted up the prop, detached the fuel line, and ran the motor dry of fuel. We unloaded our gear, laid out our sleeping bags in the warm beach sand under several small, scraggly trees about twenty feet from the water, built a fire ring with some river rock, gathered some wood and river water, and proceeded to cook our supper. In no time two nice steaks were slowly roasting over red alder wood with several large baking potatoes and onions wrapped in tinfoil roasting in the coals, spiced with fresh garlic and real butter. A can of coffee sat at the edge of the coals and was soon merrily bubbling, sending its aromatic steam into the nostrils of anyone willing to take it in. Sitting there with the sound of the river in my ears and the smell of meat sizzling over the alder coals on a small grate, it was easy to imagine myself transported to an earlier time. Trappers, explorers, mountain men, and Indians had all passed this way before for sure. I wondered what they had looked like, how they had lived, and how they had died. I also wondered whether anyone in their families back in civilization ever knew that they were dead, how they had died, and where their final resting place was, or if they had even cared. Did anyone who knew of their deaths pass those stories down in their family history to next of kin, and did anyone today remember these chaps from so long ago? Hell, for all I knew, Herb and I might be sitting on a spot where others as far back as the early nineteenth century might have rested from their canoe-paddling toils. I smiled at that thought and continued to dream.

Herb's voice brought me back to the twentieth century with the words "Supper's ready." No palatial dinner ever tasted better than the food we had that night. It really doesn't get better than that, or so I thought: good friends, good food, and the sounds of life swirling around us. After we finished the main course, I dug out a small, fresh-blackberry pie my bride had made earlier in the day with one of her world-famous crusts. Taking the pie out of its waterproof container, I let its aroma waft around our campsite. "Boy, that sure do smell good," mentioned a grinning and still-hungry Herb. I proudly cut the ten-inch deep-dish pie in half and ladled Herb's portion into his outstretched dinner plate. "Be sure and include that bit of crust from my portion that you left in the pie dish," he remarked offhandedly. I grinned, knowing that my wife's piemaking reputation had been spread by warden John Finnigan. It seemed that every time John came to the house, Donna had a piece of pie for him, and I was sure John had talked to Herb, another "pie face," as my wife was quick to call us pie lovers. Let me tell you, a piece of homemade blackberry pie after a steak dinner alongside the cool of the Klamath River is like no other experience. The aroma alone, fifty miles from God and everybody in the wilds of a river canyon, is out of sight! After dinner I scoured out our eating gear with several handsful of sand from the river as men of old had done and then made another pot of coffee for Herb to merrily boil and again fill the air with its great smell. After that, Herb and I just sat around the fire and talked shop while we waited for the "witching hour," now fast approaching.

Dark was more than upon us in those deep river canyons as we loaded up and lashed our gear in the bottom of the boat to the struts supporting the seats. We both wore all-black clothing and black navy watch caps to help conceal us with the cover of night. With pistols lashed tightly to our waists, extra rounds of ammunition in our front and rear pockets for quick retrieval, and me ready to kneel in the bow with an oar to push us off from overhanging cliffs or in-stream boulders in case we lost control of the boat, Herb nodded that we were set. I pushed us off from our friendly sandbar and into a *real*-life adventure, which was quick in coming. *Zip*, down the Klamath River's swift current we went, side to side and over often-heard but unseen small waterfalls. God, what a rush—literally! The velvet-black darkness in the bottom of that river canyon was punctuated only by the phosphorescence of the boiling whitewater around the boulders to act as our guide. Herb steadily, strongly, and calmly rowed the boat backward to slow us down in this river's magnificent power, while his faithful novice knelt in the bow, fending off the rocky overhangs that reached out as if to ruin our evening, all the while trying to stay low so Herb could see better where to steer. When we slammed into the long, swift-flowing but quiet pools characteristic of the Klamath, the silence was almost deafening. During those moments Herb would rest and just let us drift as we both got our wind. Damn, this is an experience of a lifetime, I thought through a grin that had to be from ear to ear. In the silence of those long pools, I was amazed at the sound my heart made as it pushed the blood into my head. This experience, challenging the river in the dark in a twelve-foot rowboat, was one damn heady narcotic! Even today I can still feel the chill and the heart-stopping thrills as the bottom of the river dropped out from under me in almost total blackness and I waited to hit the river below with a surprising, spine-tingling *thud!* No sooner would we have recovered from one such drop than we would do it all over again. You won't find any ride like that at Disneyland. ... Work of this kind gets into a law enforcement officer's blood as well as the depths of his very soul and stays there until he dies. What it really does is build the strength of purpose needed to carry a conservation officer through the long hauls, and ultimately through that very thing called survival. That was how it worked for the two crazy men on the river that evening, anyway!

The roaring of big whitewater was beginning to reach my ears again. Louder and louder rose the noise of violent water working its constant battle against boulders until there it was! I took a quick look at Herb to make sure he wasn't sleeping and observed a large, thrill-formed grin on his face for my trouble. Another hundred-yard chute of whitewater, boulders, and the mist created by the constant collision of moving water with unmovable rocks awaited us. I kept thinking that the river was totally different than it had been earlier in the afternoon. I truly didn't remember the water being this rough or dangerous going upstream. Throughout the years of wildlife law enforcement that followed, I found that theme always to be true: what you see during the day is not what you see during the night. A law dog reading these lines should know that a good tip of the trade is to look your area over in the light and then look it over at night *before performing any serious activity such as serving warrants*. Doing so will ultimately allow you to fulfill the first rule of the law enforcement officer, which is to come home every night. ...

Down that watery chute in a blur of speed we went, making for high excitement during the moment and feelings of immortality after the danger had passed. The moon was now high in the sky, turning the river from black velvet to silver on the quiet stretches and brilliant white on the rapids. Farther downstream I could again hear the steady roar of the river getting more and more throaty. I looked back at Herb and he had another big grin on his face and a look in his eyes that had to reflect mine. Bracing my knees even harder against the inside of the bow, I waited for the fast water that by now was announcing its presence with the sound of a freight train. Then I could feel the grab of the current through my knees and the increasing wind on my face as the god of water tried to whirl our little boat every which way but loose. *Down* we went through a deep water chute with a speed that reminded me of my younger days sledding down a particularly steep hill in my hometown of Quincy. Spray hung heavy in the air at the bottom of the chute and gathered on my clothing as I successfully parried a small but menacing boulder in the center of the current. Then, as if in anger at having lost a chance to sink the nighttime invader, the angry current hurled our boat like a shot out of a cannon into a large, quiet pool about a hundred yards long and equally wide. The roar and hiss of the chute began to lose its menace and intensity as we sat motionless and let the mighty Klamath carry us farther downstream to our evening's destiny. Not a word passed between us as we both savored the preceding hair-raising moments and then placed what they represented in the annals of our minds. When two friends share such an experience, they are moments *of* a lifetime *for* a lifetime.

Drifting through the silvery pool and down through faster but deeper water, we rounded a bend in the river just above our suspected gill net sandbar. Sitting lower in the bow to reduce my silhouette, I scanned all along the sandbar and the water surface in the adjacent pool, looking for the telltale float line of a gill net. There it was! A fine line of white floats gently arching out into the water and supporting the death-trap gill net hanging below greeted our eyes in the soft moonlight. Quickly checking the sandbar for anyone who might be sleeping there to guard the gill net, Herb and I through a quiet exchange of glances confirmed that the sandbar and adjacent bank were clear of any sentinels. We gently landed the boat on the upstream side of the sandbar and quietly dragged it out of sight into some thick brush along the river's edge. Moving surprisingly silently for two fellows our size, we marked the net rope with some yellow fingerprint paste, which would remain unseen except under a black light. Then Herb whispered that he would go back to where the boat was hidden and spend his stakeout time there. I was to go immediately below the net and hide among some rocks, where I would not be seen but could quickly move in on the folks running the gill net from the downstream sandbar side. Herb said that when someone came to tend the net, which was usually just at daylight, we would wait until they had the net in hand or were busy removing a salmon from it, and then and only then would we would spring the trap. When I heard Herb start the outboard motor, that would be my clue to run along the riverbank to where the net was anchored and close off any escape attempt by the net tenders. That way we would have the culprits between us and guarantee their apprehension. We went to our respective hiding places and were soon lost in our thoughts and expectations as we waited through the night, surrounded by the river murmuring its approval of those trying to protect the hardworking, migrating salmon. All through that long, dark night, I stood in the folds of my boulder pile, dropping in and out of fitful sleep, all the while remaining in a standing position.

The dark of the canyon and river slowly gave way to the god of light as the morning approached. I couldn't see or hear anyone from my place of concealment, but I could smell coffee brewing and alder smoke from a campfire some distance away. The smells told me that the gill net fishermen were only a short distance away, causing me to tremble in expectation of the moment to come. About seven A.M., I heard voices coming down the riverbank to my left and upstream from where I was hidden. I thought, I hope Herb is awake and listening to the same sounds I am. But I quickly forgot that thought as I heard a boat, which we had not seen the afternoon before because it was hidden in the deep brush along the bank, being dragged over the sandbar and into the river. I still hadn't seen a thing because I had not dared, in my inexperience and fear of discovery, to take a peek at the events now occurring less than twenty feet from where I stood. I have since learned that anyone who is not looking for you will not see you. Over the years in my career, exercising that fact learned so long ago, I have crawled right up to people in the dark using only eight-inch-high grass for cover and was never detected until I rose up out of the earth, often at a distance of less than ten feet!

Now I could hear muffled talking between what sounded like an old person and a younger man. Good, I thought; at least you are able to use some of your senses. Finally, unable to stand it anymore, I took a quick look along the bank to make sure no one was watching from that quarter and then slowly poked my head around the pile of rocks to look at the scene unfolding before me. The muffled talking was taking place between an older Indian man and an Indian lad, probably in his teens. Their backs were to me, so I stuck my head out farther and was rewarded by the sight of the two of them poling alongside the floats on the net and dragging it over the bow of their small boat. After running several feet of empty net over the bow, they discovered and removed a dead silver salmon from the net and placed it in the boat. Good, I thought; we now have them breaking the law of the state of California with the illegal taking of a salmon with the use and aid of a gill net.

At that moment I heard the growl of an outboard motor announcing another life-form from a hidden position upstream. The two gill netters froze at that sound, not expecting any company in such a remote piece of the river at such an early hour of the morning. Springing from my hiding place, I raced on cold-numbed and unlimbered legs to the end of the net anchored at the edge of the water on the sandbar. Down the river came Herb, piloting his boat at a pretty good clip right to the Indians' boat and grabbing it by the gunwale to prevent their escape. Our trap was sprung, and we had two gill netters in it just as soundly as they had trapped the salmon in their net. Herb identified himself and pointed to me, unseen by the Indians until that moment, identifying me as his partner and another game warden standing behind them by the net stake. He escorted both men and their boat to the shore and told them that their two salmon (one taken before I had peeked around from my hiding place) and gill net were going to be confiscated for violation of state law. We asked the two men, who were not under arrest at that time (we never arrested without good reason and unless we were prepared to transport the lads to jail), to sit on the sandbar while we unhooked their gill net from the net stake and rolled it up for confiscation. As Herb took the identification from the two men, I stored the seized net in our boat and affixed an evidence tag to it. As Herb began to record the information in his citation book, I got my first real look at Yurok Indians. The old man had to be at least eighty years old and probably weighed in at no more than ninety pounds. The young one, probably his grandson, in his mid- to late teens, was another ninety-pounder at most. They weren't the real bad guys I had expected, but I couldn't tell that to the two dead gill-netted salmon in their net.

The old man was very polite and responded to Herb's questions without any rancor or fanfare. The young one, however, was very upset, and I could see that his eyes were tearing up, especially when he learned that we were going to seize his grandfather's gill net. Herb patiently explained the process, including how to get the net back if the court case went their way, and instructed them to cease and desist fishing this way until the courts decided who had the right to do what and who had the right of regulation, be it the state of California or the Yurok tribal authorities. Once Herb was finished, he asked if they had any questions, and both said no. They went back to their camp a few yards from the bank of the river, and Herb and I loaded our boat and headed back upstream to camp. Going back up through the canyon with a motor instead of oars was a revelation. The river was a whole lot more dangerous and foreboding than I remembered from going up the evening before … a whole lot more dangerous. With that realization in my eyes, I looked back at Herb, and he smiled in recognition of my newfound awareness.

Arriving back at camp, Herb gently nosed the boat onto shore, and I jumped out and pulled it farther up onto the sandy beach so it wouldn't drift away in the current. Herb got out, and the two of us walked over to our concealed campsite and sat down on our still-rolled-out sleeping bags with twelve hours of tired in our bones. Soon those hours of river damp and lack of sleep began to manifest themselves, and Herb suggested that we build a fire and cook some breakfast. Sleeping would have to wait, he said. Being green, I did not really understand the reason but without thinking further got up and began gathering dry driftwood while Herb split some small sticks into kindling with his knife and started a fire. Then we just stood around getting the damp cold out of our bones and watching downriver in case the Indians decided to follow us and cause a ruckus. Pretty soon we heard the growl of an outboard motor coming upriver, but it turned out to be several white fishermen going upstream to their secret fishing hole. The heat from the fire, our tiredness from the long night, and the lack of food again began to affect us, and Herb and I walked over and hung our pistols and holsters in the tree limbs over our sleeping bags. I got the coffee can and walked the twenty or so feet back down to the river to get water for morning coffee. About that time I heard the growl of another outboard motor coming upriver, and I stood there with the coffee can full of water in my hand to see who it was. The boat rounded the turn in the river below our camp and continued upstream in the middle of the river. Just another fisherman, I thought as I turned and started back to our campfire with the coffee water.

"Look out!" I heard Herb yell. I looked back just in time to see our young Indian lad run his boat full bore right up onto our sandbar and, without shutting off his motor, grab a Winchester lever-action rifle from the bottom of the boat and sprint toward me at a dead run! Before I could take any defensive action, he slammed the business end of the rifle barrel hard into my stomach, cocked the hammer, and said in an emotional voice, "I want my grandfather's net back." Tears were starting to come down his face, and he was shaking like a dog crapping peach pits, he was so full of pent-up emotion. I knew right then and there that if he discharged that rifle, accidentally or intentionally, I was a goner. Even if I survived the shot, there was no way to get me those many miles downriver to our Jeep and thirty-seven miles farther down a highway to a second-rate hospital. I was a dead man if this kid went one micron further with his intentions. Actually, less than that if one considered the length of a trigger pull on a Winchester rifle, with the trigger probably already half pulled at that. ...

I saw out of the corner of my eye that Herb had retrieved his pistol from its place in the tree branches and had a steady aim on the young lad's head. That action by our best pistol shot, plus the survival training I had had at the academy, started kicking in. We were taught at the academy that in a life-threatening situation we should try to keep the assailant talking or, best of all, listening. As long as you were talking and he was listening, you were living and you could try to come up with a plan for your survival and possibly have the time to execute that plan (no pun intended).

Looking the kid right in the eye, and with a whole lot more calm than I had expected to be able to muster in a situation like this, I said, "See that man over there with the gun aimed at your head?"

The kid's eyes took a darting look and then quickly refocused their attention on me with the shaking words, "I want the gill net back." More tears, shaking, and emotion.

I knew I had to come up with something really great, *fast*, and that would be a real challenge for a rookie with very little in his life-experiences barrel. Nonetheless, I let fly with what I could mentally grab hold of in that crazy and dangerous moment of time. I said, "Son, that fellow over there with a gun aimed at your head is the sixth-best pistol shot in the state. Just before he kills you, you will see a chunk of lead smash and tear right into your eye, followed by all kinds of bright lights, followed by eternal darkness. I don't know if you know it or not, but when a bullet hits you in the head, you will be unable to pull that trigger and kill me before your body falls to the ground. Also, when that bullet hits the bone in your face, many parts of your brain and skull will fly all over me and this sandbar. When that happens, your kinfolk will not be able to gather up all those parts so you can be buried with a whole body. Do you remember what that means in your culture, to be buried without a full body for the Great Spirit to take?"

The boy's eyes never left mine but I could now see a look of wonder starting to cross his face. I continued to draw on my wide reading in Native American culture. "Without all your body parts, you will be condemned to wander the earth forever looking for the rest of you. Your family will be aware of this and saddened for the rest of their lives. In fact, I am sure the ravens and magpies will find your brain parts and eat them, precluding you from ever going to the Happy Hunting Grounds." With that, I calmly turned and walked to one side of the lad before he realized what I was doing. Being split up and with Herb still aiming his pistol at the lad, we now had the advantage. "If you try to swing your rifle at either one of us now, the officer with the gun pointed at your head will kill you in an instant! Drop the rifle, son," I commanded in a voice loud enough to get his attention.

The kid was fortunately confused and not as dedicated to killing someone at this point in his life because he now didn't have the advantage. I was sure that the part about wandering Mother Earth forever had a part in his hesitation as well. He said, but without as much conviction as before, "I want my net back."

I said, "Put down the rifle now!" The barked command had its effect, and he quickly laid the rifle down on the sandbar. Walking to it, I picked it up, let down the hammer, and unloaded it. It had only three 30-30 shells in it, but one had been in the chamber ready to go if he pulled the trigger! Sitting the lad down and with all our thoughts of breakfast melted into the air, we broke camp and extinguished our happy but unused fire.

We took the boy's rifle, and the two boats headed back downriver. Herb beached our boat and the Indian boy landed his on the familiar gill netting sandbar. Herb then marched the lad up the bank and back to the campsite. Waking up the grandfather, who was asleep beside their campfire, Herb explained what had occurred upriver. The grandfather showed little facial expression, but the look he gave his grandson was not of this world. Herb then explained that we were giving his grandson back alive and that the grandfather should try to talk some sense into him before he flew off the handle again. Herb told the grandfather his boy was more important than a gill net. I hadn't said anything to that point, and Herb turned to me and said, "Well, Tiny, any last words, or do you want to cite him for brandishing a firearm in a threatening manner?"

Looking at the grandfather, I said, "This morning the Great Spirit has given your grandson back to you so he can live a long life and take care of his grandfather in his long years. Honor what the Great Spirit has done."

The tears in the old man's eyes told the whole story, and since everyone on the river would soon know we were there, Herb decided to head back downriver to our vehicle and leave. As Herb turned to leave, I reached out and shook the hand of the surprised Indian lad before he had a chance to think about this gesture of friendship. There was surprise in the old man's eyes for just a moment, and then he said something in Yurok to me. Assuming that what he had said was at least civil, I said, "Thank you," and with that we parted company, they with the Winchester and I with the three 30-30 shells in my pants pocket, of course.

Herb and I quietly motored down the Klamath River until we reached our landing spot, both lost in thought. After our gear had been loaded in our Jeep and the boat on the trailer, we stood ready to go. Without knowing why at the moment, I walked to the edge of the river and listened to the sounds, smelled the Earth's smells, and drank in the natural beauty of the area. God, it was beautiful, and the whole area as well as the rest of my world really seemed to be very intense and in focus as I had never experienced before. The good Lord, using Herb as his instrument, had more than likely just saved my life. The life around me in that canyon that day, including my own, came to me in a rush of thanksgiving.

Turning, I could see Herb looking at me with a softer expression than I had ever seen in him. He too realized just how close the event had been to that final crossover. Without a word spoken aloud, my eyes told Herb, "Thanks." Without a word, Herb acknowledged my thought, and we both loaded up and headed for home, our job on the river done for the day.

I went on to enjoy thirty-two more years of life in the wildlife law enforcement fast lane under the guiding hand of the Great Spirit. Herb contracted cancer of the colon a short time later and died a death unfitting a man of his spirit. One of the last times I was with him, he brought up our river trip. He said, "Tiny, do you know what that old Indian grandfather said to you?"

I said, "No," and tears began to flood my eyes as I realized how close Herb was drawing to death.

"He told you to walk the Red Road," Herb replied, with a seriousness I had never seen in his eyes before.

I said, "What does that mean, Herb?"

"When you walk the Red Road, you will know what it means," he replied with a smile now softened by the tears in his own eyes.

When Herb died, he weighed about ninety-five pounds, but he still had the smile he wore when he talked to me about walking the Red Road. I have never forgotten Herb for giving me another day with my family, or for the opportunity to walk the Red Road, an expression I now understand. Herb, I have been blessed and continue to walk the Red Road to this day. May you also. ...

3

To Kill a Duck

IMMEDIATELY SOUTHWEST of the northern California town of Arcata is an extensive natural lowland pasture area surrounding a portion of Humboldt Bay. This area was once home to the mighty redwood, but of late it has been mostly inhabited by dairy farmers and cattlemen. Over time this marshy pastureland, locally called the Arcata Bottoms, had developed into a nesting and wintering ground for all manner of migratory birds, especially members of the shorebird family and countless numbers and species of waterfowl.

For as long as I lived in the Arcata area, both as a college student and later as a state Fish and Game warden, numerous wildlife violations had occurred in the Arcata Bottoms, most commonly the late shooting of waterfowl by locals during the hunting season. This was especially true for a grass-eating duck called the wigeon or baldpate. This species really liked its grass and just about anytime, especially during the evening hours, could be found feeding with relish, in great numbers, on these lush pasturelands. Why someone would want to shoot a wigeon in the first place, much less one that was feeding heavily on grass, always caused me to scratch my head in wonderment. I'm somewhat of a cook, and in the eating department I would place a grass-feeding wigeon right next to the last part of a skunk going over a fence.

Anyway, for the waterfowl hunters coming in from their long day of hunting along the edges of north Humboldt Bay and finding the air filled with hundreds of low-flying wigeon after legal shooting hours (which ended at sunset), those ducks were just too tempting a target to pass up. This was especially true for those hunters who had had a poor shooting day on the bay or its adjacent waterways. If they lingered for about thirty minutes past legal hunting hours, it was possible to easily kill several of these wigeon winging into the fields to feed. The shooters still had plenty of ambient light to shoot unless it was foggy or storming, so if they had the courage to break the Fish and Game laws in front of God and everybody, a duck dinner (albeit a nasty one) would be their reward. However, being tagged by the hardworking game wardens could also be their reward if the devil put a hitch in their giddy-up and they were a little slow in leaving the field of battle. The lumber industry being what it was in those days, with the low pay, intermittent work, and all, it wasn't uncommon to find numerous lumbermen in the bottoms past legal shooting hours, shooting waterfowl to feed their families or just for the thrill of killing under unusual circumstances. To be fair, it also was not uncommon to find local high school kids, members of the farming or dairy community, or college kids hammering away at the night-feeding waterfowl. Bottom line: when the waterfowl were present in the Arcata Bottoms in decent numbers during the fall migration, so were outlaws of every color of the cloth.

A major part of the late-shooting problem was the glare of the lights from the town of Arcata. The illumination would arc up into the perennial rain, mist, or low-lying cloud cover typical of temperate rain forests and then be reflected earthward. This phenomenon created enough artificial light to easily shoot waterfowl on any given day for up to four hours after legal shooting hours. The game warden would have his work cut out trying to locate and catch those illegally shooting waterfowl in the semidark of the night on a vast, grassy shooting area. Sometimes the culprit would be a farm dweller who would just step a few paces out his back door and bang away at the low-flying ducks winging into his fields to feed. After a few shots the farmer would gather up his ill-gotten gains and retreat into the farmhouse, often before the game warden could echo-locate and move in on that particular shooter. Other times locals aware of the many small ponds favored by the ducks would sneak up to the edges and blaze away at the birds loafing on the water in plain view. For that brief interlude of shooting, if the game warden wasn't right there or looking in that direction, the illegal duck shooters would win the round, gather up their ducks, and head for home. And so it went on into the long nights for the ducks, the outlaws, and the game wardens.

As a new game warden I used to take great delight in roaring through the bottoms, chasing and apprehending these chaps for their late-shooting violations every time they reared their heads out of the primordial ooze. Pretty soon it got to the point that I could just about zero in on anyone shooting in those bottoms because of my intimate knowledge of the landscape and the late shooters' favorite places to hunt. Once I reached that point of expertise I gave as good as I got and started to make a real difference in the night-shooting crowd. Soon the illegal shooting began to diminish, and citations were fewer and farther between. Now, some of you probably think a game warden's time might be better spent than chasing people trying to kill a few ducks during the night. Well, you might be right—especially if there were other bad guys going after endangered species, the always vulnerable migrating salmon or the like. However, endangered species were scarce in that area in those days, and by that time of year the mighty salmon had spawned and gone on to the Great River in the sky. The law is the law, and I have found over my career that wildlife outlaws are a lot like coyotes: they will take any wildlife they can get if the opportunity presents itself. So I just figured I would stop the outlaws where I found them, and the Arcata Bottoms were as good a place as any to expend my energies. In addition, there are good biological reasons for the laws to include shooting-hour limitations. The critters need some time for feeding and resting. Also, people shooting at night tend to wound a lot of birds, which end up being wasted except when found by other meat-eating critters such as foxes, skunks, and raccoons. Plus, late shooters have difficulty finding the birds they have killed in the dark, which makes the waste factor even higher. Our wildlife populations are considered a renewable natural resource, but they aren't infinitely renewable!

After several months of many successful and liberal doses of the game warden, night shooting of waterfowl in the bottoms dropped off by about 90 percent, another clear example of how the tool of law enforcement can be applied in the overall wildlife management scheme of things. But, as always seems to be the case, I had one bunch of shooters I just couldn't catch. No matter how hard I tried, they would outfox me every time. It seemed that every good late-shooting night, there would be hunting around the sewer ponds belonging to the town of Arcata. The area covered by this sewage facility was only a few acres and easy to work. However, night after night when the late shooting of waterfowl was in full swing on the sewer ponds, even after a good stalk, I would come up empty-handed. It was almost as if God were on the side of these rascals rather than standing behind the sweating, hardworking game warden! I stalked these lads many times under the cover of night, but every time I got within forty to sixty yards of them in the main sewer ponds area, they would stop shooting and disappear.

Now, the sewer ponds and adjacent buildings were illuminated with large banks of lights, and it wasn't as if I just walked up to them in front of God and everybody. No way. I would crawl the last hundred yards or so before I even got close to the illuminated area and then would get even lower to the ground, imitating a pitcher's mound because of my substantial size. But my repeated failures were uncanny—it was as if I had a beacon tied to my tail end! I would slowly rise up out of the mud and intensely look for these lads with my binoculars in the direction where I had last heard them shoot, but always to no avail. They always shot their ducks from inside the sewer pond levee, which meant I had to go up to the edge of the levee and look down into the area for the shooters. But when I poked my head up even the littlest bit, the game would be over. These folks really had my number, but it was just a matter of time before the game warden got more devious than the bad guys.

After being outfoxed for about the tenth time, I sat down and carefully went over every single angle and event. It was always two individuals shooting what sounded to me like twelve-gauge shotguns. Their shooting was not constant but spaced and calculated; it sounded to me as if they didn't shoot unless they were guaranteed a kill. With spaced shots they were less likely to draw unwanted attention, such as a game warden, into their game. Each time I had tried to creep up on them, once I felt I had blown my hand through discovery because the shooting would abruptly stop, I would stand up and quickly walk over the entire area looking for clues to my shooters' location. I would always find freshly killed ducks on the levee, laid out as if they were going to be retrieved later, and spent, freshly fired shotgun shells scattered everywhere. But no culprits. Damn! Finding the lads who were pulling the trigger was getting to be a real challenge. But I was determined to stay with it until they were mine or I died of old age. That was a dangerous state of mind for me to be in, especially if you were the bad guy shooting the duck!

After another evening of frustration and nothing but another goose egg at the sewer ponds, I met the Arcata game warden at his home. This fellow was a legend in his time, and what a time it had been. John Finnigan had thirty-four years' experience, all in the north coast area of California, during an era when wildlife law enforcement was as rough-and-tumble as it got. He was good—not pushy or the like, but he genuinely liked people, and they liked him. For these reasons he had a system of informants that wouldn't quit and possessed a nose for the bad guys that was legendary. It was only natural for me to turn to this father figure and friend for assistance in my time of need. I said, "John-O, I've got these chaps in the bottoms almost every night late-shooting ducks until all hours, and I can't catch them. These lads let me get within yards of them and then just disappear, gone, *kapoof,* just like that. It's almost like the ground swallows them up!"

John looked at me and said seriously, "Terry, only leprechauns can disappear just like that."

I said, "John, be serious. I can't catch these bastards, and it's driving me up a wall, not to mention that they're killing the hell out of the ducks, especially the canvasbacks coming into the sewer ponds at night to loaf and rest." Keep in mind that the canvasback duck had suffered a tremendous population decline over the previous twenty years, and no one knew why except possible overshooting in all its wintering areas. In California during that period there was a total shooting closure on these birds to aid their population recruitment. Hence my extreme interest in their welfare, as well as the fact that they are a unique species of wildlife.

John said, "Terry, I *am* serious!"

Overlooking John's Irish nature, I continued, "There are lights out there everywhere; the sewer pond itself is very well lit, and as a result the ducks really pour into the watered areas. That makes it a bit dicey to try and sneak up on these chaps, but I'm sure it can be done. I just can't seem to find a way to successfully do it."

After listening to my tale of woe, John said, "Well, Tiny, let's give her a rest and try it several days from now. By Thursday we're supposed to get a storm, and that would be a natural for these lads under the lights of the sewer pond."

I agreed and we parted company, but not before John had offered and I had accepted a deep glass of Old Bushmills Irish whiskey. It burned going down just like the gall I had had to swallow over not being able to capture a couple of late shooters without some assistance. But I did feel better now that I had a Plan B and a damn good partner.

The following Thursday found the German-Irish team of Grosz and Finnigan quietly sitting in a darkened patrol car hidden alongside an abandoned shed next to the sewer pond. We had come through several "friendly" yards to arrive at our hiding spot, and it was a good one. John knew the folks who owned the property we had sneaked through without any lights, and he had alerted them to our plans. They were more than comfortable with the scheme and had gladly agreed to our use of their land. From our vantage point we watched every duck entering and leaving the sewer ponds like feathered cannon shot, and we weren't likely to be discovered unless the lads who had been doing the shooting stumbled over our hidden car en route to the sewer pond. Sitting back as the light rain drummed musically on our vehicle roof, we waited to see if we were going to have some mystery guests for the evening.

Sure as God made little green apples, though we hadn't seen anyone arrive, the shooting started about eight P.M., at least three and a half hours after legal shooting time had ended! Over the next several minutes, John and I watched small flocks of ducks whistling into the sewer pond area to rest, only to watch one or two fall each time to the guns. Finally six canvasback ducks zipped up over the levee from Humboldt Bay and quickly landed out of sight on one of the sewer ponds. Three quick shots and no birds leaving the pond told us they had been shot on the water and more than likely all killed. That did it! As if on cue, John and I quickly jumped out of the car. Moving quickly on foot to the edge of the levee surrounding the sewer ponds, staying behind one neighbor's tall wooden fence and then another neighbor's laundry hanging on an outdoors clothesline, we entered the fenced-in area of the sewer pond. John quickly moved up onto one side but below the top of one levee, and I took the other side. Now by damnit, there was no way out for the lads, I thought. We had seen them, or at least their shotgun muzzle flashes, on the bay side, or southwest side, of the sewer pond levee from the patrol car just moments before. I believed that the only way out for these lads was to plow through waist-deep mud (if the tide was low) or to swim out (if the tide was high) into the bay. As we moved down along the levee edge and out of sight toward the southwest edge of the pond, the shooting continued as if these were the last ducks in the world and they had to be killed before they migrated to Mexico. Through my binoculars as I lay on the outside edge of the levee in tall grasses, I saw a vague human shape on the far south side of the sewer pond in the misting rain and dancing shadows. He became especially visible when he shot because the flash from the end of his shotgun barrel clearly gave away his position.

My observations were interrupted when John called me on the portable radio and asked if I was ready to hit the top of the levee and put a stop to this foolishness. I told him, "More than ready; let's go." With that, up onto the levee in full view we went, not more than forty yards from our targets. With our appearance in front of God and everybody, the shooting immediately stopped, but it was too late for these chaps. John was on one side of the sewer pond, I was on the other, and Humboldt Bay with the tide running out was on the southwest end. They were ours unless they chose to swim across the north bay, I gleefully thought. If they tried that, they would more than likely drown in the cold water or be towed under in the tidal currents. John and I smugly walked down the sides of the main pond, but when we met at the end, we discovered that the bad guys weren't in the bag. We looked for half an hour all along both sides of the levees and into the bay, but to no avail. As usual, the levee was strewn with freshly killed ducks and spent shotgun shells, but no one was there. Looking out into the sewer pond itself, I spotted six dead, floating canvasbacks not twenty yards from the shore. Damn, I thought; they sure as shooting had killed every one of the bunch John and I had seen flying in from the bay minutes before. They had done it again—no tracks, no boat on the south side to float away from us, nothing but the carnage left behind by a couple of pretty savvy outlaws who were apparently nonexistent!

I looked over at John as he muttered something about leprechauns and said, "John, ain't no way Jack these chaps could have gotten away from us. No way, leprechauns or not." Leaving John and his leprechauns to guard the southwest end of the dike, I went back to the levee near the middle of the pond and started slowly walking back toward John, carefully shining my flashlight along the edges of the pond and into the large clumps of cattails along the bank. I had done this many times in the past with no result, but I just had to find these chaps before they drove me nuts, so another try was in order. Suddenly, with the beam of my flashlight at the inside edge of the pond where the tall grass was folded over from its leafy weight and touching the water, I spotted what looked like a floating head. *There was a goddamned human head in the sewer pond with its eyes closed!* I could hardly believe my eyes, but there it was, partially hidden under the tall grasses. Hell, I damn near jumped out of my skin when I first saw it, thinking someone had cut a person's head off and tossed it into the sewer pond.

Getting my wits back and my hair laid down on my head, I took another careful look, and there was the solution to the riddle in plain view. These guys had been eluding me by slipping into the sewer pond full of human waste up to their necks under the inside levee-bank grasses. Here they had remained in hiding, waiting for me to tire of the game of hide-and-seek and leave. They knew full well I would give this putrid area only a cursory glance at best. After all, who in their right mind would go swimming in a sewer pond in the dead of winter? After I had left on those other nights, they would come out, gather up the dead ducks that I had missed or they had hidden earlier, and go their merry ways with probably more than several duck dinners in hand.

Without letting the lad know I had spotted him, I called John over for a look. It was really amazing to see this fellow standing there up to his neck in human waste at midnight with his eyes closed and grass pulled over most of his head, all for a few lousy ducks. It was like burying your head in the sand—and bad-smelling sand, I must say!

John took one look at the floating head and, after he got himself and all his leprechauns in order, yelled, "Hey you—you in the sewer pond. Get your ass up here right now." The eyes and the head did not move. John added, "If you aren't up here within the next few seconds, I will consider you dead and start shooting at your head with my pistol for target practice."

That did it. The eyes on the floating head opened, and a twenty-one-year-old kid dragged himself, slowly and with much effort, out of the sewer pond and up onto the bank. He was absolutely covered with sewage. It was awful! He had chunks of human effluent matted in his hair and smeared on his face, and his chest-high waders were almost completely full of the best of what the sewer lagoon had to offer. He was so large owing to the full waders that he looked like the Pillsbury Dough Boy, but with a slightly worse color and smell! Shaking my head in disbelief as the first lad hoisted himself out of the sewer basin, I went looking for his partner. It took only a few moments now that I knew where to look before I found the second man just a few feet from his evil-smelling companion, also in the "soup" up to his neck with both eyes closed. In short order he too was ordered out of the pond and up onto the levee. Once we got control of the situation and had their ducks and shotguns all laid out, we took a really good look at our cold late shooters, who were now shaking like dogs crapping peach pits: two damn dumb kids with human effluent plastered all over their bodies and duck weed draped here and there for additional decoration. What a fine picture they made. We had them strip down to their shorts and gather up their gear and then walked them back to John's station wagon. Loading them and their filthy clothes and gear onto the extended tailgate of the car, we took them to the Arcata firehouse, where several firemen sprayed them, their clothes, and their chest-highs down with the hoses. After a couple of phone calls two embarrassed moms from Arcata came to the firehouse with clean, dry clothes, and the lads were then taken to the local clinic for a few shots in the hind end for whatever diseases might lurk in that pond full of "human essence." They also got a few "shots" in their wallets for late shooting of waterfowl, possessing over-limits of ducks (thirteen over), and taking a closed-season species (canvasbacks). They each paid $150 for the late shooting, $135 for the over-limit, and $100 for the closed-season taking of a protected species, or $385 for their night's outing. That may not seem like much by today's standards, but in the 1960s it was a bundle. As a game warden, I was making only $516 per month before taxes.

It amazed me that these men wanted ducks so badly that they were willing to go up to their chins in sewage to avoid being caught. This case taught one very green game warden to learn to expect the unexpected. I'm still alive today after more than thirty-two hard, exciting years as a game warden and special agent, so I guess little lessons like this one must have sunk in and helped me survive.

These lads turned out to be juniors at Humboldt State College majoring in wildlife management. After being found guilty of these wildlife violations in the Arcata Justice Court, both changed their majors. They must have known that getting a job in the wildlife management field, which was hugely competitive at the time, was now all but impossible. Before they were able to graduate and partly owing to poor grades, they were drafted into the U.S. Army. Maybe there, I grimly thought, they would be able to make good use of their swamp experiences in the sewer pond. But apparently that wasn't the case because neither man came home from Vietnam. Both were reported killed in the Mekong Delta as they worked their way neck-deep through a swamp toward a Vietcong stronghold. Apparently the VC were better than I at detecting people hiding in swamps, and at shooting them like sitting ducks. ...

May the good Lord take a liking to them. Even though they gave me and the late-flying ducks fits, they deserved better than that.

4

A Rainy Night and a
Bleeding Trunk

THE JARRING RING of the telephone brought me from my deep midnight sleep to the instant stage of readiness that comes from being a Fish and Game warden. Grabbing it before it could ring again and wake Donna, my bride of just three years, I quietly said, "Terry here." The matter-of-fact voice on the other end was the Humboldt County sheriff's office dispatcher, telling me that Warren Duke, another North Coast Squad game warden, needed me to give him a hand apprehending a spotlighter he was currently watching from afar as the poacher carried out his deadly business. Through the dispatcher, Duke was asking me to come into the area from behind the poacher, thereby covering his escape route and preventing a high-speed run for home once the spotlighter discovered he was being watched. Duke wanted me to slowly patrol my way without the use of lights up from the Snow Camp area (not far from the town of Blue Lake) and through a wide spot in the road called Korbel, crossing over the Mad River and heading toward the Kneeland area, just east of Eureka. In the process I would drive the interconnected county back roads and numerous dirt feeder roads in the area in a classic pincher movement.

Earlier in the evening Duke had been staked out high in the Kneeland prairie area looking for spotlighters (hunters who take deer illegally at night with the use of a high-intensity spotlight and a rifle, usually a small-caliber gun because it makes less noise).

Because he was high enough to overlook and hear any activity in the Snow Camp area, across the Mad River from where he was sitting, his patience had been rewarded with the sight of a vehicle working a light and the sound of several rifle shots coming from that side of the mountain range. He said that if I could move toward him from the Snow Camp side of the mountain, "flushing out" the interconnecting roads, it might sweep the night shooters ahead of me and into his arms for capture. Failing that, I might run across them as they tried to gut their kill or double back with their ill-gotten game and catch them myself. From his position, Duke could warn me if he saw from their headlight movements that these fellows were doubling back, and on which roads, so I could be alerted before having to make a head-on car stop (the most dangerous kind). Either way, the shooters would be discovered and, if in violation of the law, arrested and hauled off to the county slammer for their misdeeds—a classic Christians-one-lions-nothing ending. It sounded like a good plan to me, and since I had nothing else to do but sleep I gave the Humboldt County dispatcher my estimated time of arrival in the Snow Camp area and hung up.

Rolling over to gently kiss my sleeping wife good-bye for the thousandth such crazy time in the morning, I was surprised to find her gone. A light in the kitchen told me that she had risen and was fixing me some food. She knew full well that I might not have another opportunity to eat during the next twenty-four hours. There aren't many women like her in this world, if any, I thought; and just think, I was the one lucky enough to marry her. As I swung my legs out from under the warm covers, those feelings were intensified by the good smell of her home cooking now emanating from the kitchen. Thanking God for my outstanding cook (even better than my mom, who was at one time the world's greatest), I shoveled my carcass into my uniform. Putting on my heavy leather boots in case I had to run someone down through the forest and strapping on my service belt containing my handcuffs, extra ammunition, and Smith and Wesson .44 magnum pistol (purchased for me by my bride in 1963), I moved to the bathroom to comb my thinning hair and try to clean up God's creation. One must look his best for the poachers, I thought, even if God failed to provide any assistance in that department. Maybe He had put so much energy into creating my wife that He was a spent unit by the time He got to me, at least in the beauty department. I headed for the kitchen and wrapped my arms around the cook as she busied herself by the stove, giving her a great big bear hug as only a man my size could before settling down for a quick breakfast of six eggs, a loaf-sized helping of spuds, a pound of side pork, and two thick slices of Donna's great homemade bread (the world's best) loaded with peanut butter and mounds of her homemade blackberry jam. With this repast fit for a king, or at least a larger-than-life game warden, and another big hug for the blue-eyed cook, out the door I went with the words "Please be careful" softly trailing me. God, how I loved that woman, and still madly do to this day after only thirty-nine years of married life. There really is a heaven on earth for some of us *really* lucky ones!

Cranking up my patrol vehicle, I checked the fuel gauge to make sure my gas tank was full (a good game warden fills it at the end of every day just in case) and slowly moved out into the darkened, rain-wet street. Taking a shortcut toward Snow Camp on the back roads, I grabbed my radio mike and went 10-8 (on duty) with the Humboldt County sheriff's office. Then I hooked up with Duke on the Fish and Game car-to-car short-range radio frequency to see if he had heard any more shots or had any change in the plan. Normally I would not have been able to reach him if he was more than a few miles away because of the low-powered radio frequency, but because he was high up on the mountain, he could reach out farther on his car-to-car frequency and make contact with me on a fairly secure channel. He told me that he had heard several more shots and it appeared that the shooters had moved from the Snow Camp area and were now traveling down through the vast Mad River valley floor between our two positions. Visualizing these details in my mind, I calculated that the poachers were moving closer to his stakeout area. He hadn't been able to locate their headlights or spotlight because of the dense stands of timber they were in but had made a good echo location on the last series of shots and was pretty sure of their current, albeit moving, position. Damn, I thought, that meant an additional dozen or so roads I would have to run out one at a time in order to try to trap these fellows if they kept moving away from me toward Duke. Duke also said he now had Humboldt County Deputy Sheriff's Officer Glenn Ragon with him.

That was a good move, I thought. Warren and I were both green rookies, and having a sage backup like Glenn in our camp was a damn smart idea. Glenn was a sawed-off son of a gun, but none came tougher. He was an ex–navy diver who was very experienced in dealing with people, especially hard cases, was strong as a bull even at his age, and was not inclined to take crap from anyone, especially if they were on the wrong side of the fence! If the bad guys were moving toward the Kneeland area and were wrong as far as the law went, they had chosen the wrong pond to paddle around in. This was Glenn's assigned area as a sheriff's deputy, and he didn't cotton to anyone breaking the law in his backyard. Pound for pound, the only thing tougher than Glenn was a rhino, and you had to piss off the rhino to get him to Glenn's level of tough when Glenn was just at "idle." In addition, Glenn knew that entire backcountry like the palm of his hand. If anyone was back there doing what they shouldn't be doing, it was just a matter of time before they were brought to ground by this tenacious officer. Last but not least, whenever Glenn shot a rifle, riot shotgun, or pistol, something dropped. If the detail we were now working came down to that, it would be good for Duke to have Glenn in his corner because Duke was one of the poorer shots in the squad and couldn't hit his hind end with a hand ax, or with his service revolver for that matter.

Finally reaching the Snow Camp area, I switched off my headlights and used my cut-off switches to turn off all my other lights (so my brake lights wouldn't go on when I hit the brakes, giving me away as I stealthy closed in on the unsuspecting poachers). The absence of all artificial light would let my night vision develop until it was almost as sharp as a ring-tailed cat's. Letting my eyes start to adjust to the darkness under the moonlit and intermittently cloudy sky, I put in a mouthful of good old Redman chewing tobacco, applied the gas, and scuttled down the road with a flourish and a hunting grin of expectation.

There is nothing like hunting the most dangerous game, your fellow man. Modern-day humans have lost much of their primal hunting ability, but they still retain the age-old commitment to being the ultimate predator, and today's technology makes that pursuit a deadly one. It doesn't take much to send species skidding into the black hole of extinction, and it seems that much of humankind is intent on heading everything, eventually including our own species, in that direction. However, the one thing most poachers have forgotten or don't give much thought to is the hunting skill of those of us representing the "thin green line." We routinely chased those on the other side of the legal fence and in the process sharpened our primal skills starting from our first day on the job. Over time those of us who really get into the bowels of this profession become almost as good as feral cats at stalking and catching those whose survival skills are a little bit rusty. But not all poachers are slow on the uptake; many are so efficient at the game of killing that it can take years and a lot of lads carrying badges to run such chaps to ground. ... Tonight, however, it seemed that I was stalking the plain old garden-variety poacher out to have a good time rather than the (potentially more dangerous) serious commercial market hunter or smuggler of wildlife. Man, was I soon to be jerked up by the stacking swivel for harboring those less than cautious thoughts.

Moving through the Humboldt County backcountry was always a joy, day or night, even when I was distracted by the nasty business of chasing outlaws. The country was pretty much logged over, the giant redwoods, Douglas fir, and Sitka spruce having fallen to human saws since the late 1800s. But the land still had a beauty I have never seen equaled or enjoyed as much in my world full of experiences and travels, which have been considerable. From mosses and lichens through mare's tails to the remaining redwoods, it is truly a land of enchantment carpeted with green, yellow, and brown hues. Even the few old remaining redwood stumps with ferns, salal, huckleberry, and many other plants growing out of the rotting wood of their remaining greatness lend a magical essence to the temperate rain forest. The climate is mostly exceedingly wet, and tonight was no different. Small patches of fog greeted me as I spun along the dark, wet back trails and roads. A ring-tailed cat zipped across the road, and dozens of mice followed suit according to their pleasure along the many miles of dirt and asphalt I traveled. My still developing night vision hinted at a small, waddling dark form in the middle of the road, and I quickly flicked on my headlights to reveal a mountain beaver, a unique, shy, small furred creature (totally unlike the common beaver) that many people do not even know exists and would not recognize if they saw it. Drinking in that rare experience, I turned off my headlights while the beaver safely ambled off the road into greener pastures, then sat there for several moments letting my eyes re-adjust to the velvet darkness. Once again comfortable with my night vision, off I went, remembering my original mission. How-ever, Mother Nature continued to entertain me. At one point a black bear ambled down the road in the partial moonlight in front of my patrol car. He was large (maybe 450 pounds), and his fat rolled from side to side with each rocking step as my headlights glistened off the luster of his coat and reflected a blue glint from his eyes when he plunged off the bank and into my zone of memories. All my windows were rolled down so I could listen for any close-in shooting as I moved from one adventure to another and smell the many odors of damp, rotting vegetation, perfumed with the ever-present musk of the occasional striped or spotted skunk. Topping off the list of smells was the pungent aroma of the bracken ferns that cloaked the area. Damn, it was good to be alive, and though it was early in the morning after just a few hours of sleep, I appre-ciated that God-given fact.

Regardless of my joy in the moment, I had a job to do and com-menced searching as I came to the first intersection of a spidery network of ranch, logging, and backcountry roads. Usually without lights, I began heading down every road until I reached its end or a locked gate, at which point I would turn around and head back to the main county road, moving on toward Duke's position until I came to another side road and repeated the process. For the most part, the roads were short and easily pushed out. But some were old muddy logging roads, and when I came across the first puddle of water in the ruts of such a road I would check it with a flashlight beam let out sparingly between my fingers. If the water in the puddle was clear, I would know that no one had been through recently, so I would backtrack to the main county road. The same tactic applied to muddy roads—if the mud had not been disturbed with fresh tire tracks for some time, I would backtrack and continue down the main feeder road until I came to the next side road. When several dirt roads fingered off in different directions, I would pull an old game warden trick by gunning my engine and digging out a tire mark across the entrance of each road. Then I would go down one road at a time, returning each time to the beginning of the maze of roads, where I would examine the tire track across the head of the next road. If there were no fresh tire marks across my dug-out track, I would push on down that road, knowing no one had come out that way while I was pushing out another road. If they had, it would have been short work to follow the fresh tracks, especially if they pulled out onto the county road and left their muddy tracks on the asphalt. Then, of course, the race would be on! Keep in mind that the need for such maneuvers was pretty clear. Often a poacher will hide at the end of a deserted road until the coast is clear, or use the quiet of such an area to gut out, quarter, and hide the illegal game in his vehicle before he ventures forth. The road-cutting trick, if done correctly, is of great service to the pursuer, and the outlaws don't usually anticipate this strategy in the heat of the moment. The country I was in was pretty much empty during the early-morning hours except for a few ranches dotted here and there. So finding anyone back there at that time of day would usually lead to a stop and inspection unless I recognized a rancher coming home late or the like.

I pushed out the roads on my side of the mountain across from Duke's stakeout location, to no avail. Starting the long climb up from Mad River, I called Duke on the radio and asked if he had seen any headlights in my neck of the woods. "None other than your own," he responded in a disappointed voice. As I pushed out the roads in my area, I had occasionally turned on my headlights just for a moment so Duke could get a fix on my position before I turned them off again. With Duke on the high ground, it was easy to work the backcountry as we were doing and remain undiscovered. The only time this kind of thing got a little dicey was when you went from a moonlit patch of road to one darkly covered by the forest canopy—or found a poacher running the same road without lights as well.

Undismayed by the latter prospect and propelled by the thrill of the chase, I continued on. There were still dozens of places where the lads could slip off the roads to gut out their animals or just plain hide, and I looked forward to checking each and every one of them. However, I would be patient and take my time so as not to do something foolish.

Earlier, after turning down into the canyon below Duke's position, I had gotten that gut feeling that often comes to law enforcement officers when something special is in the wind. I don't know how to describe the feeling, but when it manifests itself it is almost physical. If the officer wants to retire in one living piece, he'd best learn to pay heed to this sensation. I had always been blessed with feelings of this nature and was now beginning to hone them through my profession. I would bide my time and let this feeling work itself out to where it needed to go. Even as new to this game of wildlife protection as I was, I had discovered that this feeling usually came with something attached. In stalking any potentially dangerous animal, one has to be patient, and right then, because of that gut feeling, I was one of the most patient and careful sons of bitches in the valley.

Several hours later, having run out just about every damn road between me and Duke, I dismissed my gut feeling as a false alarm based on the eagerness of the chase and began to relax. Coming around a turn in the road below where Warren and Glenn were staked out and not having seen anyone, I let the devil in me take over. I knew full well that I was in plain view from where Warren was staked out, so I stopped by an open meadow, took out my spotlight, and zipped the beam across the meadow like any good self-respecting spotlighter. Warren was on the radio instantly, asking for my position in an excited, high-pitched voice that betrayed his emotions. "Terry, what is your location? Hurry, what is your location?" I gave him one miles away in the canyon below. "Terry," he squeaked, "we have the spotlighter right below us, not a hundred yards away!"

I said, "Do you want me to move up faster?"

"No, no, no," he quickly replied. "We can catch this one."

I knew damn well Warren would never share in the capture of so fine a case as a spotlighter, and I laughed to myself. Warren, I thought, get greedy and the bear will take a chunk out of your hind end if you are not careful. Taking out my pistol to add frosting to the cake, I fired a shot into the air like a poacher shooting at a deer. My state Fish and Game radio really came alive then.

"Terry, he just shot, he just shot!" Duke bellowed into the mike.

Glenn had to be really enjoying *this*, I thought. "Well, catch the son of a buck, then."

"I am," he said. "I am."

Over the radio I could hear the sound of his patrol car engine racing up to about a million RPMs and had to laugh. I could see my rookie partner slamming into the turns and gunning down the straightaways, hell-bent on the capture of the hated poacher, and I had to chuckle at someone even greener than I was. Turning off my spotlight, I sped a short distance down the muddy road and zipped into a small stand of Douglas fir that hid the patrol car from view. "Have you got him yet?" I innocently asked over the radio.

"No, he disappeared, almost like he was able to hear us talking on the radio," said Warren.

"That's impossible," I said. "They can't copy our car-to-car transmissions."

"I know," he said, his voice heavy with disappointment, "but he is gone like a ghost."

By now I was just about rolling on the floorboards of the patrol car. That damn devil always managed to grab me at the worst possible moments, at least to some folks' way of thinking. ... I came out of the trees, balls to the wall, lights on high beam, and sped right past where Duke had just pulled off the road to hide again in the hope that his poacher would resurface and come by to be apprehended.

"There he goes," yelled Warren on the radio, and out from his hiding place he came, red light, siren, squealing tires, and all. I let him pull me over, and you should have seen the look on his face when he found out it was only me. Even tough old Glenn, who I later found suspected my antics, was laughing like there was no tomorrow. Boy, was Warren red-faced. Hell, I would have been red-faced too if someone had sucked me out of my hole like a snapping turtle as I had just done to Duke. I sure as the dickens couldn't figure out where our spotlighters had gone, but I sure as hell had found the local game warden.

Regrouping, we all moved back to Warren's high mountain overlook, and after a few more bouts of laughter over the preceding events we lapsed into silence, lost in individual thoughts, for about half an hour. Warren finally broke the mood and said, "I have to get. I have court later today." Glenn said he needed to be getting along as well. I told the lads to split; I was more than wide awake now and planned to stay until daylight and then backtrack my previous route. I just didn't see how I could have missed someone shooting and driving along those roads unless it was an outlaw rancher shooting off his own property or back porch. I intended to satisfy my curiosity.

Warren and Glenn worked their way out of the meadow and down the county road toward Eureka. After they disappeared the velvet black mountainside once again grew silent, and I sat there with the great joy that comes from the quiet of the night and the gut feeling I had dismissed earlier still portending things to come. This time that feeling was really on deck, more than just rattling around in my head and guts. It was strong enough to almost be a physical presence. Having learned in my short career to identify that feeling and to trust it when it reached that level of intensity, I began to get excited as I awaited the coming event, whatever it was. This feeling manifests itself in many different ways. For example, sometimes when I am driving down a highway and decide to pass someone or change lanes, the feeling that I shouldn't do so is occasionally so strong that I change my mind, and within seconds a danger will appear that would have tested my driving abilities severely had I followed my original impulse. And when someone phones my home, about 75 percent of the time I can tell Donna who the caller is, especially if it is one of our family members, before she answers. Now it is almost a family joke because she will answer the call with "Hello" and the person's name, and they will immediately ask if we have some kind of caller ID system. Those kinds of instincts are part of the reason I have always insisted that I have two guardian angels.

It was about four A.M. when the clouds began to thickly shroud the mountains around me and a misty rain, typical of the Pacific Northwest, started to fall. During that time several doe deer moved by in front of my vehicle, scarcely paying heed. A skunk walked by my door and, after closely examining my left front tire, ambled off into the night, leaving his essence in the rain-soaked vegetation for several minutes afterward. My uneasiness continued, but I began to feel as if I should move on. Since the fog and rain clouds were now obscuring the country below me, there was no use sitting there when I couldn't see. Starting up my patrol car and leaving all my lights in the cut-off mode, I slowly moved back down the road I had driven up earlier in the morning. The rain was falling a little harder as I headed down the paved mountain road toward several backcountry ranches near the Mad River. Rounding one of a series of sharp turns about forty minutes later, I caught the flash of headlights coming up the mountain toward me. I couldn't get off the narrow county road to hide and make a car stop from the rear after they passed me (the safest method—if there is such a thing when one is alone), so I stopped my vehicle in the middle of the road and waited. The other car slowed, and I could see through my binoculars that it stopped about a hundred yards below me while one man got out of the car to urinate. In a few moments he got back in, and the vehicle recommenced its rather slow journey toward me in the ever-increasing rain. My gut feeling was having a heyday, let me tell you. Once the slowly moving car swung through the last turn and its headlights illuminated my darkened patrol car, on went my red light and high beams. The other car paused and then stopped just yards away.

I was out of my car with flashlight in hand and quickly moving toward the driver's side of their vehicle before they rolled to a stop. My headlights illuminated three men, all in their mid- to late forties, sitting in the front seat of an old four-door Buick shading their eyes with their hands in an attempt to see what the hell was going on. Strange, I thought, that all three were sitting in the front and no one was using the spacious backseat. Other than the hour of the morning and the three of them all jammed into the front seat, nothing appeared out of the ordinary at first glance. However, my instinct was clearly telling me this was the one. They continued shielding their eyes because my headlights were blinding them, and now they had my five-cell flashlight beam coming in the driver's-side window as well. That was good because I needed to get a better look-see to figure out why they were in this part of the backcountry at this hour on a rainy night.

Moving closer to the driver's door but staying behind the center door post, I said, "Good morning, gentlemen, state Fish and Game warden. You folks live hereabouts?" To a man, they just looked toward the voice behind the strong flashlight beam and did not respond. Something was dead wrong here, I said to myself as the hair on the back of my neck began to stand up. Ignoring the lack of an answer, I quickly turned my flashlight into the backseat of their car. Lying there in front of God and everybody was a spotlight, a spare tire, and some tools, all on the floorboards, and a bolt-action rifle laid across the seat. Bringing my flashlight beam into their eyes again, I asked, "You fellows been hunting?"

The driver finally broke the silence and said, "No, that stuff was left in the car by my boy after he got back from target practice yesterday."

Noticing for the first time how low the rear of their car was sitting, I stepped back for a closer look and saw blood dripping out of the trunk and onto the pavement. Rainstorm soaking the hell out of me or not, it really caught my eye—it was not just dripping, it was *bleeding,* there was so much blood trickling out! The car was sitting almost down on its springs, a sure sign of a heavy load in the trunk. Damn, I said to myself; Terry, you shouldn't have missed that clue earlier. My guts were racing super-hot now as I kept my gun hand close to the magnum resting comfortably on my right hip, all the while thanking my bride for buying me a hand cannon instead of a smaller-caliber pistol.

Returning my flashlight to their eyes, I said, "What's bleeding in the trunk, lads?"

All three of the men just sat there and stared at me. I felt that the situation still wasn't under my control, and I certainly wasn't comfortable with it, not by a long shot. I couldn't know what was in that trunk, but it was bleeding like a stuck hog, and that certainly had my attention. On top of that I was alone with three very sullen men on a mountain road at four in the morning, and the land around us was private for several hundred thousand acres in each direction. I knew they didn't live here or anywhere nearby because I knew most of the area ranchers.

Moving to a safer position by the driver's-side door so I could see every movement they made, I asked again, "What is in the trunk, lads?" in a voice that told them my question had better receive a decent answer.

This time the driver, a man weighing about 240 pounds with as mean a face as I had ever seen, said, "Look, asshole, why don't you just get the hell out of our faces? We were just out for a drive and a little beer drinking until you, your flashlight, and your big mouth showed up."

"Gentlemen," I said, "this rig isn't going anywhere until I find out what is in that bleeding trunk."

The driver looked past the flashlight beam into my eyes. He said, "Look, asshole, the three of us have spent more years in prison than you are old. If you want to get any older and not have the crap kicked out of you, just bug off. You might be a big son of a bitch, but the three of us can kick your butt before you can ever get to your radio and call for help. And by the time help arrives up here in this godforsaken place, the coyotes will be eating your cooling guts." There was a short pause, and then he said, "Your move, prick."

He was right, I thought, except that he had forgotten "Judge Smith and his six jurors" hanging on my hip. As if he had not said enough, the driver continued, "Now, Mr. Game Warden, what is it going to be—a damn good butt-kicking, or are you going to move that car of yours off the road so we can be on our way?"

I could clearly smell alcohol on his breath and realized what that kind of false courage could lead to, especially if they felt they had the edge. Quickly taking a step back, I said, "Neither. You are under arrest for threatening an officer of the state of California, and quite possibly for what is bleeding in that trunk." As I spoke those words, the .44 magnum came out so fast that I don't think they saw me clear leather. The weapon naturally was aimed at the head of the driver, but over the short distance separating us I could just as easily bring it to bear on the other two. All of a sudden their eyes got as big as dinner plates. It is absolutely amazing how much white can show around the human eye under some circumstances, I thought.

Quickly stepping a little farther away for a better defensive position, I said, "Out of the car, gentlemen, and the first man to make any kind of funny move will be bleeding as badly as your trunk. Out the driver's side door with all of you *now*." I added, loudly enough for all my guardian angels to hear, "*I will kill the very first son of a bitch that doesn't follow that order exactly!*" With my hand cannon pointed at them and the rather serious tone of my voice, I achieved truly amazing results, almost magical, if you get my drift. The three fellows tumbled out the driver's door as if there were points for the first one out and stood in front of me like soldiers on parade in the cold, driving rain. If the moment hadn't been so serious, I would have laughed at the sight of three two-hundred-pounders all trying to come out the door at the same time!

I could see in an instant from the looks in their eyes that they realized I was now in a quandary. How was I going to safely search them and put them in handcuffs without one of them jumping me while I was distracted by the others? Before they could consider the situation any further, I coldly said, "Turn around."

They did as they were told, and then the driver said, "Look, prick, let us go and we won't have to kill you."

This chap was starting to get under my skin! I said, "Listen carefully because I will only say it once. All of you very slowly drop to your knees and then lie out flat on the road face down with your hands outstretched, fingers spread. If you fail to do what I just asked or deviate from the instructions in any way, expect your head to blow up like a watermelon when this 250-grain .44 magnum bullet strikes the bone and then the surface of the highway." My tone was the selling point. I was outnumbered by what appeared to be three very bad dudes to one and couldn't get to my radio, or any help for that matter, without giving them the advantage. The more I let them move around, the more chances they had at making a go for me, and then it just might be a bad day all around! I think the only thing that saved us all was that they finally realized that to err was to die on that wet road out in the damn middle of nowhere. Of course, now that I think about it, it seems that we all die out in the damn middle of nowhere. ... Down they went, grumbling all the way about the wet and cold, and we stayed right there until just after seven A.M., when a school bus came by.

I was soaked and damn near frozen stiff. The lads on the ground were in even worse shape—they could hardly move because they were in the initial stages of hypothermia. The bus driver slowed, then stopped the bus, vaulted down the steps, and ran over to me. "Mister, do you need some help?"

"Yes," I said through clattering teeth. "Go back to the closest ranch house and call Deputy Sheriff Glenn Ragon. If he is home, ask him to come down here to give me a hand. If he isn't, send me any armed rancher or cowboy you run across with blood in his eye."

He backed the bus down the hill to a turnout and was off with twenty little faces looking out their steamy windows at the drama being played out on that wet road. Ten minutes later I heard a vehicle coming at a high rate of speed, and it turned out to be a local cowboy from one of the ranches. Boy, was I glad to see him. He leaped out of his pickup with a 30-30 Winchester in his hand. Quickly racking a round into the chamber, he said, "Which one of the sons of bitches do you want me to shoot, officer?" Boy, my kind of guy, I thought. It didn't take me long to get the handcuffs and leg irons on the lads with that kind of "top cover." Once they were secured, I began to relax. Only then did I realize just how cold I was as I tried twice without success before finally resnapping my firearm into the holster. I tried rubbing my fingers back to life and began a search of my three prisoners after asking the cowboy to watch them closely with his rifle. I discovered two pistols hidden on the lads and one eight-inch hunting knife strapped to the hunting boot of the smallest of the three. No doubt about it, they were not nice people, and a subsequent check through Humboldt County sheriff's office criminal files confirmed that feeling. All three were ex-felons, which meant they were in violation of federal law by having firearms on their persons and in their possession.

Now that my cold, wet, and handcuffed folks weren't going anywhere, the cowboy and I got their car keys and checked the rifle in the backseat. It was loaded, a violation of state law. Then we popped open their trunk. Lo and behold, we found a 350-pound steer gutted out and stuffed, and I do mean *stuffed,* inside. The brand on the beef showed that it belonged to a rancher on the Snow Camp side of the mountain, and it appeared that the animal had been shot several times. I later discovered that they had killed the animal and thrown it into the trunk in order to get out of the area where they had shot it before the owner came along and caught them. Then they had driven out a road next to a darkened ranch house (which was why I had missed them; I had not checked around the ranch houses) and during a driving rain had gutted the steer *while it was still in the trunk,* almost in that chap's backyard. The trunk was still dripping when I found them because of all the slopover from the gutting process. They thought the joke would be on the rancher when dawn came and he discovered a large gut pile in his driveway. That took a lot of gall or no brains, I thought. Most ranchers in that part of the country would just as soon start shooting rather than wait to ask any questions if they came across such an incident while it was going on. ...

I told the three men they were under arrest for cattle rustling unless they could provide some on-the-spot papers showing that the animal had been properly transferred from the original owner to the trunk of their car. Three sullen faces told me that any demonstration of a legal transfer would not be forthcoming. Glenn was already on his way to pick up his prisoners, so I ordered up a wrecker to haul the vehicle with the steer off the mountain. Once it arrived, I followed it down into Eureka and the evidence lockup at the sheriff's office, with the cowboy happily riding shotgun in my patrol car with his trusty Winchester. After the lads were booked and processed, I tended to an inventory of the vehicle. I found nothing out of the ordinary except the steer, and in order to get the stiffened-up critter out of the trunk I had to borrow a chain saw and bring the beef, hide and all, out in chunks. Cattle rustling in California, as in most states, is a felony, and my three lads stayed in the Humboldt County jail to await trial.

All three were found guilty of the rustling charges and sentenced accordingly. I don't remember the amount of fines or time, but they suffered the consequences of their ways and also had to make restitution. As was typical in those days, they were not charged for being ex-felons in possession of firearms. If the crime committed had not involved the use of those weapons against humankind, those charges routinely were not stacked on top of the core charges. The county attorney did not tack on any charges for threatening a peace officer either. He told me that first of all, I was so damn big that a jury would not believe I had actually been threatened by the three smaller men. He also said that he had a strong enough charge in the rustling violation that he preferred to stick with that. It's hell to think a beef is worth more than a human being, but who was I to challenge the legal system? Maybe he was right. After all, a 350-pound beef was worth a lot of money in those days. ...

All three of the lads served their full terms in jail, and I never saw any of them in the field again. But I have often thought of that episode up on the mountain and wondered what would have happened if things had gone the other way. What if that trunk hadn't been bleeding so profusely that rainy night? What if I had been less alert? What if the gut feeling hadn't been so strong? What if I had been smaller? Hmmmmmm? Well, you know what they say about *if*: A bullfrog wouldn't bump his ass every time he jumped if he had wings.

5

Scrap-Iron Charlie

THE WAY THE MAN was hunched over, the rapid, rhythmic jerking of his arms, and his intense concentration on a point in the Klamath River told me he hadn't seen me yet. Through my binoculars I could see that he had a four-foot-long, thick-butted, modified ocean-fishing rod in his hands with a Penn Nine-Ought ocean-fishing reel attached. The very heavy monofilament line being used in conjunction with this fishing outfit, which I could easily see from my vantage point, told me all I needed to know: I had an illegal salmon or sturgeon snagger—and from the way he was working his snagging outfit, a damn good one!

A few moments later the fellow reeled his terminal tackle up from the water, and as it came into view my suspicions were confirmed. He had a half-pound lead weight attached to what must have been a 180-pound-test monofilament line, with two sets of large treble hooks attached at intervals of about six inches. It was a perfect outfit to drag across the back or belly of an unsuspecting green or white sturgeon or king salmon resting in the large pools of the Klamath River as they fought their way upstream to spawn.

I continued to sweep the area around the man with my binoculars for a clue as to how to approach from my hiding place above him without being seen. If he spotted me before I was ready to spring the trap, he would immediately cut his fishing line and get rid of his illegal snagging gear, making my case much more difficult to prove in a court of law with no physical evidence. It wouldn't be impossible because the court still took judicial notice of the word

97

of the arresting officer as a form of evidence, but it would be less neat and conclusive as far as I was concerned. In addition, since his crime was serious enough in the eyes of the courts to be known locally to the outlaws as a "hanging offense," he would more than likely "antelope" off into the forest. His capture by a larger-than-life game warden trying to run uphill would be a bit iffy if I didn't cut off his escape route.

The poacher was standing on a small sandbar that ran into the river at a slight angle before disappearing into the foamy green waters. I surmised that if he did try to escape, he would have to run toward me off that sandbar, sprint up a slight sandy bank, and then dash about thirty-five yards before he reached the cover of the conifers. The only other escape route entailed swimming the river, and that would be iffy because of the distance to the far bank and the swift current. Going that way would involve not only the escape issue but the question of survival as well.

As I swept my binoculars over the reach from where he stood to the timber's edge so I could evaluate the situation, my field of view passed over three strange-looking lumps lying partially sub-merged in the water next to his sandbar. I had passed over those lumps before it dawned on me: they were previously snagged stur-geon on an obviously homemade stringer designed to hold such large fish! I quickly moved my binoculars back to verify my suspi-cions and confirmed my initial identification. There in the eddy of the small sandbar lay what appeared to be three undersized stur-geon (less than forty-eight inches long). The poacher had run stout nylon line through the mouths of these fish and out through the sides of their gill plates, then hooked the loops to safety-pin-like metal fasteners attached at short intervals to another heavy nylon cord. Closer examination revealed that the nylon cord was attached to a heavy metal stake driven deeply into the sandbar at the edge of the water so the fish would remain alive and fresh in the water until he was ready to remove them while he continued tending to the illegal snagging business at hand.

For those unfamiliar with the terminology, snagging is nothing more than using oversize weights (to get the hooks down deeper into the water) and large treble hooks attached to a very stout fishing line. This gear is cast into a large pool or eddy known to hold the fish species the snaggers want to catch. In the West this illegal tactic is used for salmon and sturgeon when they ascend the rivers during their respective spawning seasons, and the favored spot for it is a quiet pool at the head of a riffle where the fish are likely to stop to rest after fighting their way through a difficult stretch of river. Once the line with the treble hooks is cast out into the pool, the snagger lets it settle a bit, then gives his rod a violent jerk, abruptly tightening the line and yanking the hooks upward from the river bottom. If a fish is not struck, the terminal gear is immediately allowed to sink once more, and then the jerking action is repeated until the terminal gear either reaches the shore or successfully foul-hooks a fish. If the latter occurs, the snagger reels in the critter after a fight commensurate with the fish's size. This activity is repeated until the snagger's arms get sore from the efforts of the snagging action or from the effects of landing many strong fish—or the "long arm of the law" snags the snagger, and relieves him from his labors.

I was pleased that the lad snagging so intently appeared to have no suspicion that a game warden was close by, though disgusted that he had taken three fish already (two over the limit had they been taken lawfully). His success only strengthened my resolve to hook this lad no matter how fast or far he ran. At that moment he snagged another fish, and his loud grunt as he set the hooks told me he had a really big one. It probably weighed more than three hundred pounds, and the tussle it gave him showed that it did not like having a set of hooks embedded in its back. The line really sang as it spun off his heavy ocean reel while he frantically tried to hold the rod tip up, all the while tightening down the drag with his free hand. But his efforts were unavailing as this huge fish turned sideways and headed downstream at an angle, literally dragging the snagger, locked feet and all, right off the sandbar and up to his waist in the river before you could say "boo." Realizing that he would shortly be drowned if things didn't change, the snagger quickly took a lit cigarette from his mouth and touched it to the line as it raced from the reel. The loud shotlike snap of the line told me the fish was free, with a set of treble hooks stuck deep into its back or belly for its troubles. The reaction from the release sent the snagger staggering backward out of the water and across the small sandbar, only to tumble into the eddy on the other side where the three previously snagged live sturgeon were tethered. Thrashing and splashing were the words of the day as the poacher tried to get out of the water and off the backs of his three hapless captives. For an instant I knelt in the brush, intrigued by this spectacle. Then it dawned on me that I should get my big hind end moving. Now was my chance to catch the lad while he was preoccupied with getting himself untangled!

Out of the brush I came like a mad grizzly surprised from his day bed, storming across the thirty-five or so yards that separated us. I was on the man before he could even think, much less make good his escape. Surprising even myself with my lightninglike speed, I growled, "Fish and Game warden. Don't move; you are under arrest." My sudden entry into his heretofore happy world, the size of the man confronting him, and the word "arrest" completely froze the man for a moment. Reaching out, I forcefully took the fishing rod from his hands, then lifted him out of the water and onto the sandbar by his collar. He never took his eyes off the person confronting him, who had mysteriously, albeit noisily, appeared like a bad dream. Moments before he had been locked in illegal bliss, but now he found himself reeled in like the fish he had pursued. For an instant I saw him casting a glance behind me toward the forest and liberty. "Don't even think it," I rumbled. The hard look that accompanied this command seemed to remove whatever starch remained in his carcass, and he went limp.

I was not happy with those who illegally snagged fish because of the resource damage they did, and I worked hard in my law enforcement travels to apprehend as many as I could along the major California north coast river systems. Each of those yahoos only whetted my appetite for more, and I caught a pile of them. Also, the rivers in those days were loaded with salmon and sturgeon in huge numbers, and the banks of those rivers were lined with snaggers in numbers to match. The pickin's were good if one chose to apply himself—on either side of the law. As I said, I did choose to apply myself. I treated those lads professionally, but I prosecuted every damn one of them like there was no tomorrow, as there wasn't for the salmon and sturgeon that fell prey to their lethal avocation. It was the least I could do for the poor fish being dragged cruelly from the river and sold illegally as smoked fish for $2.50 per pound—and those were the days when T-bone steak was fifty-nine cents per pound!

I looked down at my wet and now shivering capture of the moment. He wasn't much: a little bit of a man, probably weighing no more than 135 pounds soaking wet (no pun intended), with a muscular frame and a huge mustache matching his uncut mop of straggly hair. His clothing suggested that he might be a logger or someone of less than adequate financial means, and he looked like he could do with a meal, or several, in fact.

"What are you going to do with me?" he chirped.

"Well," I said, "with the illegal snagging activity, illegal terminal gear, and your over-limit of snagged, undersized sturgeon, I would say you have got one hell of a financial problem brewing. The judge in these parts doesn't look too kindly on chaps involved in the business of snagging, and her fines in cases like this very plainly reflect her attitude."

The little man dropped to his knees on the sandbar and began to sob uncontrollably. I just stood there dumbfounded. I had expected a battle royal from this lad, who had to know that the fines could approach $1,000 plus jail time, but his collapse and real alligator-sized tears were totally unexpected. Usually I got the "mouth" typical of a fish poacher in that part of the world instead of a man on his knees with his shoulders rocking with sobs.

"Now what the hell is the matter?" I growled, trying to maintain my image.

"Mister," he said between sobs, "I have been out of work for three months. I don't have enough money to get even the basic things for my family, so I thought I would catch and sell some fish. Everyone else seems to be doing it, and I thought I would get my share too. I didn't think I would ever get caught, but now that I have, I'm in even more trouble than before." More sobs and genuine tears of remorse began to stream through the fingers that were again pressed hard to his face. He swayed back and forth, his head almost touching the sand when he bent forward like a Muslim in prayer, and his whole body shook as he poured out his deep emotions. It was apparent that this man was not only a rookie in the poaching business but was truly grief-stricken over his capture as well. Standing there like a moss-covered post, I wasn't sure what to do. I was baffled because I had never had this type of encounter with any poacher. Finally, when there appeared to be a break in the man's weeping, I grabbed him by the shoulders and gently helped him to his feet. I was a rookie state Fish and Game warden and a well-trained one, but I had never been taught what to do in this kind of circumstance. This guy was one struggling human being, and I related to that, remembering what it was like as my mom struggled to raise me and my sister on the seventy-five cents per hour she received as a worker at the Meadow Valley Box Factory in Quincy, California, in the late 1940s. This guy had really screwed up under the game laws, but if his story checked out I wouldn't have the heart to stick him with four citations for his little morning of adventure. *That was mistake number one!*

Taking a picture of the fish on the stringer for evidence purposes, I happily released them, much to their happiness as well, back into their river home. Gathering up the rest of the snagger's gear, including his driver's license in case he ran at some point as we made our way off the river, I said, "Come on, let's go up to the patrol car. I am going to check out your story, and if I discover that you are lying to me I am going to drown your scruffy ass in the Klamath River right then and there!" I looked at him for any kind of body language that would give me a clue to his truthfulness or how to proceed, but there was nothing but the same sick, contrite look. He shrugged his shoulders like a totally beaten man and followed me up to my parked patrol car like a lost puppy. I locked his fishing gear into the trunk, retaining his driver's license in case I decided to issue him a citation, and we drove back to town. When we reached the mountain town of Orleans I asked him to show me where he lived, and he pointed down a dirt side street without saying anything. He had me pull up alongside a ramshackle house with a run-down, unpainted fence in front. The place was clean, but otherwise it was just like something out of *The Grapes of Wrath*. Out the front screen door tumbled four little towheaded kids followed by a frail-looking woman I assumed was their mother. She sported a homemade chicken-feed-sack print dress and a dirty white apron. It was just like pictures I had seen in old issues of *Life* magazine of the people of Appalachia.

Because I was convinced that this lad was leading me on a wild-goose chase, I did not have a Plan B or any idea of what to do if I called his bluff and turned out wrong. I believed that no matter what he said, his situation couldn't be half that bad. Man, it sure seemed from first appearances that I was dead wrong!

Being the thickheaded German I was, without any real polish or class, I blurted out to the woman standing on the porch, "Do you have any food in the house, lady?" Boy, that was a highly trained professional question from a mature officer, I thought, grimacing. What a class A dingbat! I was trying to find out how bad things really were, but instead the damn question came out like I was rudely inviting myself to dinner.

She looked kind of startled but said in a very gentle voice, "We don't have much, officer, but you are welcome to what we have." I could have kicked myself clear back to Eureka. Her words lodged in my heart like a long metal rod. Though she apparently had very little, she was willing to share what she had with a perfect stranger. Man, my heart hurt for that woman and her children. With a thin smile, she went back into the house, beckoning me to follow. I had no idea which way to turn, but since I was here as a result of my big mouth I had to go through with it. I told the poacher to lead off and followed him into his home. It was poor beyond belief: very little furniture, none of the evidences of a real home on the walls, and a bare kitchen. A single mattress served as a bed for the four little kids, and the mom and dad shared a sleeping bag on the floor in another room. A few ratty shreds of clothing hung in a hall closet without a door. There were no curtains on the windows and only one throw rug on the wooden floor, which, from the looks of the warped floorboards, had seen better days. A quiet "Thank you, Lord, for my many blessings" hurtled across my mind like a freight train.

The mom called from the kitchen that lunch was ready. What she gave me that day was a cup of pretty thin coffee from twice-brewed grounds and one slice of bread with some homemade blackberry jam (blackberries grew wild in the area and were free). I can't remember too many times that I was put in my place by the good Lord, but that day He did a fine job of teaching me a lesson in humanity. The old phrase "I complained because I had no shoes until I saw a man who had no feet" ran through my mind over and over. Finishing my bread and coffee, and noticing that the little kids and the mom didn't eat anything, I looked long and hard at the dad and poacher. He kept his eyes downcast out of pure and simple shame. Getting up from the table, I thanked the lady and told the man to follow me in a tone of voice that brooked no refusal. Out the door we went and into my patrol car, and I had the lad direct me to the nearest grocery store. That store out there in the bush wasn't much, but it did carry all the staples at the usual high backcountry prices. I filled two shopping carts with food, all the while wondering what my wife would say, since this would be coming out of our pockets and we were on a tight budget ourselves. But I knew it was a wasted thought. Donna would always share with others and worry about the consequences later. Maybe that is why I will love her forever, plus one day. We wheeled two very full carts out to the patrol car, loaded full shopping bags into the trunk, and filled the backseat as well. I kept avoiding the fellow's questioning eyes as we drove back to his house. When we unloaded the food, you would have thought I had just given those people a gold mine. Their joy and relief were so apparent that I had to look away several times because of the dust that seemed to be getting in my eyes. Their appreciation was something I have seldom seen since. After we put the groceries away, I beckoned the man to follow me outside.

Sitting in the patrol car so I wouldn't embarrass him in front of his family, I chewed his ass out. I told him I was not going to issue him a citation for snagging, but if I ever caught him on the river again he was going to jail after I broke both his legs, ripped his lips off, and fed them to the first hungry-looking magpie that came by. *I think I can log this as the start of mistake number two. ...* I could tell the message had more than registered and that I would not have to say any more. We got out of the car, and I returned his fishing pole. As I walked away I couldn't help but notice the genuine tears of thanks welling up in his eyes. As I drove off, I waved to the kids on the porch, noticing that they had found the gum and candy that had somehow found their way into the bags of groceries. I think I got some more of that damn dust in my eyes as I rounded the corner and left. ...

When I got home later that day, I gave my wife a giant hug and then let her go to investigate the good smells of homemade bread coming from our kitchen. The clean and cared-for house with its nice furniture and homey atmosphere was not lost on me in contrast to the place I had just come from. "Honey," Donna said, "Captain Gray wants you to call him right away. He has an assignment for you and John Finnigan up in Hank Marak's district." I nodded an OK as I continued my quest for a piece of the world's best homemade bread. Donna always made bread when I was on the road just so such depredations would not happen. I was glad I had caught her off balance, so to speak, as I shoveled a second piece of still-warm bread coated with peanut butter into my mouth. "*Terry,*" came her voice from the living room in a tone that told me my bearlike rampage in the kitchen had just come to an end. With an impish peanut-butter-smeared grin, I obeyed. Damn, I really love that woman.

A phone call to the captain revealed that he had a patrol assignment for John Finnigan and me in the eastern outback of the district. We were to work the salmon and sturgeon fishermen in the Willow Creek and Hoopa areas of Humboldt County and the Burnt Ranch Falls area of Trinity County. I told the captain that would be fine and agreed to contact John, who was the Arcata warden, for the details the captain had relayed to him earlier. Hanging up the phone, I wondered what kind of adventure this new assignment would bring into my life as a game warden. What a lesson in life and my profession I was about to get!

John was a great friend, and I was glad to be working with him again. He was a dyed-in-the-wool Irishman who had taken a liking to me from my very first day on the job. Like me, he had some problems with the captain, so it just seemed natural for the two of us to fall into a friendship that lasted until the day he died many years later. He was a good old man and knew most of the coast area like the backs of his weathered hands. The area we were going into had at one time been part of his Arcata district before the district had been divided, with Warden Marak assigned to the eastern segment. That old familiarity was probably one of the reasons the good captain had assigned us there. The other reasons, given Captain Gray's special love for us, were probably that it was hard, hot, and dangerous work that would get us out of his hair for a while. That aside, he also knew we would work the area the way it needed working. Not that Warden Marak couldn't do the job—Hank was willow-thin and strap-steel tough. He was also one of a kind when it came to an outstanding work ethic, much to the chagrin of the outlaws. When Hank passes, the critters will lose a great advocate and I a dear friend. The reason Hank was getting extra help was that his assigned patrol area was just too large for one man to work, and within that area was some of the most godawful terrain a man ever set foot on. It was straight up and down and rocky to the nth degree, possessed little in the way of roads, and was full of loggers, construction workers, Native Americans, and the rest of the in-laws and outlaws related to those groups, all trying to get more than their share. Throw just about every kind of species of wildlife into that mix, and you needed someone with a badge, gun, and "sand" to keep order in a lawless land.

"Where do you want to start working today?" John asked as we drove into the town of Willow Creek a few days later.

"Well," I replied, "I haven't had a chance to work the Burnt Ranch Falls area for snaggers, so why don't we give that area a try."

"OK," replied John. "Let's give it a whirl and see what kind of folks we can find operating outside the law." He continued down state Highway 299, and a short time later we were parking our undercover patrol vehicle at a wide spot in the road along with a bunch of other vehicles at the head of a trail leading to the Trinity River. Gathering our fishing gear, and dressed like all the other chaps fishing the area, we headed down the steep trail to what was locally known as Burnt Ranch Falls. The "falls" were a boulder-strewn spot in the Trinity River that presented an enormous problem for the salmon in their upstream navigation. The river was very constricted here, and one form of angler or another stood on every available piece of surrounding real estate. John and I stood on the high ground like a couple of rubes, watching the circus going on below. Men were lodged in every safe corner by the rocky river pass, hurling lures out into the fast-moving torrent in an attempt to catch the prized migrating salmon. Every now and then someone would hook a salmon only to lose it shortly thereafter because the fish, especially the big ones, would go back downstream in the fast current until they snapped the line. Since every place that could hold a fisherman in this limited area had one, John and I just stood as if we were waiting our turn to fish. This was the best place for wardens to be, where we could watch everything going on below.

After about an hour a lad not sixty feet away, after a careful glance our way to make sure we weren't the law, changed his terminal tackle. He removed a legal spinner, attached an obvious piece of snagging gear, and commenced to snag away in a small pool before him. John winked at me. Ever the "businessman," I kept track of the number of times our chap tossed his illegal fishing gear into the water, the number of snagging jerks as he retrieved his gear, and the number of times he foul-hooked a fish, only to lose it in the fast water. Finally he hooked a salmon small enough that he was able to get it to shore After the snagger killed the fish with a knock on the head from a short stick, John and I had a very good case. Soon we were able to work our way down to the falls as other fishermen, disgusted at their luck, left and cleared a space for us to stand. This movement allowed us to get closer to our illegal snagger, and in time, after realizing no one else was breaking the law, we grabbed our lad and his fish before he knew what had happened. Once the grab was made, it was amazing just how fast the other fishermen cleared out when they saw that the wardens were on the river. Oh well, I thought; if they can't stand our presence, so be it. That respite would give the fish a little more time on this earth to get their job done without a heavy human hand stuck in their faces all the time.

Charlie Dean Tuggles turned out to be the man who had had the misfortune to snag a fish in the presence of God and His Irish and German swords of Mother Nature. He was a smallish man, but he fairly rippled with muscle and moved with the essence of a cat on the prowl. Because of the man's menacing appearance, I stood at John's gun side as a backup while he issued a citation for snagging and the use of illegal terminal tackle. Charlie had little to say, but he studied both our faces intently as if memorizing them for future reference. John explained how the court system worked, and after he was done, since we were now known to be on the river, we grabbed our evidence fish and Charlie's fishing rod, reel, and terminal gear and began the long climb back up the mountain trail to our car. Once out of earshot of the remaining fishermen and Charlie, John said, "What do you think, Tiny?"

"A good pinch, John," was my satisfied reply.

"Do you know who that was?" he asked.

"Not really," I said, winded as we hauled our tiring carcasses up the steep terrain.

"That, my friend, was Scrap-Iron Charlie, a fish-poaching outlaw of the highest order."

"What do you mean?" I asked.

"Well, he probably doesn't remember me from my days as a warden over here, but even then he had a reputation as a fish poacher. Charlie was born in Reno, Nevada, and it is rumored among the gentry of Junction City, where he lives, that he catches and sells so many sturgeon and salmon annually that he goes to Reno and lives and gambles for at least three months every year on the proceeds."

"Damn," I said between gasps as we ascended a rather steep portion of the trail, "how the hell does he do it? Surely he doesn't make that much money just from snagging?"

"No," answered John, who was now also winded, "not entirely. I heard in the old days from my informants that he would hike down to deserted stretches of the Trinity River, camp out, and, once assured he was alone, run a small gill net in the river. The next morning he would haul out his catch, clean the gill net, and hide it somewhere along the river for use the next evening. Then he would sell the gill-netted fish in the evenings in the bars of Willow Creek, Burnt Ranch, Salyer, and Junction City to the tourist fishermen who hadn't done so well." Stopping once more to catch his breath, John added, "To the best of my knowledge, this is the first time he has ever been caught in a fishing violation. I caught him once taking quail during the closed season, but nothing else. He is very good at his trade, and I think I will have a word with Judge Bonham and see if we can't up the ante on this citation." John's smile was soon answered by my understanding grin. We finished our hike out of the river bottom and, after several long pulls on our water jugs, went into the town of Burnt Ranch to meet with the judge—and what a meeting that was to be.

Visiting with Judge Bonham was always a treat. She was a fifty-nine-year-old grandmother who had a good strong handshake and a set of gray eyes that met yours intently when she talked to you. I got the feeling she never missed anything in a conversation. John sat down and explained the situation, including the earlier years of intelligence he had gathered regarding Charlie's illegal activities, as she listened with rapt attention. After listening to the intelligent and interested questions she fired rapidly at John, I thought, Damn, this little lady doesn't miss a trick. It was apparent that she had a great love of life and of the resources in her area of responsibility. It was also apparent that she understood that it was her role to see that the law protecting such things was not only upheld but interpreted with the future of those resources in mind. My other internal questions about her were answered when she invited us into her chambers to check her law books for the answers to a couple of John's questions about the Fish and Game code. What a sight! Her entire ceiling and three walls of her office were covered with illegal snagging gear of every known kind. There were net floats, spears, and every other kind of illegal catching device in evidence as well. It was clear that this lady didn't go for those who resorted to the grossly illegal methods of taking such noble fish as salmon or sturgeon from the rivers within her jurisdiction. I marveled at this historical collection of gear, and then my eyes caught the ultimate symbol of her office and position: hanging directly over her desk from the ceiling was a small hangman's rope, noose, knot, and all! Man, I thought, this was one tough judge. She might have been a grandmother, but she could also be a grim reaper for anyone who needed a "reaping"! John's work with Judge Bonham was done, and as we left her office she thanked us for our time so sweetly that all I could manage was a grin.

I found out later from John that Charlie was fined $250 per offense, or a total of $500, for not following any hunch he might have had that morning about the two of us being who we were. He also lost all his fishing gear. That may not sound like much of a fine, but in those days it represented a month's worth of wages to even a well-paid workingman in the lumber industry. I could just imagine where his illegal fishing gear ended up. ...

As John and I continued our river patrols that fine, hot summer day after our meetings with Charlie and the judge, I learned from John that Charlie had come to be known as Scrap-Iron either from his numerous fistfights in the area's bars or from working in a steel mill in Michigan right after the war. After listening to John's story, I thought the most probable link was barroom based. It seemed that Charlie had a very high tolerance to pain and never quit a brawl until the other chap was on the ground with a face looking like hamburger! This tough local lumber-mill worker was said to hit like the kick of an army mule, so anyone unfortunate enough to offend him and foolish enough to start a scrap was in for a rather rude and painful awakening, especially after having his nose or jaw broken early in the fight. John also said it was rumored that Scrap-Iron would soak his fists in seawater if he could get it, or strong saltwater if he couldn't, for at least an hour a day to toughen them up so they would be like cured leather. That way, when he hit someone, it was like being hit with a board, plus Charlie's hands would not be cut as easily when striking a bony head or face. I now realized how accurate my observations of this little man's catlike movements and muscular body had been. Charlie was a fighter, pure and simple. His muscular frame and lithe movements clearly identified his nature, and woe to the man who did not see that before starting a barroom brawl with him. This type of history was one of the great things John had to offer a green officer like me. He was older than dirt and had been a warden in the area for more than thirty years. Anyone who listened could learn a lot from this old man, and I did listen. ...

After several more days of climbing up and down the steep mountains to check the fishermen, with me getting a damn good case of poison oak on my last part over the fence, John and I headed for home. How the hell does a guy get poison oak on his bottom? I was always very careful, but just as sure as God made green apples, I had a raging case! In fact, it got so bad that I went to a fisherman friend called High Tide and asked him for the cure he used. Now, High Tide was a rough-and-tumble sort of chap who always got a rash from poison oak as he fished up and down the north coast rivers for the elusive salmon. However, his rash usually seemed to last only a few days, so I took my poison-oaked bottom to his house for some of his mysterious homespun relief. I had cited High Tide early in our relationship for an over-limit of king salmon and was not sure he would help me, but after hearing my tale of woe with a big grin of enjoyment, he did. He went out to his garage and took out a gallon jug of the secret stuff he used and gave it to me. At that point, even if he had had a dozen salmon over the limit in his garage, I would have let him go without a citation. Well, maybe not ...

"What's in it?" I asked.

"One half seawater and one half full-power Clorox," he replied with another grin. "Now be careful the first couple of times you put it on—it will get your attention if you don't. Also, be aware you are going to smell like a fresh load of laundry every time you use this as, in your case, 'butt rub.'"

Brother, was he right! However, my bottom was much better after a few "howling sessions," if you get my drift. ... As for the smell, well, it was better than having to slide the patrol car around every corner in order to have an excuse to slide an itching bottom across the seat for some relief. ... As if our hot, tough detail had not been enough, my darling wife also got a good case of poison oak all over her hands and arms from handling my clothing when she washed my sweat-encrusted shirts and pants. I was glad she hadn't gotten the rash where I did because then all my kitchen delights might have stopped! After that experience, I was the one putting my clothing into the washer, but the stream of homemade breads, pies, tarts, cookies, and other treats still came from her skilled hands, so I guess all was forgiven.

The following week I was in the Trinity River area by myself as John worked through a pollution problem involving the pulp mill in Eureka. Wanting to check Burnt Ranch Falls again, but realizing that many of the locals would now recognize me, I took to doing a lot of creeping around and watching the fishing activity from a distance with my binoculars. On one of those days I heard from the Forest Service folks in the town of Salyer that a great number of salmon had moved into the Burnt Ranch Falls area and that snagging was now going full tilt along that portion of the river. I gathered up some grub, water, and a sleeping bag and headed for the place where John and I had caught Scrap-Iron Charlie. I waited until nightfall, then parked the undercover truck out of sight among some deserted buildings about a hundred yards from the Burnt Ranch Falls trailhead. Since the area was loaded with rattlesnakes, I went carefully down the trail, making liberal use of my flashlight until I got to a spot off to one side of the falls where I knew I would be able to see most fishing activity through my binoculars once the fishermen got started in the morning. The spot was right next to a large stand of blackberries and poison oak but out of the way of anyone going down the trail. I rolled out my sleeping bag, took off my uniform shirt, and hung it on a nearby bush. Then I ate my cold dinner of sardines and crackers in the quiet of the dark. For several hours I just sat there on my sleeping bag, listening to the night sounds and soft roar of the river in the distance. A lone deer approached me in the moonlight, trying to figure out what I was. Once she winded me, there was a stamping of front feet and a loud snort, and I heard her *thump-thump* through the forest for several moments before quiet returned. Tired from the heat and the day's work, I fell asleep on top of my sleeping bag only to awaken around midnight to a feeling of unknown danger. Realizing something was wrong, I moved only my eyes and right hand, looking for the danger and slowly grasping my firearm. Clasping the cold steel butt of my .45 and quietly cocking the hammer against the cloth of the sleeping bag so as not to arouse the suspicions of whatever was threatening me, I very slowly rolled over on my side. Not fifteen feet away in the pale moonlight stood a black bear weighing 250 to 300 pounds. It was on its hind legs and motionless but looking right at me. All of a sudden, with an explosive *whoooff* and crashing of brush, the bear whirled and stormed off into the night like a train off its track. I realized for the first time that my hair was standing up as if it were looking for a better view! Not surprisingly, I slept little the rest of the night. I blamed it on the bright moonlight, of course. ...

The next morning I dressed and crawled farther into the blackberry bushes where I could observe the action on the river but not be seen by any fishermen wandering off the trail. Belly down, I propped myself up on my rolled-up sleeping bag and waited for people to arrive. Soon they came, and before long I had an even dozen fishing in Burnt Ranch Falls. For about two hours everyone obeyed the Fish and Game laws, and the heat and boredom were starting to cause me to doze off. Then, as if on cue, Mother Nature provided a little entertainment to keep me awake. A rattlesnake about four feet long, belly distended from a dinner engagement with some poor unfortunate mammal, crawled into view and wriggled right up to where my elbows rested on my sleeping bag. In the shade of the blackberries, it coiled up and settled down for what appeared to be the duration. Now, having a snake that size lying within eighteen inches of my elbows was not something I really desired. Moving my entire carcass was out of the question because doing so would alert the fishermen on the river, and my time up to that point would be wasted. So I came up with Plan B, thanks to one of Ronald Reagan's B movies. In those days I chewed massive mouthfuls of chewing tobacco, so I worked up a great spit and let it fly at the head of the snake, hoping the creature would get the message and leave the scene. But I missed, and all I got was the snake riled up and rattling like there was no tomorrow. Damn, I thought; this is not how it worked in the movie. ... Working up another load of spittle, I let it go, hitting the snake's body but missing the head by a mile. The rattling increased, and I began to get a little concerned. The snake's closeness was causing me to dry up in the spit-making department, and I figured I had only one round left. This time I very carefully aimed a spew that would have made Gabby Hays proud, and *kapoo,* right on the head of the snake (and part of the sleeping bag) went the spittle. With that, the snake struck the sleeping bag between my elbows so fast that I never saw the strike coming—and then I *moved!* Not enough to alert the chaps fishing on the river, but enough to give that damn snake a harder target to hit. However, after that spit shot the snake moved deeper into the shade of the blackberries, and I reclaimed my sleeping-bag position, all the while keeping a wary eye on my reptilian friend.

Satisfied that my crawling partner was set for the moment, I took another gander at the fishermen with my binoculars. *Damn!* There between two boulders was a fishing rod whipping the water to a froth as the holder was "pure-dee" snagging. Soon the fellow hooked one of the massed salmon in the pool at his feet and a few moments later reeled in his catch. As he bent over to gill his fish (that is, pick it up by putting his fingers under the gill plates from the back side), I was stunned to see that it was none other than Scrap-Iron Charlie! He carefully looked around before putting a small cord through the salmon's mouth and under the gill plate, anchoring it to a stake at his feet. Then he commenced to snag again. Since he was now out of sight except for the tip of his fishing pole, I took off from my hiding place and steamed toward the spot where I had seen him. My fast trip to the river was perfectly timed: everyone on the shore was so engrossed in watching another chap legally catching a large salmon that I was upon them before they knew the law was in country. Scrap-Iron had his back to me and didn't see me until I walked right up behind him and identified myself. He almost crapped! Quickly reaching over his shoulder, I grabbed his fishing rod and reeled it in before he could hang the illegal terminal gear up on the bottom of the river. With his recently snagged salmon and a stunned Scrap-Iron in tow, I went back up on the bank and commenced to write him a citation for snagging and the use of illegal fishing gear. He never said a word, just stood there all red in the face and fumed. He was so stunned that I thought he really had not expected to see a game warden back at his fishing hole such a short time after his first apprehension.

My business done, I gave Scrap-Iron his copy of the citation, seized his fish and fishing gear, and bade him good-bye. With that, I walked back to my sleeping gear, retrieved it after making sure the snake had not taken up residence anywhere nearby, and started my long, steep walk back up the trail. Taking one last look back at the river, I saw Scrap-Iron just standing there watching me. It was apparent that he was still stunned by the recent events, not to mention a bit concerned over the legal action that would follow in front of the same judge after such a short lapse of time. Then a notion dawned on me: this was his second fishing violation in about as many weeks. If he received one more citation for a fishing violation, the state of California could revoke his fishing privileges for a three-year period. If he was as bad a character as Finnigan had said, man, what a boon that would be to the fish runs! With a grin and a new lightness in my tired step, I came up out of the canyon and headed for Judge Bonham's court.

Scrap-Iron was on his best behavior in court one week later and this time paid $500 per offense, twice what he had paid per offense for John's citations. Furthermore, Judge Bonham told Charlie that his appearance in her court in the near future for a like violation would guarantee him at least thirty days in jail to think over the error of his ways. From the look on Charlie's face, I could tell he had had enough of this judge and that he was determined it would be a long time before he came through those gates again!

As I left the courtroom, Charlie brushed by me and said, "You will never catch me again, asshole."

"I hope not, Charlie, because if I do it will mean another round with this judge and a trip to the jail, and I don't think that would be wise for even as good a fighter as you."

He looked long and hard at me before moving to his vehicle and leaving the parking lot in a cloud of dust and flying gravel. It was a good feeling to have taught one so hard on the fishery resources that there really is a God. ... I bet his trip to Reno to gamble this year will be a bit less fancy, I thought smugly. *I think my arrogance could be counted as mistake number three!* I hope you readers are keeping count. ...

Two weeks later I was working the Klamath River, several canyons across from the Trinity River, looking for snaggers of salmon and sturgeon in the Weitchpec area of Humboldt County. That area of northern California is extremely rugged, with numerous deep, rock-filled canyons that are so damn steep in some places you just about have to go hand over hand to reach the more remote places on the river. These canyons are full of wildlife of every kind, including lots of rattlesnakes, as well as early California mining history—and adventure. Did I mention that it never seemed to get cooler than 100 degrees during the summer months in that neck of the woods, and that the entire canyon area along the river was blanketed with poison oak? Damn, you might have thought a game warden could pick a nicer place to work. Oh well, when you are young, trying to prove yourself a "good hand," and immortal (ah, youth), you do crazy things. I certainly was off and running in the right direction.

I had chosen a particular spot along the river that Hank Marak had told me tended to host numerous local outlaws. Quietly moving into an area where I could overlook about a mile-long stretch of the river several hundred feet below me, I sat down, carefully avoiding the poison oak nearby. Sweating like all get-out after my rather strenuous descent, I sat there in 103-degree heat by a rock face, which provided some cover, and "melted." Fishing below me were four individuals who appeared to be doing what the state required. After several of the lads had moved on without breaking the law, I began to lose interest as the heat of the day and the early hour I had risen started to take their toll. Lying back for just a few minutes to "rest my eyes," I awoke to find that two hours had passed and it was now late afternoon.

Remembering my original mission, I sat up and quickly scanned the river below, only to find that it was now deserted. I stood up, stretched my legs and tired back, and began to walk out along the deer trail that had led me to my observation point. As I slowly moved through the dangerous rocky overhangs and narrow spots along the trail, I kept my eyes roaming along the river under me, alert for anything out of place. Working through an extremely narrow spot where a misstep could send me to the rocks two hundred feet below, I suddenly caught a flicker of movement by a large pool, about a hundred feet below me.

I stopped when I reached better footing and focused my binoculars on the suspicious movement. Nothing. I watched for a few moments, and there it was again! I could just barely make out the movement of the tip of a fishing rod behind a large rock located at the head of a wide pool. Sitting down by some buck brush, I double-checked the movement with the binoculars resting on my knees so I could steady them against my labored breathing. Sure as hell, I was able to confirm that a fishing pole appeared to be going through the motions I had come to associate with snagging. I scurried farther north until I reached a safer sitting position on a rocky face overlooking the river, and then I was able to obtain a partial view of a fisherman hidden between two boulders. I no longer noticed the heat, sweat, or poison oak as I started to work my way down to the river via a small draw covered with scrub oak. When I was about thirty-five yards away from the riverbank, I sat down behind a pile of driftwood logs to examine him through my binoculars. Wiping the sweat from my forehead so it wouldn't drop in the eyepieces, I took my first close look. The man had his back to me, and sure as God made cow slobbers, he was snagging salmon. I watched him go through numerous snagging motions with the fishing rod, haul up and clean leaves off obvious illegal terminal gear designed for snagging, and cast it back out across the pool for another try. After about twenty minutes he snagged a fish and after a pretty good tussle successfully landed about a twenty-five-pound king salmon.

By now I had taken my Super Eight movie camera out of my rucksack and was filming the event. Damn, it was great. I had a direct line-of-sight shot on the fellow as he was doing his thing. How sweet it was! The camera recorded him hauling the salmon up onto the sandbar with large, illegal treble hooks clearly embedded in its back in front of the dorsal fin. Zooming up to the fellow, who still had his back to me, I continued to film as he removed the hooks from the back of the fish. Then he turned to see if anyone was watching, and I damn near fell off the log I was lying against to film the event. The face was none other than that of my man Scrap-Iron Charlie! Charlie was now confirmed, in my mind at least, as one of the most notorious fish snaggers in the north coast area. He just couldn't leave the blood sport alone. John's information that Charlie spent several months every year gambling and living it up in Reno sure appeared to be right on the money I just couldn't believe this guy. He couldn't get snagging out of his system even after being tagged hard twice in the past few weeks for the exact same thing! I shook my head as I began to speculate that this contact, especially in light of my most recent apprehension of this lad, just might mean a real "hoorah," physical or otherwise, before we were through. ... I hope Charlie is a thinking man, I thought, because to assault a state Fish and Game officer would land his tail end in the slammer for far longer than any illegally taken fish. Plus I didn't want my Robert Redford–like face altered. ...

Charlie stared right at me as I sat concealed in the log and brush pile, and I damn near ducked until I realized that the camera was in zoom mode and he was still thirty-five or forty yards away. I continued to film, hardly believing my luck. Seldom is an officer of the law able to catch someone doing something illegal twice in a row, much less getting the activity on film. God had to be a game warden that day! Charlie had been apprehended and convicted twice for violating Fish and Game laws, and if I could apprehend and convict him this time, he would not only be fined and jailed but would automatically lose his fishing license for the next three years. I was so excited I could hardly stand it, making it hard to hold the camera steady.

I told myself to calm down and get on with the job, and the camera framed Charlie beautifully as he clubbed the salmon on the head and slid it into a gunnysack that had been weighted with a rock. He then tied off the gunnysack with a rope and tossed it into the pool at the edge of the sandbar on which he was standing. He secured the other end of the rope to a wooden stake that was driven deep into the edge of the sandbar but hidden under water. The murky water fairly well hid any evidence of foul play, especially if a game warden just happened by. Damn, it was really slick, and I committed that bit of outlaw information to my memory bank for later use in my career as Charlie reeled up his line, cleaned the hooks, and cast it out again. He continued snagging, all the while carefully watching up and down the river for any sign of human activity. About thirty-five minutes later he snagged another fish, but the hooks tore out before he got it to shore. Charlie continued to swing the heavy lead weight out across the pool without much luck for about another ten minutes before *wham*, another fish felt the sting of his gear. This time he hauled it in within a few minutes because it weighed only about ten pounds and was unable to fight hard against the heavy fishing tackle. Again the camera allowed Scrap-Iron to be center stage, much to the glee of one rather large but well-concealed game warden.

Charlie carefully removed the hooks from the fish, knocked it on the head, and slid it into the gunnysack with the fish he had caught earlier. He carried the gunnysack behind a set of boulders, and I could no longer see what was going on. Pretty soon I saw some fish guts fly out into the river from behind the boulder. Realizing that he was cleaning the fish in preparation for leaving, I carefully sneaked over to where he was intently working, all the while with the camera up and ready to continue filming the episode. Rounding the boulder, I found Charlie with his back to the camera, so I got set and then said, "Hello, Charlie. Care if I check your fish and fishing gear?"

At the sound of my voice, he jumped like a bug on a hot rock and whirled around. His eyes immediately focused on the uniform and the chap wearing it. Without a moment's hesitation, he grabbed the fishing rod and reel lying at his feet and flung them far out into the river, getting rid of the terminal-gear evidence. This all occurred on film, of course, under the slow-motion setting. In fact, that little action got him two more tickets: one for failure to show his fishing equipment to an officer of the law and the other for violating Section 5652 of the Fish and Game Code—littering! Charlie leaped for the fish to provide them a watery grave in the river as well, but he found himself knocked to the ground with a well-placed trip throw, advised that he was under arrest, and handcuffed before he could recover his senses, all in one fell swoop. I will admit that the handcuffing was a bit of a to-do. Charlie was strong, and if I hadn't been all over him before he realized what was happening, I would have had my hands full.

Charlie said through a mouthful of sand, "I want my lawyer."

I said, "Charlie, no problem. We just have to walk out of this place, and after you are booked in the jail at Hoopa, you can call him with your one call."

He just glared at me like a man thinking bad thoughts. The quick throw and handcuffing seemed to have taken his usual options away, though. ...

I picked up the fish and the rest of my gear, and we spent the next hour walking up out of the river canyon to my hidden patrol vehicle. Nary a word was spoken between us during the trip to the county jail, and it was just as well because he would have detected the glee in my voice at catching one of the worst salmon poachers on the north coast of California.

The next day in the Eureka Fish and Game office there was much cussing and discussion of the previous day's events. I got lots of pats on the back for finally catching Charlie with enough goods to put him off the river for at least the next three years. I drank in all this praise with gusto. After all, why shouldn't I? I had worked hard to catch this lad. I deserved some praise and darn sure was not going to turn any away. *I am not sure what number this mistake would be owing to the fact that there were so many by now. ...*

Several weeks later I was advised by the county attorney that Scrap-Iron Charlie had pleaded not guilty and demanded a jury trial. That really surprised me because I had filmed the entire event. For the next couple of days I ran the case through my mind and could find no weak points. I had my testimony, the film showing Charlie's snagging action and his use of illegal gear, the foul-hooked fish, and his disposal of the gear in the depths of the river. There was nothing left. I had him by the throat, and he knew it. It was a great feeling.

The day of the trial found me sitting in the Hoopa courtroom with a very happy county attorney. He too had reviewed my case, including the film, and had not found it wanting. He was prepared to ask for $1,500 in fines, three months in jail, and revocation of Charlie's fishing license for three years by the court. He decided he wasn't going to wait for the Fish and Game Commission to revoke the license sometime down the road; he wanted it done now and was heading in that direction like a bull terrier on the prod. Sitting on the other side of the room was Charlie with some castoff, skinny, raggedy-ass attorney. The looks on their faces gave me even more confidence regarding this outcome. Then, in a surprise move, Charlie's attorney stood up and requested a trial change. They had decided they did not want a jury trial after all and were requesting a trial by the sitting judge, Judge Bradburn (another hanging judge and grandmother). My spirits really soared at this request. A jury trial can really go crazy because many jurors don't know their hind end from a hole in the ground. In addition, they often know the person being tried, especially in small towns, and you can guess what that means.

The trial commenced as routinely as the winter rains in a temperate rain forest. I got on the stand and exhibited my evidence against Charlie (film and testimony), overwhelming I might add, and right off the bat the trial was going my way. I had even gotten our simple forensic laboratory in Sacramento to check the two fish to see whether any hooks had ever been in their mouths. There wasn't any evidence that the fish were fairly hooked, and that was another nail in the lid of the coffin.

Then Charlie's attorney asked for a short recess in order to bring in a surprise witness with new information, and the county attorney and I looked at each other with questions in our eyes. When the mystery witness appeared, boy, was I floored! It was the fellow I had caught weeks earlier from the town of Orleans—the one I did not write a citation to for snagging sturgeon, and the one for whom I had purchased several shopping carts of food. The man got on the stand and testified that he was Scrap-Iron Charlie's first cousin and that I had caught him snagging sturgeon and with an over-limit several weeks earlier and had not written any citation for those illegal acts. The silence in the courtroom after that statement was fraught, to say the least! The judge's cold, steely gaze met mine, and I could tell I was in trouble for being judge, jury, and executioner out on the river that day. Charlie's scruffy attorney rose and demanded that the court find Charlie not guilty and dismiss all charges against him. His basis was that if the state of California found it fit to let one person go for an even worse offense, surely Charlie should be set free as well.

Before I could say anything, the judge had dismissed the case against Charlie and ordered the return of his fishing equipment and fish. Talk about a reverse of fortunes. I couldn't believe what was happening! We all rose as the judge suddenly left the courtroom. The bailiff came over to me and announced that the judge wanted to see me in her chambers, and she meant right now!

Scrap-Iron Charlie walked past me and said out of the side of his mouth, "Better luck next time, rookie." I felt the burn start and go clear to the top of my head.

As if that was not wounding enough, the out-of-work fellow I had let go earlier came by and said, "Blood is thicker than water. But thanks for the free food anyway."

By now I was livid! Needless to say, the county attorney was fit to be tied. He just folded up his trial notes and walked out of the courtroom without saying anything to me. I knew I'd be hearing from him later, though, in the confines of his office. I stood alone in the deserted courtroom, feeling the anguish of total defeat on a very personal level. My first inclination was to harden my heart in the future if I came across anyone breaking the law in their time of need. But then a calm came over me and I knew that in reality I would still treat others as I wanted to be treated—but with a little more common sense regarding the courts and their side of the legal responsibility. In other words, I would let the judge decide whether to release a violator, with as much help as I could give with a guiding word behind the scenes. My job was to apprehend and present; it was the judge's task to decide the legal course of action. With that idea firmly driven home, I went into the judge's office to face the music. It turned out to be a full-fledged symphony, to say the least. Before I walked out of the judge's chambers with a hitch in my giddy-up, she said in a softer voice, "Terry, I know you feel badly about this one, and to be quite frank, I dismissed this case for one reason and one reason only. You have a great career ahead of you. But you must realize there has to be a balance of power in this business; otherwise many people will be damaged beyond repair by officers of lesser character. I just figured I would make that point with you early on relative to a very important case so it would be cast in stone in your mind. That way, when it really counts, you will have the guilty party by the throat and the people will have their due."

I looked long and hard at her, still pissed over the turn of events. She was right, of course, but what a way to learn a lesson about life. I still thought I had done the right thing with the fellow on the river, the one with the family in need. But everyone would have been better served if I had let the judge release him instead of me. She walked over to me, stood on her toes, made me bend down, and gave me a kiss on the cheek. Then she said with a twinkle in her eye, "Now, get out of here and bring that bastard Charlie's head back to me on a legal plate and I will show you how it is done in accordance with the laws of the state of California. I will make Henry the VIII look like a piker."

I managed a weak grin and walked out into the summertime heat. I had learned a real lesson, one I never forgot throughout the next thirty-two years of my law enforcement career. After that I always let the courts make the decision regarding a person's guilt or innocence, with my active input, of course, and I had few wrecks from then on. This case was one of six that I lost during a career that included several thousand investigations. But it was worth it except for the second raging case of poison oak I got trying to sneak down to where Scrap-Iron Charlie was snagging salmon. At least that time I had the cure ready.

I never again saw Scrap-Iron Charlie or the fellow I let go for snagging sturgeon. Lord, how I looked for them over the next year, as you can imagine, but to no avail. Scrap-Iron quit his job at the sawmill and just flat disappeared. As for the out-of-work man at Orleans, he moved on to greener pastures.

I guess all I can say is, thank you, Scrap-Iron, for a damn good lesson in life. It has served me well—but I can't say it has done the same for all the other poachers I ran across. ...

6

Eric

THE PERSISTENTLY RINGING TELEPHONE obviously wasn't going to quit, so I rolled over in bed and picked up the receiver. I had been up all night working an illegal set-line case on the 2047 Canal in Colusa County and, after apprehending and booking the two offenders, had hoped for a few hours of uninterrupted sleep before hitting the trails again. Fat chance with that damn phone ringing off the hook, I thought as I prepared to speak to my caller.

"Good morning," I responded in a falsely cheery tone.

"Terry, this is Captain Jim Leamon," said a familiar voice.

"Good morning, Captain," I replied. "What's up?"

"I just talked to Dave Nelson, and he needs some help checking the fishermen in the high country. It seems a horse fell on Clyde Shehorn while he was working the backcountry, and he is laid up with a lot of torn muscles and a strained back. Since the area needing work is part of your old stomping grounds when you were a kid, I thought maybe you would jump at the chance to go there and keep the fishermen in line."

"You got that right, Jim," I responded quickly. "Anything to get out of this heat and humidity in the Sacramento Valley would be just fine with me." All of a sudden I was wide awake, bright-eyed and bushy-tailed. The prospect of working in the high Sierras was always an adventure, and it is hard to find any prettier backcountry in the summer, except maybe the Rockies.

In the summer of 1967 I had transferred from the North Coast Fish and Game Squad to the Valley Squad in the Sacramento

Valley. What a change! From the towering redwoods, Douglas fir, and Sitka spruce in a temperate rain forest with salmon, sturgeon, Columbian black-tailed deer, and many ocean species to the heat, humidity, and agricultural lands of the Sacramento Valley with its millions of waterfowl and mosquitoes. The Valley's natural resources—fish, fowl, mammals, and everything else imaginable—were immense, and I had plenty of work to do, but I welcomed an opportunity to spend a few days in my old stomping grounds in the Sierra Nevada Mountains, where I had grown up. As an outdoor-minded lad was wont to do in those days, I had explored every nook and cranny of several Sierra mountain counties, fishing, hunting, and hiking, and I was happy to return to those glorious, carefree days of yesteryear.

"Fine," Jim replied. "Call Dave and set it up. When that is done, let me know when you are going and where so I can reach you if we need you back here for anything unusual that hits the fan."

"OK, Captain," I replied. "By the way, if I get the time, should I give Gil Berg a call and see if I can swing by the lakes in his district and give him a hand as well? It never hurts to show another face up there, one the outlaws don't know, and come at them from another side." Gil was a warden and friend in my squad, and a close friend of the captain as well.

"Good idea," Jim replied, "but see to it that Dave's needs are served first. Then if you have any time left, give Gil a hand."

"Yes, sir," I responded. Hanging up, I rolled over and tried to return to my dreams. No such luck. Tired or not, my mind was racing with the prospect of a new adventure. A few moments later I was dressed and on the phone to Dave Nelson, the captain in Paradise, California. Dave was a tall, thin "drink of water," an excellent Fish and Game captain, and an all-around good man. He was a very hard worker who was totally dedicated not only to the resources but also to the well-being of his officers. I never knew a man worth his salt who didn't think Dave was one of the very best.

Dave's "Marine Corps" voice came through the phone loud and clear in response to my greeting. "Good morning, Terry. Want a little extra work?"

"You bet," was my instant reply. "What's up?" Bear in mind, I didn't lack for work. Colusa County was a resource-driven area any time of the year, and I never had a day when my plate wasn't full and running off the table and over onto my shoes, if you get my drift. But the officers in Dave's Fish and Game squad were always helping us Valley wardens when they got snowed out in the high country, and this was a good opportunity to pay back a few favors in addition to getting out of the Valley's humid summer heat. Dave described how Clyde Shehorn—the Blairsden, California, warden and a very close friend—had been injured while working deer poachers in the backcountry. Clyde had been crossing an old wooden bridge on horseback when the bridge had given way, and the horse had landed on top of Clyde after both of them had gone through to the creek bottom below. Clyde was lucky to be alive, I thought as Dave's voice droned on with the proposed patrol plans. Dave said he would cover the larger lakes, and he wanted me to cover on foot the smaller high-country lakes in the Elder Lake basin. That way he could remain in radio contact with the rest of his squad in case something blew up and still do the easy back-country work that the resident officer would normally handle.

"That would be no sweat," I responded. "My dad took me fishing many times in the Elder Lake basin as a kid, so I know the area well."

Dave, in his usual wordy style, said, "Work out the citation administration with Clyde, and I will see you when you get there." With that, he was gone. Great, I thought. I could visit Donna's and my folks in Quincy as well as catching some bad guys. It was an unbeatable combination, especially because our folks always cooked up some great meals when I visited.

After finishing my evidentiary work from the previous night's set-line case, I drove into Colusa and filed the paperwork with Bonnie Grussenmeyer, the clerk of the Colusa Justice Court. "Terry," came Bonnie's voice as I started to leave the clerk's office, "Judge Weyand will be out of town for a few days. I will hold up any action on this case, if you don't mind, and let him review it when he returns."

Man, it was great having that lady as the clerk of the court, I thought as I returned to the counter. She was always on the ball, and apparently something in my set-line case had caught her ever-sharp eye. "What's up, kid?" I said, looking at her closely.

"Well," she replied, "Judge Weyand just had a drunk-driving trial on one of these fellows while sitting in for another judge, and this person really gave the judge a bad time during the sentencing." Her dark eyes flashed as she looked at me for any hint of opposition. Not finding any, she continued, "So this may be a case where the judge might want to *personally* manage this citation through his court." The impish look in her beautiful eyes told me I had better let her do her thing.

"Your call, kid," I answered with a knowing grin as I reflected that my chaps running the set lines might be in for a lesson on the wisdom of using such illegal devices in Colusa County after Judge Weyand got back. With that thought and a smile, out the door I went, knowing full well that Bonnie would take care of the Colusa Justice Court home front while I was away. When I returned days later, I discovered that $500 fines per offense and loss of equipment was the word of the day on my two set-lining chaps, and as usual, Miss Bonnie had been right on the money with her decision to wait until His Honor returned. It always amazed me just how far the long arm of the law could reach!

Shadow, my 110-pound, all-teeth-when-she-had-to-be retriever and field partner, sensed preparation for an upcoming adventure and showed it by not leaving my side no matter where I went. She figured if she constantly stayed underfoot, I would have to take her just to stop her from tripping me. Damn, what a great dog and companion. Donna had purchased the dog earlier in our marriage, and neither of us had realized at the time what a friend she would turn out to be. Both Donna and I enjoyed her for the years she was with us, as did my kids. That dog made such an impression on me that I still miss her twenty-five years after she died of cancer. I have never had another dog since, largely out of respect for her memory and the great times we had together as a team. I still get misty-eyed when I think about her and her devotion to me.

I finished loading the gear I would need to covertly work the trout fishermen in the high country and cleaned up the last of my administrative duties. Then I swung by the Colusa County sheriff's office to let the lads know I would be out of town for a few days and ask them to keep an eye on my house and family during my absence. I was a state Fish and Game warden in an area where many people didn't much appreciate game wardens or the work they did. The Sacramento Valley was a mecca for commercial market hunters (people who killed migratory waterfowl in mass quantities for sale in the commercial markets), and as a result of that level of illegal activity, game wardens were understandably not really welcome. In addition, some of the game wardens who had previously been assigned to Colusa County had been less than stellar in their work ethics and personal behavior. In fact, when I first moved into the town of Colusa, I rented a shack to live in and had to pay three months higher than a dog's back rent in advance because the landlady wasn't sure how long I would last in light of the fact I was a game warden. I even found it difficult to pay for the gasoline I used in the state patrol truck with a state credit card at several local gas stations! Needless to say, I had my work cut out for me to get the local chaps in line and obeying the laws of the land, not to mention respecting the long arm of the law. However, I was young, of substantial mass, could be ornery as well as professional if necessary, had a double dose of guardian angels, and most importantly had a wife who was an expert at patching me up, emotionally and physically, so I could return to the "wildlife wars" in fine fettle. I figured that with that chemistry I would set an example for the people of Colusa County, and let the chips fall where they might. But I still worried that my family was vulnerable when I was away and unable to defend my home. After a few months in the county, I found that the sheriff's office was filled with professional officers who were also damn fine human beings. They took it upon themselves to look out for Donna and our children when I was gone, and I never had a problem from the seamy element because of the dedication of the men and women in the sheriff's office. When I was gone, my home was a regular part of their patrols, and sometimes even members of the city of Colusa Police Department would cruise by when the sheriff's officers were tied up or shorthanded. In return, I made sure that when those officers went into "battle," no matter what the odds, they had a game warden at their side, for better or worse. If nothing else, if things got *really* bad, I was big enough that the officers could have shot me and then lain down behind my cooling carcass to fight back, as Custer did behind his horses. ...

The next morning, after kissing Donna good-bye, "Dog" and I headed off into the Sierra Nevada Mountains for another adventure. Leaving Colusa County, I climbed into the foothills via the city of Oroville. As I traveled, I let my mind wander through the paths of history I was crossing: early settlers, explorers, trappers, the gold rush, outlaws, stagecoach routes, and the like. I have always been a student of my country's history, and any time I traveled, my enjoyment in being alive and free in America was always doubled by my sense of the presence of history. I drove up through the Feather River Canyon, so named by the early Spanish explorers because of the vast quantity of feathers always floating on the waters, deposited there by the many Indian tribes living along the river from the waterfowl and other birds they took as food. Then I passed along the Feather River Highway, built in part by convict labor in the early days and paralleled by a railroad of immense wonder. The railroad had been a dream of such greats as Collis P. Huntington, Charles Crocker, Leland Stanford, and the like— men with the money and power to back that dream, including the knowledge of the profits to come as this great country of ours was slowly woven together. Greed and ego were also driving forces for such men, like those I made a career of chasing more than a hundred years later. But how often does one have the opportunity to link the nation as they did with the iron rail, the "iron horse," and their own iron will? After many failures in the unyielding granite mountains, and after trying every labor force known at that time, these men broke tradition and hired the comparatively tiny Chinese laborers at the instance of Crocker (who would later become president of the Crocker system of banks). These men were called "Crocker's Pets" until they went to work with a zeal hardened in the crucible of racism. Many came directly from China to build a better life for those they left behind. What iron men they became! It was only appropriate that they helped the "iron horse" come to represent the lifeblood of the nation. Hanging from the cliffs, suspended by ropes in wicker baskets, they drilled holes with single-jack hand drills and hammered into the granite faces for blasting. Still hanging in those baskets, they lit the fuses and hoped they would be drawn up in time before the explosion sent them into their idea of heaven. Many survived, but many fell into the canyons as a result of fast-burning fuses and slow-moving baskets. Shovels, picks, pushcarts, and strong backs matched by their will to succeed pushed the iron rails ever farther through the granite mountains toward the railroad builders coming from the east—all for just six cents a day and a ration of rice. Those "little giants" of industry may not be thought of as building this great land of ours, but their courage and hard work certainly contributed in no small measure.

Up past the old mining towns of Dame Shirley and the stage stops used by the likes of Black Bart and Mark Twain I went with my usual sense of awe for those who braved those times to build a better life as they settled an untamed land. I reveled in the beautiful scenery and my thoughts about days of old until I arrived several hours later in Quincy, California. Quincy was also a domain of history: lived in by the earliest peoples, explored by the Spanish, traveled over by the fur trappers, settled by the very first pioneers, grazed by the cattlemen, and turned upside down by the miners in '49. Even after all those years of use and abuse, Quincy was still a beautiful little town snuggled in a high mountain valley. I had lived there starting in 1947, and it was and still is home to my soul even though most of those I loved who lived there have passed across the great divide.

I had traveled all around Quincy as a boy with limited means, no father because of divorce, a hardworking mother, and a heart and eye for the land as big as any that came before me. I knew every fruiting bush, apple tree, and cornfield that at various times of the season could supply food to a growing boy who was always hungry. I knew almost every trout stream so well that I could predict where the fish were and thus caught many an unwary trout. I also knew where every mountain quail territory was, and I took as many of those tough little speedsters for my mom as I could. She loved pink-meated trout and white-meated quail, and I saw to it that she never lacked those things, in season or out. As for the deer, I knew many a buck's bed, and for many it would be their last. Maybe that was why I was now a game warden: God plain and simply had me doing penance for my earlier ways. Well, I couldn't think of a better way to spend my life than married to Donna and my natural environment.

I drove past the area where I had killed my first buck at the age of eleven, using a .32 Winchester special borrowed from a boyhood friend, Harold Tweedle. I had gutted the little forked-horn buck with a straight razor (I didn't own a knife) and brought it home strapped over an old girl's bicycle that my uncle had given me the previous Christmas. Man, was I proud!

I stopped the patrol car in my folks' driveway and was greeted by my dad (in fact my stepdad, but he was such a wonderful man that I always called him Dad), Otis Barnes, and my mom. Mom gave me a hug and then took over in the dog department, giving Shadow a piece of fresh fried chicken that I could smell cooking. Damn, the dog was more important than I was! I was home.

The next morning at first light, Dog and I lit out for Blairsden and Clyde Shehorn's house. I had known Clyde, the resident game warden, since I was a young man. He was as kind and good a man as ever crapped between a set of boots and was respected by friend and foe alike. He had been in that area for years, and everyone around could tell stories of this legend of a man. I reached his home, surrounded by hundred-foot-tall ponderosa pine trees (unusual in mining country because of all the logging a hundred years earlier to provide timber for the mines) and knocked on his front door. It was quiet for the longest time, and then I heard a shuffling sound before the door slowly swung open. There this "man of the mountain" stood, or perhaps I should say leaned, in a stooped position, held upright by a cane.

"Morning, Clyde," I said.

He just looked at me through pain-filled eyes and quietly beckoned for me to follow. Man, was he a mess. It was plain as he shuffled back to the living room that the crash through the bridge had done a number on him! A lesser man, or one without strong guardian angels, would not have survived such a fall, I thought.

I sat down, took a long look at my friend, and said, "Clyde, you look like crap!"

"I love you too," came his equally crusty response. At least I had gotten him to break a smile. We discussed his recent mishap and I made light of it by calling him a cowgirl and promptly got my ears pinned back. After this exchange of pleasantries, we got down to the brass tacks of why I was there. Clyde outlined some areas for me to check where he had been having problems with over-limits of trout being taken along with the illegal use of chum in some of the high-mountain lakes. Chumming is nothing more than tossing food (worms, salmon eggs, cheese, etc.) into the water in an effort to attract more fish to the location and your hook. No two ways about it, it is an unfair and unsportsmanlike way to take fish, easily leading to overharvest; hence the law restricting such practices. I made mental note of the areas of concern and told Clyde I would spend several days on foot in those parts and then swing across to give Gil Berg in Sierraville a hand checking his fishermen as well. I parted company with Clyde with an admonition to take care of himself and said I would get back to him if I found anything out of the ordinary. With that, Dog and I were off to the Elder Lake basin.

The Elder Lake basin is a unique geographic area loaded with early California history. It comprised high-mountain meadows and numerous lakes surrounded by massive granite ridges, peaks, and valleys; in fact, it seemed that in every mountain meadow there was a lake with its numerous little snowpack-supplied feeder streams. The lakes ranged from a few acres in size to larger, and in those days they were all chock-full of rainbow trout, German browns (Lochlevan, as they used to be called in that neck of the woods, having been transplanted from Lochlevan, Scotland), and brook trout. Few of those lakes could be driven to in those days, so it was "shank's mare" or horseback if you wanted a truly unique fishing experience or just a panful of frying trout and an eyeful of scenery second to none. It wasn't uncommon for fishermen to go to a trailhead, pick the lake where they wanted to fish from the ever-present wooden Forest Service sign, and start their hike. Most of the lakes were one to five miles from the trailhead on the old miners' foot trails and were scenic natural jewels to enjoy after you reached them. It was a perfect setting for a game warden because many people were already fishing in the area and would have no idea the warden was coming until I arrived. In addition, the thick stands of snow brush and other high-mountain meadow plants gave even a guy as large as me a place to hide until I wanted to play my hand. The fishing was almost always good because most of the lakes were inaccessible to vehicles, making for moderate fishing pressure. This remoteness, excellent fishing, spotty coverage by the local game warden, and the usual human ego and greed all provided the chemistry for several days of my kind of enjoyment.

Hiding my patrol car down an old abandoned logging spur, I gathered up my sleeping bag and other overnight camping gear, including my fishing rod (so I would look like one of the boys), and walked half a mile back to the trailhead. Picking the trail that led to Wade Lake, Grassy Lake, and Rock Lake, Shadow and I ventured into a geographic and historical time that was nothing short of great for the soul and the eyes. As I started up the trail, enjoying the musty fragrance of the mountain stream–splashed soil and plants surrounding me, I let my mind wander back over the earlier time when I had roamed this neck of the woods. I had been all over the basin as a kid, not only fishing with my dad and Uncle Lanois but as a "pack mule" hauling out cast-iron scrap metal. The entire basin area had been the scene of furious gold-mining activity in the middle and late 1800s, especially during the heyday of the California gold rush. Everywhere you looked were the remnants of old hard-rock mines that had extracted $50 million, $75 million, or even up to $100 million worth of gold apiece! Also dotting the countryside were the old stamp mills that had crushed the ore so the gold could be more easily extracted from the rock and converted into bullion.

My uncle knew the owner of these properties, a man named Colonel Lunde. The good colonel was a wealthy World War I veteran who, after returning to the States from the battlefields of Europe, had purchased many of these old, supposedly worthless mining claims for peanuts. He had continued to mine a few of them in the hope of striking it rich but was unsuccessful in that pursuit, as far as I know. Little did he know that these purchases would yield him and his descendants millions more in the form of real estate "gold" fifty years later! Meanwhile, in those early days of my youth, scrap cast iron sold for 1.5 cents a pound, and many of the old stamp mills had huge cast-iron flywheels to drive the stamps used to crush the gold ore. The mills were set up so that raw chunks of ore were dumped down a chute onto a table covered with cast iron, or later steel, and crushed by cast-iron hammers, or stamps, moving rhythmically up and down on a crankshaft driven by a flywheel. The flywheel was driven first by natural water power and later by belts driven by steam boilers fueled by wood taken from the surrounding land. I had heard that large stamp mills could be heard hammering the ore from miles away. Once the ore was crushed down to sand and powder, the gold would be extracted through various recovery methods, many of which poisoned the land and waterways for years afterward with mercury, a chemical commonly used in the amalgamation process.

My uncle had contracted with Colonel Lunde for the scrap metal in the stamp mills, and we blew them up to obtain it! God, how I now regret that chapter in my life. To make a few bucks we demolished the historical stamp mills that had been there for at least a hundred years for the cast-iron riches they held, without a thought of the history we were destroying. After blasting the cast parts into manageable chunks, we would "walk" our Jeep pickups into the area, load up the chunks of scrap, and haul them down the old wagon trails (if there were any) to the road, where a larger truck was parked. Once that truck was loaded, off it went to Reno, Nevada, to sell the scrap metal to a junkyard while we continued to blast every chunk of stamp-mill history in the area to pieces. After all these years, I understand why the buffalo almost disappeared. ... Humankind has little or no sense of history, and I am sad to say I am only too human.

Thinking back, I remembered that some of those flywheels weighed many tons and stood over twelve feet high. Those early miners must have used dozens of oxen or mules to sled that hardware into their rugged mining camps after the snows came, often working against terrible odds. Thousands of hours of backbreaking work had been scattered across the countryside in a millisecond with our 20 percent sticks of dynamite! Crowding that piece of contemporary history out of my mind, I let my eyes wander the area for pure scenic enjoyment. Dog foolishly chased chipmunks, and I began to break a sweat under the load I was carrying, thanks to the climb, the unaccustomed elevation, and the intense mountain sun beating down through a cloudless azure sky. Not a breath of wind stirred, making it possible to smell the perfume from just about every wildflower I passed. God really did work his magic that day in many wonderful ways.

Arriving, I believe, at Wade Lake (after all these years I can't remember which one came first, Wade or Grassy), I quickly scanned the shore and lake for fishermen. There were several on the east shore with kids, but they seemed more interested in playing in the water than catching fish. Moving my attention to a two-person inflatable raft on the lake, I saw that it contained a man and a woman. That combination was always a good bet because the men would often take the women's limit and then fish for themselves, thereby taking an over-limit. With that perhaps biased but more often than not accurate thought, I walked out of sight as if I were a fisherman heading for another lake, then quietly backtracked into a large stand of snow brush along the shore. Taking off my backpack and getting out my binoculars, I began to observe the two in the raft. The first glance through the binoculars revealed a middle-aged man and an obviously younger woman. Both seemed engrossed in their fishing and were catching fish at a pretty good clip.

Shortly after I began to watch and count the number of fish each was catching, the man reached over the side of the raft and pulled up a gunnysack that had been attached to a piece of rope. He took out two Lucky Lager beers, opened both, and offered one to the lady. No problem; a cold beer would taste good right now, I thought. About fifteen minutes later the lad finished his beer, looked all around as if he were looking for someone, and then casually held the empty can over the side of the raft to let it fill with water and sink into the lake. That rascal, I thought. It was a violation of the Fish and Game Code to deposit any litter within one hundred feet of the high-water mark, and I duly made note of the time and action in my notebook. The man continued to fish and do quite well, approaching what was then the daily limit of fifteen trout per person.

The lass finished her beer and, like her male friend, looked around before sinking her empty can over the side of the raft as well. Good, I thought. If nothing else, both of these folks would get a citation for littering. Maybe the surprise of finding a warden in such a remote area would break them of "sucking eggs" and littering the bottom of a very beautiful lake! Anyone else who saw these folks receive a citation would pay heed as well and maybe be a little better citizen in the backcountry after that.

About that time the group of fishermen and kids on the far shore packed up and left without committing any violations that I could see. Excellent, I thought. With those folks gone, maybe the two in the raft would catch an over-limit since they believed no one was around to observe them breaking the law. No such luck. They just continued to drink a lot of beer, sinking the empties over the side. After about an hour of this activity, the lad pulled up the raft's anchor and paddled over to shore, not thirty yards from where I sat hidden in the snow brush. They both came out of the raft and began to relieve themselves after a careful look around to make sure no one was looking. Then the fellow commenced to get amorous, and after a few moments they walked into the snow-brush patch where I was hiding and had sex. Damn, I thought. All I needed now was an over-limit case and I would have experienced it all! Back to the raft they went and out onto the lake for more fishing.

After a couple more hours of fishing, they headed back to shore. They had not caught an over-limit, so all I had them for was littering (twelve cans dumped over the side into the lake), but I definitely planned to address that issue. After they got to shore and started to deflate and unload their raft, I sneaked out from my brush pile so they could not see where I had come from and made a casual approach. Walking over to them, I introduced myself, exhibiting my badge.

"What the piss do you want?" the surprised man said belligerently.

Ignoring the lad's obviously beer-affected language, I calmly said that I wanted to check their fish and licenses. The woman complied, but the man continued to give me a lot of guff, and after taking about all I wanted, I turned and asked him in a professional tone, "What is your problem?"

He let me know in no uncertain terms that he didn't like being checked by a game warden and that he considered us lower than any other life-form he could think of. As I addressed a question to his companion, using the name on her driver's license, he unloaded on me again with even more abusive language. Again, knowing it was mainly the beer talking, I let it go.

After I finished checking the woman, I asked for the fellow's fishing license, but he just stared hard at me. Again, in a pleasant tone, I asked for his fishing license. "Don't have one," came the arrogant reply.

Tired of his mouth, I said, "May I see your driver's license, please?"

"Don't have one of those either. Besides, I am not driving," came the sneering reply.

"Then I don't have any option but booking you into the nearest county jail," I said sternly.

"Oh, give it to him, Roger," said the woman. The man continued his hard stare at me, but after a long moment he reached into his back pocket and took out his wallet and a driver's license. With his license in hand, I told them I was going to issue each of them a citation for littering and an additional citation to the gentle-man for fishing without a valid fishing license. He went into orbit again, colorfully punctuated by his logging-camp jargon. Ignoring the knothead, who continued to rant and rave about what a hind end I was, I turned to the woman, opened my citation book, and began to take the necessary information. I entered at the bottom of the citation as evidence, "4 Lucky Lager beer cans sunk in lake and a handful of toilet paper deposited on the shore." I didn't normally write someone up for depositing toilet paper on a shoreline, but I did it this time to make a point. ...

Over the continuing loud noise coming from her partner, I explained what was on the citation and what was required of her legally to address it. As she read down the paper, I could tell when she spotted the words "4 Lucky Lager beer cans sunk in lake and a handful of toilet paper deposited on the shore."

"What is this toilet-paper thing?" she asked in a measured tone.

Without batting an eye, I told her I meant the large wad of toilet paper she had thrown into the bushes after having sex with her partner.

She froze, her widening eyes not leaving mine. She said incredulously, "You saw all that?"

"Yes, from about ten feet away," I said, trying to sound detached.

She whirled to face her male friend and told him in her own pretty logging-camp terms to shut his mouth and settle up on the ticket so they could "get the hell out of here." The fellow was shocked and started to respond, but she leveled him with the words "Want any more? If so, shut your mouth right now, or else."

"Mouth" went to "wimp," and that was that. I issued the citation to him for fishing without a license and littering, and he was only too happy to take the ticket and retreat. Damn, being observant can sometimes do wonders for a game warden, especially when the moment comes to write a ticket. Off went the two fishermen, one still very red over the revelation of her secret and the other doing what he was told just like a lap dog. Nothing personal, lady, just doing my job, I mused as I watched them walk down the trail and out of my life.

Shadow and I continued our hike, working our way up an old wagon trail cut into the granite rock en route to Grassy Lake. Grassy Lake was a beautiful spot surrounded by granite bluffs and sloping granite ridges. As the name connoted, it was full of vegetation and numerous species of aquatic grasses growing along the shore. There were a few fishermen along the shore, but they didn't look like the violating kind, and the fish weren't biting because it was the hottest time of the day. After watching the lads fish for an hour or so and noticing that the hour was getting late, I started my hike up to Rock Lake, a few miles farther up the trail.

Rock Lake was appropriately named: it was contained in a deep, rocky basin surrounded by high granite bluffs on all sides except one. Here the water level ran right to the edge of the bluff, and then a small stream carried the overflow over the edge to the rocks below. I had fished here as a small boy and still remembered the numerous big trout that used to reside there. In fact, I remembered one trip here with my dad in which we had caught eighteen rainbow trout that collectively weighed more than seventy-five pounds! In those days the limit was fifteen fish or forty-five pounds of fish per person. I would bet a month's paycheck that those limitations are not in the regulations for California today. My, how times have changed.

Working my way up onto a high bluff, where I could see into the lake but remain camouflaged from view by some snow brush, I looked over the rocky edge. No one was fishing below. Since it was a Saturday and was now getting late, I decided we would stay for the night, work Rock Lake in the morning, and then hike to some other distant lakes during the afternoon. That way I could cover a lot more ground in the backcountry and scare the hell out of those who believed they were safe from the game wardens. Moving back over the lip of the rocky ledge, Dog and I hiked down to a small valley at the side of Rock Lake where a little trout stream loudly flowed over the rocks and out of sight into a thick patch of willows. Taking my backpack off and letting the air get to the sweat on my back, I took a long, well-earned stretch and drank in the magnificent view. Then I got out my fishing pole, a gob of worms, a number six Eagle Claw hook, and two small split shot, and it didn't take long to catch six nice, plump brook trout running about a pound to a pound and a half each from my little stream. They were really thick across the back, and when I opened them up, their flesh was dark pink, heralding a terrific dinner. After gutting and washing the fish, my partner and I found a little bench area along a granite cliff and tossed out my sleeping bag on a deep bed of moss and grasses. Gathering up some wood, I built a fire ring and a small fire and fed Shadow her can of dog food and a Snickers bar (her favorite candy). Then I took a stick and poked around the coals of my fire, spreading them out a bit before tossing in a tinfoil-wrapped potato and red torpedo onion. The onion had been peeled, coated with real butter, and liberally sprinkled with garlic powder before it was wrapped. The potato, well, what can one do wrong with a potato? It had been washed, poked full of holes, smeared with butter, wrapped in foil, and now was sitting contentedly in the coals hissing out steam. In a few moments the hot snow-brush fire was sending off smells that only God and a good cook (which I was, of course) could make. Out came my old ten-inch cast-iron frying pan, and into it went a glob of butter. After the butter had melted just a tad, I dropped in two of the freshly caught trout, which I had sprinkled with lots of seasoning salt, garlic powder, flour, and pepper from a plastic bag. Within moments the smell of woodsmoke mixed with cooking onion, a steaming potato, and fresh trout; the sound of a happy brook moving to the Pacific Ocean; and an orange-and-red sunset were capping my day. The only thing I missed was having my bride alongside me so she could also enjoy the elements that made up the basic tenets of my soul.

I kept turning the onion and potato to avoid burning and the fish once to avoid shattering, all the while enjoying the last of the day and the beginning of the evening. A light, cool breeze drifted across the campsite, and with it came the voices of ghosts from the past. Before I could get too far into the world of historical wonder, my fish were done. Placing them on a bare rock to cool, I added more butter and two more seasoned trout to the skillet for a repeat of the action. When they were finished, so were the onion and potato. Removing them from the coals, I set them aside to cool in the now rapidly chilling high-mountain night air, regreased the frying pan, and set the last two trout to cook in the coals for tomorrow's breakfast. No greater meal was ever eaten by any king than the one I ate that evening. There is really something to be said for eating in the great outdoors, especially if it involves fresh-cooked brook trout! Once the last two trout were cooked and cooled, I wrapped them and one left over from dinner in a piece of aluminum foil and laid them in my pack. Removing my boots and socks so the night air could dry them, I sat back, broke out a cigar, and listened to the sounds of the night. As the fire died down, so did the day's "fire" in me, and I prepared for sleep. Hanging my pants and shirt on a nearby bush, I took my Colt .45 out of the holster, placing the gun beside my sleeping bag where I could reach it in a hurry if the need arose. Then I slid my frame, more tired than I had realized, into the cold sleeping bag. Within moments it began to warm from my body heat as slight night breezes began to dance around the campfire's embers. Lying on a soft bed of plants and looking up, I marveled at the clearness of the sky and the stars that hung there. The snoring of Shadow, who lay beside me, reminded me of the next order of business, and it was only moments before I joined her.

Shadow's deep, rumbling growl brought me from a deep sleep and told me all was not well at the campsite. Opening my eyes and moving only slightly, I slowly slid my hand over the comforting cold steel butt of my pistol. The continuing rumble told me I had a visitor that was not wanted by the dog, and probably not by me either. Moving ever so slightly, I picked up my flashlight and carefully started to raise myself up so I could see what the problem was and defend myself if necessary. Looking over the dog's head in the direction she was looking, toward the embers of the dying campfire, I turned on my flashlight with one hand while I cocked the hammer of the pistol with the other. Not ten feet from the edge of the fire, standing on all fours, was the massive form of a huge, glossy-coated black bear, probably weighing in at four hundred pounds or better! The beam of the flashlight combined with a loud holler from me sent that critter down the hill at a speed that surprised even me. A splash and immediate crashing in the brush told me he had crossed the creek where I had caught the trout and had gone into the willows on the far side in his efforts to escape.

Shadow, trained as she was, stood her ground as the bear departed. Now that the intruder was gone, I reached over and put my arm around the dog to give her a thankful and reassuring hug. When my arm went around her, I noticed that her hackles were standing straight up from the back of her neck to the tip of her tail. Damn, she was ready for battle, no matter who the opponent! Giving her one more hug, I lay down, put away my gear, and tried to get some more sleep. After viewing the stars for a while, I became aware of the deep snoring of my protector and soon joined her again. This time we remained undisturbed until dawn's light.

A faint rustling in my rucksack, combined with the early-morning light, woke me. Dog was still snoring, but I was more than awake after glancing over at the quiet noises coming from my backpack. I watched the now moving bag holding my food and last night's fried trout and was soon rewarded with the sight of the most beautiful coal-black mink I had ever seen. The mink backed out of the pack dragging what was to have been my breakfast, the aluminum-covered packet containing the three trout left over from the night before. It commenced to tear the foil apart until the trout were exposed, then wolfed down my breakfast, bones and all, while Shadow slept through it all. Damn, what a great moment and experience! That little chap gobbled down the trout not three feet from where I lay watching, explored the bag for any more of the same, and then headed for the creek. Once at the water, the mink paused to look around, took a long drink, and disappeared into the willows in the blink of an eye and a single bound.

A smile creased my face as I crawled out of the warmth of the sleeping bag. Grabbing my shirt and pants, I put them on and felt the cold damp from their all-night exposure to the chill of the high-mountain air. On went my cold boots and into the holster went my .45 as a long stretch of my back muscles completed the start to my morning. Dog woke up as I began moving about and ambled off to the creek for a drink. Once there she winded the mink and had to explore that new smell before she tended to other important dog business. Opening another can of food for the dog, I placed the contents on a nearby rock, then wrapped the two smashed-flat dog food cans in a plastic bread bag and put them back into my pack. I dug out a Snickers candy bar and slowly ate my breakfast, all the while letting my nose, eyes, and ears drink in the sounds of the unique waking world around me.

One of the sounds I heard in the distance was unmistakably that of human voices. I had company, I thought as I hurriedly finished cleaning up my camp and then scrambled up to my Rock Lake overlook. Sure enough, below me at the lake's edge were three fishermen who had just arrived. Man, I thought, these chaps must have left the trailhead early to get here at this time in the morning. That told me they were really serious about their fishing. I wondered how serious they were about staying within their daily limits. … I slid into my covered position behind the snow brush as the idea of any more breakfast became a dying thought. I put my binoculars on the fishermen and discovered two men, a boy in his early teens, and what appeared to be a five- or seven-person inflatable raft being inflated with a foot pump. As the older of the men pumped up the raft, the other assembled three fishing rods and the boy played about at the water's edge. Once the raft was inflated, they pushed it out into the lake, and all three got into it. The dog lying close by my side started snoring again as the three lads finished assembling their terminal gear with Ford Fenders and what appeared to be a Dave Davie's. Good, they were going to troll around the lake. Having fished this lake before, I knew that kind of activity would produce the best results if they wanted to catch not only big fish but lots of them. It didn't take long to figure out their method of operation for the day. One of the men rowed, and the other man and the boy tended the three fishing poles. It wasn't a bad plan except that it was a violation of the Fish and Game laws. In those days you were entitled to fish with only one fishing rod: your own. You could not attend to more than one, and it was now appearing that I would have at least one violation before the day was done. I couldn't do much with the kid because he appeared to be under the legal age (eighteen) for receipt of a citation, but I could ticket the men, and I would if they continued to fish in this manner. It didn't take long before they were hooking and landing lots of pretty nice-sized fish. In fact, during their first hour of fishing, I don't think I saw them land any fish weighing less than two or three pounds!

This pattern continued, with the same man rowing and the other tending to their two fishing poles while the young lad tended his own. Before long the adult tending both fishing poles had exceeded the limit of fifteen fish per day and was starting on the rower's and the boy's limits. That was OK, I thought, because I still had about eighteen blank citations left in my book and would have no trouble adding another name or two to the "book of fools." After about three hours of fishing the three had their forty-five fish. As I said earlier, they were damn nice ones. There is a huge granite bluff at one end of Rock Lake, and every time they rowed by that end of the lake it seemed that several big fish would appear on their lines simultaneously. Damn, these lads had the process down pat and sure knew how to fish this lake.

As they headed toward the lower end of the lake to unload and clean their fish, I slipped out of my hiding place, keeping cover between us, and headed their way. Coming in from the bushy side of the lake, I surprised the lads as they deflated their raft, cleaned their fish, and talked excitedly about the day. "Good morning, lads, state Fish and Game warden. How did you do?"

The man who had been rowing was so surprised by my unexpected appearance that he jumped out into the lake, landing in water up to his knees. "Damn, man, don't sneak up on us like that. What the hell, did you think that we are outlaws or something?" he said as he stormed out of the icy waters and back to shore.

"No, I don't think you guys are outlaws, but you did violate the law," I said. You would have thought the adults had been hit with a large stick.

"What do you mean?" asked the rower very slowly.

"Lads, I have been watching you since daylight and keeping notes on your fishing operation. You rowed the boat the entire time," I said, pointing to the rower, "and you and the boy caught all forty-five of the fish," I said, turning to the others. "That is a violation of the Fish and Game laws, and you, the one who caught the fish for yourself and your partner, are going to get a ticket for an over-limit and fishing with two poles."

I could see that I would get no argument, and I duly issued the two citations to the one adult for his violations. I then seized the thirty-seven fish he had caught that morning (his limit, his buddy's limit, and seven of the boy's limit) and sent them down the mountain after informing them that their fishing was over for the day. First, however, I explained to the youngster why we had bag limits and why fishing as they had done that morning damaged the health of the fisheries in those high-mountain lakes. From the look on the father's face, I could see that my message had cut two ways. The rower, however, just stood there and glowered, pissed at having been caught with his hand in Mother Nature's cookie jar. When they had left and walked out of sight, I carried the seized fish to my campsite, finished cleaning them, and then loaded them into my pack in a large, heavy plastic bag I had carried to keep my clothing dry in case it rained. I now had one hell of a load (once weighed, the fish came to just over a hundred pounds), so instead of heading off for other lakes to check fishermen, I packed the fish in snow from an unmelted drift and headed down the mountain.

Once out of the lake basin, I left my evidence at Clyde's house and then returned to the backcountry for several more days of checking fishermen. My remaining stay in Clyde's district was uneventful, with the usual run-of-the-mill violations. Finishing up my stint for Clyde, I moved into Gil Berg's district and continued my pattern of hiking into the backcountry and checking fishermen. Gil's district, like Clyde's, produced only ordinary violations of over-limits, no fishing licenses, and littering, all of which I dutifully addressed. Finishing up my three-day detail for Gil, I loaded up Dog and we began our long trip home by a different route.

Rounding a bend in state Highway 89, not far from Sierraville in the Tahoe National Forest, I passed a wide turnout where three vehicles were parked. Always curious, I left Shadow sleeping in the patrol car and followed a well-used trail up from the edge of the highway until I discovered a small high-mountain lake quite close to where I had parked. It has been so long that I don't even remember the name of that little lake, but it had two lads fishing from the shore and another in a small green six-foot wooden boat out on the water. Using some snow brush for cover, I sneaked over the hill and settled in behind a large sugar pine. From that hidden position, I used my binoculars to look over the two lads who were fishing from the shore. They didn't look too interesting, so I shifted my view to the fellow in the boat. He was an old guy with short-cropped white hair and the worst "scrootched-up" face I had ever seen. Suddenly his face went from scrootched-up to "regular."

What the hell? I thought, really crawling into my binoculars to check out that facial behavior. There, he did it again! Now my interest was really up, so I steadied my binoculars by leaning them against the pine tree. *There, he did it again!* This time I saw a small splash before him where his fishing line entered the water. What the hell? This pattern of the scrootched-up face and splashes in the water continued for a few more minutes while I continued to observe the fisherman, trying to figure out what the hell he was doing. Then I saw him reach over and pick up a jar of yellow salmon eggs from the bench seat in the boat. Looking all around to make sure no one was watching, he tipped his head back and dumped the contents of the jar into his mouth! He waited a few moments, took a look around again to see if anyone was looking, and began to spit the salmon eggs one at a time into the water where his fishing line entered the lake. Each time he spat out a salmon egg, he would scrootch up his mug. The lad was chumming in a manner I had never seen before. Unfortunately for him, that practice was illegal and was now being seen by a rather large lad with a badge lurking behind a tree.

Reaching into my "war bag" (a small canvas bag that held my extra enforcement gear), I took out my Super Eight movie camera and began to film the events unfolding below me. I let the man in the boat catch a few fish to close the ring on the case, then left my hiding place and walked down to the lakeshore. I hailed the lad, identified myself, and asked him to row ashore so we could talk. The lad had just refilled his mouth with salmon eggs, and I saw him swallow hard in an effort to conceal that oily gob of evidence before he came ashore. I had to chuckle as he gagged a few times in order to keep his secret from me. It looked like Mother Nature was already starting to get her due. ... He rowed ashore without any problem, and I asked him what he had been doing with the salmon eggs, spitting them into the water and all. He just looked at me and said, "You saw that?"

"Yes," I said, "and not only did I see that, I filmed it as well."

His eyes quickly darted to the camera in my hand, and with that, he rolled over and admitted that he had been chumming for trout. By the looks of his fish stringer, it was a pretty effective method of catching fish. I asked for and received his driver's license. His name was Eric Oostrum, and he lived in a nearby mountain community. He was a very old man, seventy-nine at the time, if I remember right, and very polite. The only reason I remember this ticket was the date: it was June 22, 1968, my birthday. I thought, what a nice birthday present as I wrote the man a citation for chumming. We parted company shortly after that, I with his fish (since they had been taken illegally he could not keep them under California law) and four empty salmon-egg jars for evidence and Eric with a fishy taste in his mouth, fishy breath, rolling guts, and a ticket in his wallet.

The next few months sped by with the usual amount of violations and work for a game warden assigned to the Sacramento Valley. Early the following summer Captain Jim Leamon called to ask if I would go back to Sierra County and give Gil Berg a hand with his horde of summer fishermen. I said sure because, as usual, anything that took me out of the Sacramento Valley heat and humidity was my idea of a good deal. The following week I met Gil and got lined out to work in one part of his area while he worked in another. During the following days Gil and I worked the trout fishermen throughout his district, and then after supper we worked spotlighters illegally killing deer in the high-mountain hay meadows. It was a fun time: running all day and burning the candle at both ends, working with a fellow officer I really liked who was chock-full of game warden war stories, and working in an area where there were lots of bad guys to catch. We managed to turn up several dozen fishing cases, mostly over-limits and littering, and caught two spotlighters with a doe deer as well. All in all, we managed to pay for the "gas and oil," as some officers used to say, and then some.

After finishing that detail, Gil and I shared a lunch along a high-mountain meadow one day, drinking from the cold snowmelt waters of the stream (we didn't worry about *Giardia* in those days). Then we topped the day off with a few hours of trout fishing of our own during which we each caught a limit of fat brook and rainbow trout. After cleaning the fish by the side of the stream (carrying out the entrails in a plastic bag) and placing them in ice chests lined with unmelted snow from the previous winter to keep them from spoiling, we parted company.

Heading down state Highway 89, I decided I would go home via Graeagle to East Quincy, where my folks lived, and load up on some of my mom's home cooking. The day was super, made all the better by my recent successes in the citation department and topped off with a pleasant few hours of successful fishing. My mother really loved trout with pink meat (indicating a high-protein diet), and I was bringing her as nice a mess as one could find. It made me happy to be able to do something nice for her once in a while, and a gift of trout would be just the cat's meow.

I was so deep into daydreaming about my previous few days and the homemade meal to come at Mom's that I almost missed it when I passed a small high-mountain lake that, based on the number of parked vehicles, was experiencing great fishing. Quickly checking my mental list of all the lakes recently stocked by the department's fish division, I realized this lake was one of them. With visions of over-limits dancing in my head, I turned around and headed back to have a look-see. Parking my rig among all the others, I grabbed my gear and sneaked up to a rocky point where I could observe the activity without being seen.

Sure enough, there were about a dozen people along the shore and two boats on the lake, all intently fishing and catching recently stocked fish. Stocked fish aren't too smart, and these were showing it by biting everything thrown at them in the form of bait, much to the glee of those fishing along the bank. I could see that the lads on the shore would probably "control" each other as far as over-limits went because of the number of people fishing alongside one another. Shifting my gaze to the lads in the boats, I saw that one boat had already limited out on the stocked fish and was starting to head in. The other contained a lone individual who continued fishing. I watched that chap for a while and saw that his fishing line and hook must have been inside a bottle on the bottom of the lake. He wasn't catching a damn thing.

Losing interest in him, I returned my gaze to the lads on the shore and saw that many had finished and were in the process of cleaning their fish. Not seeing anything out of the ordinary, I half-heartedly returned my binoculars to the lad in the boat, only to see a fisherman with a "scrootched-up" face. Wait a minute, it couldn't be—it *was!* Eric was the lad in the boat, and he was fishing with his trademark mouthful of salmon eggs, chumming for the trout. Sure as hell, he was spitting the salmon eggs over the side, and in a few minutes he had a trout on. After he bagged that one, it seemed he had barely tossed the hook, line, and sinker over the side before another trout was on. For the next twenty minutes or so Eric alternated between landing fish and filling his mouth with salmon eggs from the jar. I had to chuckle. He was going to get another ticket for chumming, just as sure as God made little green apples! Finally I had had enough of Eric's antics, so I rose from my hiding place on the rocky bluff and walked down to the lakeshore. Upon seeing me walking toward him, Eric swallowed the mouthful of salmon eggs and then almost puked them back up right in front of God, the game warden, and everybody. I let him finish his dry heaves, then called him over to the shore and, when he arrived, greeted him by name.

One look at his eyes, still tearing from trying to puke up the re-cently swallowed salmon eggs, told it all. He didn't say much, but I could tell he knew this was not going to be his day. It was evident that he recognized me. After all, one does not meet many three-hundred-pound game wardens in any state. Forgoing the usual greetings and other remarks we game wardens make when we have someone "in the net," I asked for and received his fishing and driver's licenses. After he handed them over, I asked, "Eric, when are you going to learn?"

He looked at me with eyes showing stubborn resignation and said, "Just write the ticket, please."

I got out the citation book and commenced to write him a ticket for chumming for game fish in the waters of the state. That wasn't the unique part of the situation. I was now in the process of writing a fisherman for the same violation, on the same lake, and *exactly one year later to the day!* It was June 22, 1969. Only once in my career, with more than ten thousand citations, have I written a chap for the same violation two years running on the exact same date at the exact same place! Poor Eric was my first and only. Again, the only reason I even remembered the previous citation was that it had been written on my birthday.

When I got back to my vehicle, I had to chuckle. What are the odds against this happening? I asked myself. They had to be astro-nomical. It went to show what a really small world we live in, I mused. Occasions like that had a way of bringing that point home when one least expected it. For Eric's sake, I hoped he had taken that point too!

I am sure Eric has passed on to his reward by now, as I am writ-ing this story some thirty years later. I hope that wherever he is, chumming is legal. ...

7

The Commercial Froggers

S ITTING AT THE DESK in my reloading room, where I manu-
factured rifle, pistol, and shotgun ammunition for hunting
and target practice, I went through my stack of official state mail
for the day. There were the usual bulletins announcing regulation
changes, a memorandum from the captain about a change in reporting hours worked, several documents on various state Fish
and Game meetings around the area, and one that looked omi-
nous to me as soon as I laid eyes on it. It was about a proposal from
some members of the commercial fishing community to allow the
commercialization of bullfrogs, that is, live-catching these critters
throughout state waters and then selling them to biological supply
houses. In theory, the frogs would be injected with red and blue
dye to show the arteries and veins of the circulatory system and
would then be used as a teaching aid for high school and college
students studying biology, zoology, and anatomy.

That proposed regulatory change made all of my commonsense and reality-check red flags shoot up! First of all, the major
rice-producing county in which I was stationed was loaded with
bullfrogs, not to mention every other kind of frog. That meant
I would have my hands full with licensed "outlaws" raping the
amphibian resources in every body of water in my district. Also, it
didn't take a rocket scientist to realize that the prices paid for
bullfrogs would be far higher in the restaurant industry than at
the biological supply houses. It took me only a microsecond to
realize that this group was trying to get a regulation changed

under the guise of a benefit to science when in reality it would benefit only their bank accounts once the frogs were sold to the highest bidder! The loser, of course, would be the amphibian community, the role the frogs played in the balance of nature, and ultimately the American people once the critters were practically hammered out of existence.

Boiling out of my office and getting on the phone, I began calling my squad mates, and soon we were all voicing our concerns to our captain. Most wardens stationed in the Sacramento Valley had vast numbers of frogs in their districts. We realized that this was a little-understood and fragile resource that should be managed more carefully by our agency. We also knew from past experience that there were many markets for amphibian flesh in the form of frog legs. Soon those markets in the populous Sacramento Valley and San Francisco Bay area would be a bonanza for the commercial froggers as they sold their squirming catches to the highest bidders. Other wardens scattered throughout the state where there were large populations of frogs also began to raise hell about the prospect of creating illegal markets and the consequent decline of the animals' beneficial population status.

All our hollering was to no avail. The state of California, hell-bent on exploiting this new revenue source, ignored all the red flags being raised by the apparently know-nothing game wardens. It seemed that the amphibians didn't have many people who loved them—they lacked wildlife biologists who understood the frogs' fragile population dynamics, commonsense leadership at the top, a good political lobby, or all of the above.

Soon the new regulations were adopted, allowing commercial frogging throughout the state. The only restriction was a requirement that commercial froggers must call and personally advise a warden when they would be working in his district. Another regulatory clause stated that anyone caught violating the laws under the new regulations upon conviction would automatically lose their commercial frogging license for a year. These restrictions were nothing but a bone thrown to the still-fuming game wardens by the administration, which didn't have a clue as to the Pandora's box it had just opened. But it was a bone I was soon to turn into a thighbone of monstrous proportions!

I called some of my Humboldt State College classmates who were working at several of the Bay area's largest biological supply houses (they couldn't find a job in the field of wildlife management and had to eat) and was shocked at how little they were paying for live frogs compared to the underground restaurant markets in Yuba City, Fresno, San Francisco, and Sacramento! In those days, according to my sources, including several damn good informants in the commercial fishing business, it was almost a ratio of three to one restaurant dollars over those from a biological supply house! I could see nothing but problems with this new regulation before all the dust had settled. Asking my friends in the biological supply house business to keep me informed of the approximate increase in numbers of frogs that became available to them with the passage of this new law, I began to set my anticipated enforcement sights on this new problem. That evening at the dinner table, I advised my long-suffering bride of the latest turn of events and how it was going to affect our lives because of the numbers of frogs in the county. Since most successful frogging takes place at night, I told her I was going to double my enforcement efforts in an attempt to somehow keep the illegal take in check. She just grinned, knowing her husband was on another of his vision quests, shook her head, and served me a second piece of her outstanding homemade pumpkin pie. Man, how I did *love* that woman, I thought as my tongue tasted the spices. When I look back over the years at her way of addressing my crazy work ethic, I somehow think she had as good an understanding of the resources and their needs as I did!

Figuring it would be a few days after the passage of the regulation before I ran across this new form of market hunter, I got down to the basics. I spent the next few nights carefully running almost every known "froggy" canal in my district, and there were a pile of them. Carefully logging in my mind those that had heavier populations, I vowed to keep a sharp eye on them to prevent their pending mass destruction. I even went so far as to contact many of my landowners, advising them of the change in the regulations, and noted in a book those who were going to post their lands and waterways against this kind of problematic harvest. I also asked them to call the sheriff's office if they suspected that their waterways were invaded with this latest flood of hunters so the dispatcher could notify me in turn, at home or on the state radio. I read and reread the new regulations, looking for any loopholes to help me in my efforts to protect the resource, and found none. After about the tenth reading, it became apparent that the commercial fishing industry had had a hand in how they were written. The only handle I had was that I could snap them up if they didn't notify me that they were going to be frogging in my district before they arrived. That seemed like a pretty weak hook for an enforcement officer to hang his hat on, but a drowning man will grab even a spear if it is thrown to him. And since that appeared to be what the higher-ups in Sacramento were throwing at me and my kind, I promptly put on a glove. ...

As I expected, the flood wasn't long in coming. According to the Fish and Game Department news releases, twenty-six commercial fishing licenses to harvest frogs were initially issued for northern California. Nine days after passage of the regulation, I found my first commercial fishermen frogging on the 2047 Canal, smack in the center of my enforcement district. I was checking some catfish fishermen that evening on the banks of the canal, and they told me a boat had just passed them, heading upstream with two men frogging. The men had observed what appeared to be at least six gunnysacks full of frogs in the bottom of the boat. The sport-fishing limit on frogs in those days was twenty-five per person. Six gunnysacks held a heap more than the allowed fifty between the two fishermen in the boat, so I figured they must be "commercial." I quickly scrambled up the bank of the canal, got into my patrol truck, and called the Colusa County sheriff's office on my radio to ask them to call my residence and find out from my wife if she had been called and notified that any commercial froggers would be frogging in my district. Some of you may be wondering why the call would have been made to my wife. In those days, as is still the case today, many of the burdens of Fish and Game wardens fall on their spouses, especially wives. They are the ones who are usually home, so they're the ones who answer the phone. These women became skilled in every kind of Fish and Game matter and in most cases could accurately respond to the public. They did this work at all hours of the day and night and *were never compensated by the state for these valuable services!* When you're a public servant, it doesn't take you long to realize that everyone in your family will soon be impressed into service. ... In a few minutes Colusa called back and told me my wife had received no such call. Hot dog! I thought. Here go a couple of knotheads into the toilet in short order for not notifying me of their commercial frogging activity in my district.

Moving upstream along the 2047 Canal on the levee road without headlights, I soon overtook the boat full of frogs and the two fishermen. I hate like hell using the word "fishermen," but unfortunately, they were licensed as commercial fishermen, hence my use of the expression. May all you good readers who are fishermen in the truest sense of the word forgive me for using the term and dragging the good name through the mud.

Through my binoculars I could see that they had a unique setup. One man lay in the bow of the johnboat (a flat-bottomed boat designed for shallow water) on top of some padding. He wore a powerful spotlight strapped to his head, leaving both of his hands free. Two wires led from the spotlight to the terminals on a car battery sitting in the center of the boat. The man in the bow was extended a few feet over the leading edge so he could reach out and grab the frogs before they spooked from the presence of the boat's wake. In the stern the other frogger ran the boat quietly and slowly, so as not to spook the frogs. When they spotted a frog, the driver would slowly move the lad leaning over the bow right to the frog for an easy capture. Plain and simply, it was a slam-dunk! The light was so bright that the frogs just froze in its glare until captured. Then the boat driver would back the boat off, and the man in the bow would cast his spotlight back and forth at the water level along the canal banks until he sighted another frog and the process would be repeated. The man in the bow had a boxlike structure at his elbow that was nothing more than a wooden chute with two spring-loaded doors in the front. Once caught, a frog would be quickly shoved through the spring-loaded doors and released. As the man pulled his hand back out, the two doors would spring shut, preventing the frog's escape. Attached to the other end of this foot-and-a-half-long wooden chute was a gunnysack into which the live frogs tumbled. Once the sack was full, it could be unfastened, knotted shut, and then placed out of the way while another gunnysack was attached to the wooden chute. And so it went.

Watching these guys in fascination, I couldn't believe how deadly efficient they were. I could tell they had been doing this for some time. They were like a live-frog vacuum cleaner! I followed them for about half a mile, and *they never left a live frog of size on either bank of the 2047 Canal the entire way!* Finally they came to a dam crossing the 2047 on the northeast side of Delevan National Wildlife Refuge. Knowing the dam would stop their upstream progress unless they got out and horsed the boat over it, I made sure I was there waiting.

The boat idled up to the west side of the canal and anchored. Both men got out to relieve themselves not ten feet from where I was kneeling in the dark. When they finished, I stood up and said, "Good evening, gentlemen, state Fish and Game warden. How are you fellows doing this evening?"

There was a bit of a shock at being surprised by the local game warden in such a remote area and at such an oddball hour, but they soon recovered. "We are fine, sir," came a measured reply.

"Are you boys commercial froggers?" I asked. If they weren't, with the limit of sport frogs at twenty-five and with seven gunny-sacks of frogs in the bottom of the boat, they would be in a heap of trouble. If they responded as commercial froggers, since they had not notified me of their activity in my district, they were also in a heap of trouble. Either way, checkmate. ...

"Yes, sir, we are commercial frogging under the new law and have our licenses right here to prove it, officer," the man from the bow responded.

"May I see your licenses, please?" I asked.

Both lads handed me their licenses, still in the envelopes in which they had received them from the state just days before. Reviewing both documents, I noted that a copy of the current regulations had also been enclosed. "Did you lads take the time to read the regulations that accompanied these licenses?" I asked.

They gave each other a questioning look, and then the man from the bow said, "No, not all the way through."

"Well, gentlemen, prior to any frogging activity under this license, you must contact the local game warden and let him know you are going to be operating in his district."

"We did that," said the stern man, "and he said it would be all right."

"Oh, who did you fellows call?" I asked.

"We got ahold of this Terry Grazzy, and he said it would be all right to frog in his district," replied the stern man.

"Well, gentlemen, I don't know any Terry Grazzy. I know a Terry Grosz, but not a Grazzy."

"That's the one," said the stern man. "It was Terry Grosz."

"Well, if you contacted him and he said it was all right to frog in his district, I guess it is all right," I said.

"Well, we sure did, mister. We don't want any trouble with the law, so that is why we called," replied the stern man with a big grin, which was soon to change.

"You talked to him direct, now, is that right?"

"Yes, sir, we know what the regulations say when it comes to that."

"Well, gentlemen," I continued, "I am Terry Grosz, and I sure don't remember any phone call from anyone, and neither does my wife, regarding any commercial frogging in my district this evening."

The stern man just froze, as did the bow man. Then the stern man stuttered out, "Well, we did contact someone before we came."

"Did you fellows call a Warden Chuck Monroe?" Chuck was the Williams warden and the only other one in the county.

"No, it wasn't anyone by that name. I am sure it was Terry Grosz."

"Well, I am here to tell you that no one, since this new law has passed anyway, has called me regarding commercial frogging in my district. That being the case, both of you gentlemen are in clear violation of the law."

Both lads just looked at me like a couple of trapped cats in a culvert, and me holding a cherry bomb with a lit fuse. They were in the very heart of the county, and there could be no mistake as to where they were. They had just screwed up royally, and now I was going to see if the state had the guts to enforce the loss-of-license provision under the new law. "I need to see your driver's licenses, gentlemen," I stated slowly.

"Why?" asked the stern man.

"Because both of you are going to receive a citation for commercial frogging without notification to the area warden."

"That is pretty chickenshit," said the stern man as he reached for his wallet.

"I don't make the laws, fellows, just enforce them, and both of you are clearly outside this one." I issued citations to both men and then went to their boat to take a look at their catch. There were seven very full gunnysacks of live frogs of every make and model. After listing "seven gunnysacks full" on the citation and photographing the bags, I had the lads sign their citations and gave them a copy. Then I removed the sacks of frogs, opened two of them, and let the contents out in the 2047 Canal. Brother, did that elicit groans from my lads standing there watching all their hard work going down the drain. Knowing that was a pile of frogs for one area, but also knowing they would quickly migrate out into the adjacent rice fields, I wasn't worried. Then I took the remaining sacks of frogs, hauled them with difficulty up the levee, and dumped them into the adjacent flooded marshes of Delevan National Wildlife Refuge. I knew Ed Collins, the refuge manager, wouldn't object, and neither would the frogs. Both lads were pretty sullen, and when I asked where they had put their boat into the canal, they remained silent. When I repeated the question, they sullenly answered that they had put in by the Highway 20 bridge. I sent them on their way and left the area through the road on the north end of the Delevan National Wildlife Refuge en route to the Four Mile Road area to the west.

I hadn't gone half a mile north on Four Mile Road when my mind began to race regarding the fellows I had just cited. Stopping, I sat in the middle of the darkened gravel road, which was abandoned at that time of the night. My gut instincts were reporting that there was more to be done in the area I had just left. Hell, I thought, there was no one else there to check, so why the strong feeling? Then it dawned on me! Damn, what a knothead you are, Terry, I thought. Spinning the patrol truck around, I headed back to the area where I had recently left the two commercial fishermen. Stopping a hundred yards from the 2047 Canal on the north end of Delevan Refuge, I got out and quietly shut the door. As I walked toward the canal, I could clearly see the beam of a spotlight bounding off the waters and shooting skyward. Sure as hell, my two froggers, incensed at being caught, had stuck their hands right back into the cookie jar after I had left. Arriving high on the bank above the canal, I could see the fellow in the bow of the boat reharvesting the two sacks of bullfrogs I had dumped out not twenty minutes before! It was pretty obvious that they hoped to reclaim some of their lost financial ground. The only problem was, they were going in the wrong direction, as would shortly be proven when I got through with them once again. Quietly walking a few yards downstream from their hectic activity, I crept down the bank of the canal and sat at the water's edge. When the lads came to my side of the canal to retrieve some of the released frogs bobbing in the water at the bank's edge, I hit them with the beam from my five-cell flashlight. Surprised at my return and realizing what the consequences would be if they were caught again, the stern man reversed the motor and moved the boat out into the middle of the canal, obviously making ready to get the hell out of Dodge.

"Hey," I yelled, "I know who you are, and if you run I will beat you to where your car is parked. When you finally arrive, I will arrest both of you for failure to show and throw your hind ends into the slammer!"

There was a pause and a hurried conversation out in the middle of the canal. Then the boat slowly idled over to where I stood as the bow man started to dump some of the reclaimed frogs over the side.

"*Hey,*" I yelled again, "dump one more frog overboard and you will go to jail for destruction of evidence!"

With that, the man resigned himself to the problem at hand and sat down in the boat. In a moment the boat touched shore at my feet.

"Hand me the sacks of frogs, gentlemen," I commanded in a tone not easily misunderstood. I was handed one and a half sacks of live, squirming frogs. Damn, I thought. Money for frogs must be pretty good for them to try something as stupid as this. Placing the sacks up on the bank for safekeeping, I said, "Well, gentlemen, are we commercial frogging again?"

"No, you know damn well we aren't," gruffly replied the stern man.

"How about you?" I asked, looking at the resigned man in the bow.

"No, I am not commercial frogging. I already got a ticket for that from an asshole," he replied.

"Then I guess you boys are sport-frogging, is that it?"

"What else is there?" replied the bow man.

"How about you?" I asked the stern man.

"You're damn right, and I have a sport-fishing license as well, so stick that where the sun don't shine!"

If I hadn't known better, I would have said my two fishermen were a little unhappy with me. ... "May I now see your sport-fishing licenses?" I asked. Both licenses were forthcoming and were in order. "Now, gentlemen, we have a slight problem," I told them.

"What this time?" blew off the stern man. "Do we need to contact you if we are going to sport-fish for frogs as well?"

"No," I replied, "you can do that anytime, but you must stay within the limits, and these two sacks of frogs tell me you fellows might just be a few over."

You would not believe the look I got in reply. The bow man stood up and threw his headlamp down into the bottom of the boat with such force that it shattered into a million pieces. The stern man just sat back and said, "You got to be shitting me!"

"No, I don't usually do that," I replied as I got out my cite book and laid it at my feet. Then I got up and started counting the actual number of frogs in the gunnysacks, and as I counted them, I gently threw them into a small feeder canal on the wildlife refuge to preclude any further attempts at capture. With the daily limit of twenty-five frogs per person, I found the number of ninety-four in the sacks a *bit* over. I issued both lads citations for possessing over-limits of frogs and handed them copies of their citations as a re-minder of an evening gone bad—*really* bad!

After I finished with the lads, they headed downstream and left me sitting on the darkened canal bank with the ever-present mosquito to savor my evening's successes, my "save-the-day" gut instinct, and a stinking Toscanni cigar. The ferocity of the mos-quitoes cut short my celebration. Where were those frogs with their sticky tongues when I needed them?

I never heard a peep out of Sacramento on the first two com-mercial froggers out of the bag getting caught just a few days into the program, and both had their licenses revoked. In addition, they each paid a $150 fine for commercial frogging and not advis-ing me in advance and a $235 fine for their following over-limits of frogs on their sport-fishing licenses. All in all, a good evening ...

For the next several weeks, it was pretty quiet in my district as far as the commercial froggers went. After that I would get a call about once a week notifying me that someone was going to be commercial frogging in my district, and that was it. Afterward I would scout out the areas just worked by the froggers and find no frogs, or no more than one or two, left in the entire drainage. These guys were just like the buffalo hunters and beaver trappers of old. They took everything and left nothing in the ecosystem for reproduction. Good old Sacramento and the wise decision to allow commercial frogging and the resulting extermination of the frogs in the areas these lads went through like vacuum cleaners ... I stayed with them, though, since the bullfrogs had no other voice in their support—and believe me, I could be heard clear across the Valley!

I tried to keep track of the approximate percentages of frog population reduction in the areas hit by the froggers and reported the numbers to Sacramento via monthly reports and every other chance I got. However, the higher-ups and the biologists remained strangely silent throughout my flood of reports and general squallin'. I guess they felt they had the usual uneducated nut-case game warden on their hands, though that wouldn't have been a wise thought. Most game wardens today possess at least one college degree, if not two or more, and they are out in the field every day experiencing the real world of wildlife, not just the view through an office window or the screen of a computer. ... The bottom line was that I would be there to check the froggers every time they were in my district, and they knew I was out and about. I ran those on private land off the waterways, and those landowners wanting total protection of their frogs got it. I knew I was not alone. My counterparts were also out and did not miss any opportunity to check the commercial frogging fraternity.

One hot summer day I got a call from a pair of commercial froggers who said they would be working in the northwestern part of Colusa County in the Willows area. I informed them that it was not my assigned area, nor was it in Colusa County, and they would have to call Warden Wally Callen and let him know. I gave them his home phone number and thought nothing more of it. Later that evening, one of my rare stay-at-home nights, I got a call from the Colusa County sheriff's office to tell me that a fisherman had called from Sartain's ranch on the northeast side of my district and said a boatload of froggers had just gone down Butte Creek by the Colusa-Gridley highway bridge. That was no big deal because it was an area commonly worked by sport froggers. But when the dispatcher added that the caller had said the froggers had gunnysacks filled with frogs in the boat, my blood pressure and hind end got with it! Man, I was up and out the door in a flash, to be called back only to have my badge pinned to the clean shirt I was hastily trying to put on and to be given a kiss by a rather understanding bride. ... I vaulted into my patrol car, and Shadow, my Labrador retriever, leaped into the bed of the truck.

Racing up to the bridge in question, I soon located the fisherman who had called the information in to the sheriff's office. The froggers had gone downstream, and the fisherman had seen them taking frogs from both sides of Butte Creek (the east bank was in Butte County; the west bank was in Colusa County). I got on the state radio and called Warden Fred Brown, the local warden stationed in Gridley. Now, there was a catch dog if there ever was one. Fred was one of those unusual officers who not only ate and slept the job but had the damn fine instincts needed to catch the bad guys, especially those who crossed the line by using set lines, taking over-limits of ducks, or taking a deer or two illegally out of what he considered *his* natural resource larder. He was a big, raw-boned man but smooth as a schoolmarm's thigh.

"Come on, Fred," I said out loud to the radio, impatient for his return call. Finally, after my second call, he responded. It happened that he was tied up on a deer-spotlighting investigation, but he told me he hadn't been contacted by anyone wishing to commercial frog in his district that evening. After a short explanation of what I figured I had going, I thanked him and signed off. Excellent, I thought as I bailed out of the truck and let the tailgate down for Shadow. After a drink of water to offset the Valley's summer heat, off we went. Walking a mile or so down Butte Creek on the Colusa County side produced nothing but a sweat-soaked shirt and a zillion welts from the ever-present hordes of happy mosquitoes, so I headed back upstream, got into my truck, and drove down the Colusa-Gridley highway until I hit the levee road going south through Sartain's ranch. I headed south on that levee toward the White Mallard Duck Club, continuing to look for the bouncing light beams off the water typical of a frogging operation. Seeing none, I drove off the levee just below the White Mallard and started for the Butte Creek Farms area. Stopping to get a cold soda out of the ice chest I always kept in the back of the truck, I saw a bouncing beam of light shoot through the air on the south side of some of Sartain's rice ground. Pop forgotten, I jumped back into my truck and began a without-headlights stalk on the canal where I had seen the light beams bouncing off the water. Parking in some shrubbery at the base of a small levee road, I walked up to the edge of the canal, and there in all their glory, not forty yards away, were two froggers. They had apparently slipped out of Butte Creek and crossed into Colusa County via the many connecting waterways and from the looks of it were now having a very successful evening catching frogs in one of my better-populated canals!

I watched them for a while through the binoculars as they took frog after frog from this little-known canal. I could see that the froggers were working their way toward a canal crossroad where they would have to get out and carry the boat over, so I decided to set up my ambush there. About thirty minutes later the two lads were at the road berm. Getting out of their boat, they dragged it up out of the canal and onto the road in preparation for dumping it into the canal on the other side. That was when I chose to make my presence known. "Morning, guys, state Fish and Game warden. How you doing?"

One lad jumped like a bug on a hot rock, but things quickly settled down. "Fine," replied the shorter of the two as he continued to drag the boat across the road as if my presence meant nothing.

"Why don't you hold it right there?" I said. "I would like to check your licenses and gear if I might."

"Sure," replied the short one, whereupon he pulled out his commercial frogging license and handed it to me. The other man did the same, and as I was looking at their licenses they again started dragging their boat. Damn, I thought, in a hurry or what, boys?

"You boys want to hold it up a bit?" I asked.

"We need to get going if we can, officer. Burt here has to be back at work by eight," said the short one.

"Well, this will just take a moment," I replied. "I see from the sacks of live frogs and your commercial frogging licenses that you boys are in the business at hand. Since you are in Colusa County, I am wondering if you called anyone this evening prior to starting your commercial frogging endeavor to let them know what county you would be working in?"

"Yes, we called Terry Grosz, and he gave us the number of another warden, but he wasn't home," replied the short one, who was called Jim Stacey.

"Well, you are in another county at this point in time, and I should have been the one called if you were going to frog way over here."

"Isn't this Butte County?" Jim asked.

"No, Butte County is a mile or so that way," I responded, pointing to the east.

"Oh, does that mean we are in trouble?" Burt asked.

"Yeah, if you were to follow your own frogging regulations," I said. "Besides, gentlemen, I called the warden from this area, and he said no one called him regarding commercial frogging in his district either."

Suddenly I was startled to hear a gunnysack right next to me in the boat *quack!* Looking down at the dry sack, I could see duck toenails sticking out the sides. No wonder these lads were anxious to get the hell on the way; they had a live duck in the bag. "Well, what have we here?" I said as I lifted the *quacking, wiggling bag* out of the boat. Because of their uneasiness, I had planned on really shaking down the boat anyway, but now that I had an entry, I took it. Untying the knot at the top of the sack and looking in, I was greeted by a flopper hen (a bird so young that it cannot yet fly) mallard duck standing on a pile of dead ducks looking up at me.

"I told you to wring that bastard's neck instead of taking it home for your little girl!" Burt hissed through clenched teeth.

Letting the duck go over the edge of the boat before it damaged its still growing primary feathers any more than it already had in the sack, I turned to the lads and just stared. It was obvious to me that they had used their strong spotlight to fix the nonflying ducks roosting in the canal in their tracks before grabbing them and wringing their necks. Neither man said anything as I emptied out the sack to discover another twelve dead mallard ducks. "Well, lads, we have a bit of a problem since duck season is still three months away!"

Neither man moved; they just looked at their shoes and then at me.

"May I have your driver's licenses, please?" I politely asked. They handed them over, and I wrote out citations for possessing migratory game birds during the closed season. Normally I would have booked these lads for the duck episode, but I decided against it so I could continue to work the east side for any other folks wanting to step across the line. When I finished the duck citations, I started to write each of them another citation for their evening's work frogging.

"What is that ticket for?" asked Jim. "You already wrote us for the illegal ducks."

"Gentlemen," I said, "now you are being cited for not notifying me you were going to be commercial frogging in my portion of the district of Colusa County."

"What kind of crap is that?" yelled Burt. "It is so damn dark out here anyone can get lost on his bearings."

"That may be true," I said, "but you called a warden in another county and were unable to contact him. Then you took off and commercially frogged in two other counties without notifying either of those officers. So you now must pay the piper for those indiscretions. Besides, gentlemen, Butte Creek is an excellent county boundary and is clearly shown on any map." I could tell they were pissed, but nothing like they were going to be when they saw the fines handed down along with the loss of their commercial frogging licenses!

Several weeks later Bonnie Grussenmeyer, the Colusa County Justice Court clerk, notified me that each of my early-season duck catchers had paid $500 for the duck offense and that Judge Weyand, having heard lots of complaints from fishermen that all the frogs were disappearing because of the commercial froggers, had upped that portion of the fine to $250 each. It made me feel good that the local populace was finally getting up in arms, but that still didn't do the frog populations any good. The commercial froggers had discovered Colusa County and its froggy bounty and were pounding the hell out of it regardless of what I did to slow them down. Now there were many nights in which I would have three or four commercial froggers in my district at a time, going at it with a vengeance! The only good thing about it was that I had now caught four of the commercial froggers, and the word was getting around to be on the lookout for the large, fat game warden in Colusa County. In addition, there weren't twenty-six licensed commercial froggers in the northern part of the state anymore; it was down to twenty-two. It seemed that some damn game warden had caught four of them. ...

Throughout the remaining days of summer, I worked the froggers as hard as I could along with all the other things going on like closed-season pheasant shooting, over-limits of striped bass, spot-lighted deer, and the like. The summer was good to me, and I managed to scratch six more commercial froggers who had sneaked into my district without the required notification. It seemed a little chicken at times to use that section of the law, but looking into those canals, usually full of frogs, and seeing nothing the day following a commercial frogging escapade diminished that feeling considerably. Besides ... frog kind of tastes like chicken, doesn't it?

When the commercial frogging stopped for that year because the frogs were mudding up for winter, I had caught a total of ten commercial froggers, reducing the number of commercially licensed lads at that moment to sixteen! By then the hue and cry from the sportsmen who carried the Fish and Game with their license monies was starting to be heard in lots of strange places. Many landowners took to throwing froggers off their lands, and Judge Weyand (God rest his soul) had upped the fine for being caught illegally frogging in Colusa County to $350 per offense. That was a high fine for the old judge, who was used to and comfortable with $25 to $35 fines for wildlife offenses.

The next frogging season, just as soon as the frogs warmed up and came out of the mud, I was ready. It wasn't three weeks after the frogs were out in heavy numbers that I had my first run-in with another of my favorite customers. I was working the lower reaches of Butte Creek one evening and had just sat down with the mosquitoes for a breather when I heard the soft purring of an outboard motor coming my way. Looking upstream into the dark, I could see a strong light beam dancing off the water and sailing skyward through the trees and brush. I lay down on the creek bank and pulled Shadow down alongside me to wait. Sure as shooting, here came what appeared to be a commercial frog boat working just the Butte County side. I knew from talking to Warden Bob Hawks earlier that he had a commercial frogger out that night in the Butte Creek area of his district (Fred Brown was the warden on the north, Bob Hawks on the south of the creek), so I relaxed a little. Several times I saw the beam of light strike a bullfrog on my side of the creek, but the lads in the boat passed them by, not having notified me regarding their frogging presence in Colusa County.

As they moved out of sight, my gut instinct cut in and said they needed to be followed. Having experienced the accuracy of that feeling many times before, I followed it. Trotting out of sight along the bank of Butte Creek, Shadow and I followed the lads through the brush for about half a mile. There was a small slough running directly into Butte Creek from the west, and I was curious if they would go in there, which was Colusa County, for that oxbow's supply of frogs. Sure as shooting, in they went, but not before shutting off all their lights and just sitting there in the dark at the mouth of the slough for about forty minutes. Shadow and I sat a few yards away, listening and watching. Finally I heard one voice say, "If that puke is around, we should have thrown him by now."

There was no response, at least none that I heard. But soon I heard another voice say, "Let's give it a shot. There is no way that bastard even knows about this slough." With that, they went right into Colusa County. As they turned on their lights, the air filled with the sounds of disturbed wood ducks fleeing the scene, leaving only their fluting little whistles behind. Shadow's ears went up, and she looked up at me as if asking, Do I get to do any retrieving, boss? Petting her, I hauled myself to my feet and waited until my froggers got into the middle of the no-way-out slough before I walked to the constriction point, sat down, and waited again. As they made their way around the edges of the slough, I could see the lad in the bow working really hard and filling the maw of the frog box attached to his gunnysack time and time again. In fact, it took the froggers about an hour to clean out all the frogs in that slough. Then all the lights went out except a small beam to guide them as they started back toward Butte Creek and safety ... or so they thought!

As my froggers approached the narrows leading back into Butte Creek, I waded out to the bottom of the pistol barrel on my hip and just stood there in the middle of the little channel. Their boat was within two feet of me before they realized they had a problem with an "obstruction" in the canal. *"What the hell?"* shouted the surprised man in the bow as he turned his headlamp on full power. When he saw me, he hollered, *"Jesus Christ!"*

"Evening, gentlemen," I quietly said as I grabbed the bow of their boat. "How is the commercial frogging tonight?"

"Uh, uh, uh, it's all right," said the man in the bow, who by now had raised himself onto his knees. "Are you Terry?" he asked cautiously.

"The one and only until God decides to change me out for something else," I responded.

"Holy shit, where the hell did you come from?" asked his partner in the stern.

"Been here right along," I said with a twinkle in my voice.

"Are we in Colusa County?" the shaken man in the stern asked.

"Sure are," I responded. "I thought you folks knew that when you stopped and waited at the mouth of the slough for about forty minutes without using any lights and then headed in hoping the 'puke' wasn't around." The lads just looked at each other like a couple of gutshot owls as I said, "Fishing licenses and driver's licenses, please."

There was no argument as they dug them out from their wallets and handed them to me. Wading back to shore, I got out my citation book and wrote up both of them for frogging in Colusa County without prior notification or authorization. They never said a word other than to respond to my questions relative to the citation.

Finishing up, I asked the froggers if they had any questions, and their silence indicated that they had none. I said, "All right, let's dump two sacks of frogs overboard after I get some evidence pictures."

"*What?*" they both said at the same time.

"I said two sacks, please."

"Why?" asked the one called Darrel, almost beside himself.

"Because when you went into the slough in Colusa County you had three sacks of frogs in your boat. I figure you took those lawfully in Butte County, so they can stay. However, you now have five sacks full of frogs, so I figure two of those came from this slough. Those will be returned."

Darrel got up, grabbed one sack of frogs, and in anger just slammed them over the side of the boat. Quickly standing up, I told him to do that one more time and his little ass was going to jail for destruction of evidence. That got his attention, and the next sack of frogs went overboard in a less violent fashion. Let me tell you, when you dump out a tote sack full of frogs, you have a circus. They are trying to go every which way, and most do. But it was a good feeling to see them free and back in their home slough once again.

Randy, the other lad, then asked a question I was totally unprepared for. "Can we advise you now that we are going to be here in your county tomorrow, in fact here among other places?"

"That is the way the law reads," I said, biting my lip. "Just keep in mind that once this citation is processed, your licenses to frog commercially will be gone shortly thereafter."

"Good," said Randy. "It is now eleven o'clock. In another hour it will be tomorrow, and we will be right back here to get our frogs." He had a smart-ass look in his eye, but both of us knew he—and the wording of the law—had me! I thanked the lads and moved off into the night like a whipped pup. I went back to the area the next evening and was saddened to see that there wasn't a frog in the old oxbow or backwater. I wasn't surprised, but I guess I was hoping against hope.

This war on the froggers had taken a mean turn for the worse, I thought, and then, after a second of mulling that thought over, I smiled. Folks should remember that people don't get as big as I am by standing last in line. When I filed the citations in Colusa Justice Court a day or so later, I had a chance to tell Bonnie my little story of apprehension. I included the smart-ass commercial frogger's surprising question at the end of the evening, which had ultimately led to the decimation of all the frogs in that little slough. I saw Bonnie's eyes harden, and for some reason, instead of the usual $350 fine, both lads ended up paying $500 for the error of their ways. Sometimes you eat the bear, and sometimes the bear eats you. … Now I was down to fourteen commercial froggers still under license, and that was becoming a manageable number in my eyes.

Throughout these battles with the commercial froggers, I kept in touch with my inside contacts and informants in the biological supply houses and restaurants in the Valley and Bay areas. According to my sources in the biological supply houses, the newly licensed froggers had led to only a slight increase in the quantity of frogs coming in. Their main live-frog suppliers continued to be foreign markets and places in the Southeast that raised frogs for these outlets. Also, as reported to me, the frogs that did come in from the commercial froggers were little to medium-sized frogs, not the jumbos. However, after some tips from informants, I personally found some restaurants, especially the smaller "mom-and-pop" ones in Marysville, Yuba City, Sacramento, Oakland, and San Francisco (especially in the ethnic neighborhoods), that had frog-leg dinners on their menus for the first time. In some cases the menu change was penciled in or attached to the menu with a small piece of paper advertising the newest table fare. Surprise, surprise! I had known it would be just a matter of time before the frogs started moving into the restaurants in the Valley and Bay areas because that was where the really big money was, but I didn't figure on it being as widespread as it was. These menu additions didn't appear everywhere, but they occurred in just enough restaurants to make a difference, so I redoubled my efforts. There were legal frog-leg sources in those days (as there are today), especially foreign markets and a few from the Southeast, but before the new commercial frogging regulations, when asked for frog legs, people in the restaurants had said they were just too expensive to serve, so they had never been on the menu with regularity. The frogs may not have had a nicely dressed spokesperson with a big cigar in political circles, but they sure as hell had one on the creeksides and canal banks when the sun went down. ... And yes, their spokesman did smoke a cigar, a cheap Toscanni, but that was to keep the mosquitoes at manageable numbers so I could survive without being carried off and eaten.

I managed to keep burning the candle at both ends and with the grace, allowance, and wisdom of my bride worked many a day and night together. Daylight would find me doing everything from the administrative work associated with the job to attending court, giving evidence meat to those less fortunate, checking fishermen, and the like. Dark would find me prowling the waterways checking sport froggers, fishermen, and of course my old friends the commercial froggers. In the latter category my work was really cut out for me. The froggers, like the frogs, could be anywhere. And the very biggest and most numerous frogs were in the most out-of-the-way places. The froggers still patrolled the canals and large backwaters, but they were beginning to wipe out those frog populations and were forced to go farther and farther off the beaten track to stay profitable.

Another phenomenon was that the frogs migrated from their protective big waterways into the warm-water rice fields in the summer to feed on the minnows, crawdads, ducklings, smaller frogs, reed-nesting songbirds that fell out of the nests into the water, and the like. Then, when the rice farmers drained their fields in preparation for harvest, the crawdads and frogs would migrate back into the more stable waterways, calling them home until the next spring migration cycle. With that rush by the frogs back into the big waterways in the late summer I would have a resurgence of commercial froggers hoping to reap the fresh-off-the-rice-fields bounty of jumbo-sized frogs. Armed with that bit of information, I would almost live along the waterways, making sure the froggers toed the line, so to speak. As in any segment of society, I found the good, the bad, and the ugly. Most of the froggers I ran into in those days occupied the last two categories. ... But there is always the exception.

Turning off the Princeton Road onto the Colusa-Maxwell highway one hot, humid night, I turned off my headlights and drove down the road in the dark to get some night-driving practice. It was late, and the highway was deserted and safe as a tomb. Driving slowly for a quarter mile or so to let my eyes adjust to the darkness, I just relaxed with my arm hanging out the window and let the sweat roll off my brow as well as down the middle of my back. Damn, how I hated plastic seats, but that was all the department would buy us, so those of us in the hot, humid Valley districts just roasted in our own juices night after summer night, and tonight was no different. It was almost midnight, and it still had to be at least 100 degrees with about 80 percent humidity. Slowing down at the intersection of Four Mile Road, I turned north and had driven about one hundred yards along that road in the soft moonlight when a feral cat ran across the road and into a culvert. Slapping on my brakes, I slid to a stop just above the culvert, grabbed my 12-gauge, Model 11 Remington shotgun, and bailed out. Feral cats in the Valley in those days were just about overrunning the land. They were so numerous that I can remember killing an average of fifteen a night when the floodwaters ringed the Valley, eliminating many of their usual hiding places and forcing them out in the open on dwindling patches of land. Quickly reaching into my shirt pocket for the M-80 cannon cracker I usually carried, I lit it at the end of my ever-present mosquito-killing cigar and threw it into the east end of the culvert. Racing across the gravel road to the west end of the culvert, jacking a live shell into the chamber, I turned on my flashlight, held it underneath the shotgun to provide some shooting light, and waited. *Boom!* With the explosion at the east end of the culvert, out tumbled a wad of dazed cats far in excess of the number of shells I had. I had removed the plug from my old shotgun, one I had had since I was a boy, and killed the first five cats out of the culvert with five shots.

Then I quickly laid down the now empty shotgun, switched the flashlight to my left hand, and drew my .44 magnum Smith and Wesson revolver to kill one dazed cat right at my feet. I missed the next one as it ran off into the night outside the beam of the flashlight but killed the next three as they came boiling out of the culvert. The last cat out of the culvert was a big tom, and it was obvious he had been shot at before. He flew out in excess of nine hundred miles per hour, or so it seemed, and zigzagged back and forth like a fighter plane. I might as well have shot straight up into the air with my last cartridge instead of at that cat, but it was fun trying for such a fast-moving target. Besides, there was no one there to witness my poor shooting and the miss at the final cat, so I felt all right.

The cat lovers rolling around on the carpet at this apparently casual act of barbarism should realize that I had good reasons. A feral cat is part animal and part human. It is without a doubt one of the most efficient predators on the land because it retains its abilities as a wild animal but also knows the dangers of humankind and how to avoid people. There is hardly any more lethal killer when it comes to all the ground-nesting critters such as songbirds, quail, and rabbits. That becomes even more true when the cats are running wild in the outdoors in the thousands, as they did in those days. They are only doing what comes naturally, but they are an unnatural element in the wild of today, and especially when they hunt in unnatural numbers. Because the critters in the wild were being hammered from every angle by humankind, I just tried to help out by eliminating one of those angles. Besides, I missed two of those cats, didn't I?

Satisfied with my evening's work in the cat world, I reloaded the shotgun (minus one in the chamber for safety reasons) and returned it to my vehicle for later judicious use if more felines showed themselves. Then I paused to light up another cigar and tend to the call of nature. I was looking eastward into the Delevan National Wildlife Refuge, thinking about other things, when I saw it! Just for a moment I saw a "spot" in the dark on the refuge. Careful not to lose its location in the inky black of the night, I felt

around on the seat of the truck until my hand closed over my
binoculars. Still staring at the point where I had seen the thing,
I raised the binoculars to my eyes. I knew my eyes hadn't been
playing tricks on me; they were too good for that. Thanking the
Lord for my excellent vision, I watched a small but intense light
moving back and forth in the tall rice grasses at the flooded south
end of the refuge. What the hell? I thought. No one was supposed
to be in that area because of its refuge status and the nesting birds,
but bigger than life, there it was again. The light was almost
muted to the naked eye, but with the binoculars I could plainly
see a glow right in among the marsh plants with an occasional
sharp white flash as a light was pointed in my direction. The light
appeared to be moving very slowly in the flooded marsh area but
there was no doubt that it was there! When I lowered my binoculars, I could hardly see anything, and if I hadn't known where to
look I would have not seen it at all.

Getting into my patrol truck, I turned it around on the Four
Mile Road without using the lights and headed south. When I hit
the Colusa-Maxwell highway, I turned east until I reached the
gated road on the south end of the refuge. Quickly unlocking the
gate, I drove into the refuge and relocked the gate behind me.
Driving in about a hundred yards, but still several hundred yards
from my mysterious light source, I parked the truck, grabbed my
flashlight, binoculars, and citation book, and headed north on the
Delevan. After walking about a hundred yards, I got out my
binoculars and looked the area over once more. There was the
light again, but now it was a little clearer. What someone was
doing on a national wildlife refuge after midnight with a light
down in the marsh was a new one on me, but it wouldn't be for
long. I continued toward the light, walking along old rice checks
(earthen dikes spaced in a rice field to maintain the proper water
depth), until I found myself working my way north and east toward the 2047 Canal, which bordered the refuge. Finally I hit the
levee road paralleling the canal and continued north toward the
light. From what I could tell, someone was on the refuge in a boat
doing something with a reduced light. The marsh reeds and tall

grasses still hid the mystery, but it was man-made, and I was going to get to the bottom of it or else!

Creeping along on the raised levee road, I finally got a good look at my mystery. There were two men in a very short, shallow-draft boat doing something on the water. Moving farther up on the levee road out of sight so I could see better, I was surprised to find a johnboat anchored in the 2047 Canal with a rope leading up the canal bank from the boat to one of the many willow trees lining the levee. What the dickens? I thought. Scrambling down the bank a bit so I would be out of sight of the two fellows on the refuge, I turned on my flashlight and took a look, shining the beam through my fingers to diffuse the light and not alert the lads to my presence. It was a sixteen-foot johnboat with a small outboard motor. In the bow was an old mattress with a headlamp with wires leading back to two car batteries, and sitting quietly next to the batteries were what appeared to be three sacksful of frogs! Glory be, I thought; I have a couple of commercial froggers who did not bother to inform me that they would be in my enforcement district to practice their seamy trade. Then, to complicate matters, *they were now frogging on my national wildlife refuge!* I scrambled back up the bank and relocated the two chaps, who were still happily frogging, totally unaware of the eyes watching them. Sitting down with my friends the mosquitoes next to their tie-off rope, I just watched and waited.

About three in the morning, the light used by the froggers trespassing on the refuge went out, and I saw no more of them for about twenty minutes. I knew they had to come my way eventually, so I knelt alongside their tie rope next to a dense stand of willows. Pretty soon I could hear grunting and groaning like two people under a heavy load. Then two dark shapes appeared to the north, stopping short of the johnboat tie-down rope. For about twenty minutes they just stood there as if they were looking the area over for any unwanted guests. Finally they picked up something loglike and walked to where the rope was tied to the willows. Setting down their load, which now appeared to be a small canoe, they collapsed to the ground and whispered quietly. Never one to miss out on a conversation, especially one in which the speakers believe they are alone, I listened.

"How many do you think we got?"

There was a pause, and then a second unfamiliar voice said, "Hell, I don't know, but if you figure 150 frogs to a sack and we have three sacks, about 400 or so, I would guess."

"That will put a few bucks into our pockets, won't it?" came the first voice, now sounding happy.

"Uh-huh," came the reply.

"We'd better get our asses out of here, though, before we get caught on this refuge," came the first voice.

Good, I thought. Nothing better than a little intent in violating the law to sweeten the pot once one gets to court.

"You're right," said the second voice. "Let's get these sacks of frogs down to the johnboat, and then we can come back for our boat." The taller of the two took two sacks of frogs out of their small boat, and the other lad took the other, and they walked right by me and put the frogs in their big boat in the 2047 Canal. Then both lads walked back up the levee bank and, grabbing their canoelike boat (which turned out to be homemade), turned to head back down the bank. They walked straight into a rather large chap standing tall with a soft voice.

"Good morning, gentlemen, state game warden. Hold it right there."

"*Goddamn,*" yelled the tall one, and he took off down the levee bank as if shot out of a cannon. The smaller of the two froze. I imagine it helped to have my paw firmly clamped on his shirt collar. ...

Yelling after the runner, I said, "Go ahead and run. I have your boat and partner, and the sheriff's office is sitting on your vehicle waiting for your return. If you don't come back right now, both you and your partner are going to jail and your boats and vehicle will be impounded!"

There was a bit of quiet, and then I heard a pathetic voice say, "I am coming back." Soon a dark form walked into my flashlight beam.

You may ask how the sheriff's office knew where their car was parked. They didn't! I made it up. There was no way I could run after my sprinter, all the while hanging on to my first catch, now, was there? So I just used a good old ruse and hoped it worked. It did. In law enforcement you soon learn to use any port in a storm—just as long as it is legal.

"May I have your fishing and driver's licenses, gentlemen?" I asked and soon had both in my hands. Both men were from the Yuba City area and had been commercial frogging. From what I could figure, the pickings had been a little slim because many of the frogs had already been captured in previous visits by their fellow froggers on the 2047 Canal. So they had just helped themselves to the bounty that is normally found on the national wildlife refuge, hoping they wouldn't be caught. Well, you can wish in one hand and poop in the other, and the one that fills up first is what you are going to get on details like this one, as my two fellows soon discovered.

In the light of my flashlight, I got my first real look at my latest captures. Both were in need of haircuts and baths. I would say a hearty meal or two wouldn't have hurt either of them as well. They were dressed like a couple of rag merchants, and it was plain to see that these chaps were almost at the end of the line. Conversation indicated that both were married and had large families. Both were also out-of-work farm laborers who had been unemployed for some time. During the interview process, I discovered that they had seen a lot of frogs on the last farm where they had worked and had seen other froggers catching them. That was where they got the idea of going into the commercial frogging business, figuring it was a quick, easy way to make a buck. They told me that the boat and motor belonged to a friend and they had borrowed the money to get their commercial fishing licenses. As a result, they had little left between them. In fact, I found a cast-iron skillet in the boat and a three-pound coffee can full of flour. I asked what it was for and was told they hadn't eaten much lately, so they had been eating some of the frogs they had caught. Damn, I thought. I liked catching bad guys along with the best of them, but not a couple of chaps who were so down and out they didn't have any luck but bad.

I had the lads bring up all the sacks of frogs caught on the refuge, since they had caught the earlier ones on other waterways, and had them dump them back into the Delevan marshes. You would have thought I was killing their children. It was obvious their families were anxiously awaiting the money to come from their commercial frogging venture. It was obvious to me from the looks on their faces that things were looking kind of grim. I had the sheriff's office run the boat plates, and they in fact did come back to another chap, as they had said. I got them to tell me where their vehicle was parked (they didn't seem to notice my little lie about the sheriff's office being there) and kept their driver's licenses while I walked back to my truck and drove to their vehicle. They boated back down to their landing, and when I met them there I could see that the two of them had slept in a dirty blanket the night before, and their truck wasn't much either.

Acting on a hunch, I had the Colusa County sheriff's office call the Yuba County sheriff's office and check out these men's stories. About an hour later the Colusa County sheriff's office confirmed that both chaps were down and out, as were their families. The Yuba County Social Services Department was going to try to find a way to provide some assistance after the deputies had seen how the two families were living. As these conversations went back and forth, my two chaps just sat on the tailgate of their worn-out pickup and said nothing. I could tell they felt like crap about the fix they now found themselves in.

It was now approaching daylight, and with the information I had, I told the lads to load up; we were going for a ride. "Are we going to jail?" they asked in unison in rather sick voices.

"No," I said, "just follow me."

"Mister, we can't go far, we don't have much gas," the tall one said.

Looking back at my two ragamuffins, I said, "Just follow me anyway." I still had the passenger's driver's license and had written down the information about the driver, so I wasn't too worried about losing them. When we reached the Shell gas station in Colusa, I had the lads drive in, and I filled their truck up with gasoline. It wasn't much in those days; if I remember correctly, it cost 34.9 cents per gallon, and I paid for it out of my own pocket. Damn, those were the days when it came to decent gas prices. Then I had the lads follow me to my house on Eighth Street. I was glad Donna was off to school by that time because she would never have let the men into the house. That would have included me, as dirty and sweaty as I was. Parking my patrol truck, I walked by my two charges, parked beside my home, said, "Come on," and continued walking toward my front door. They quietly followed, not having any idea as to what was happening, but I am sure they feared the worst.

Entering the house, I showed the lads where the bathroom was and told them to go in and get washed up. Walking into the kitchen, I saw that my wife had laid out a thick package of deer steak for dinner that evening. Quickly throwing two large cast-iron frying pans onto the stove, I breaded and spiced the steak. Into one frying pan went our evening's dinner while I rummaged around in the refrigerator until I found a plastic container full of last night's uneaten mashed potatoes. Into the second frying pan went a cube of butter, followed by some chopped onions, fresh chopped garlic, green peppers, and celery. Soon the kitchen began to smell like heaven, and I was so bent on getting breakfast fixed that I forgot about my two waifs. Realizing they were still in the house, I turned to find them standing in the kitchen door, looking on in amazement. Showing one man where the plates, napkins, and utensils were, I had him set the table. I put the other one to work making coffee while I tended the stove and cut some of my bride's world's best homemade bread and put it into the toaster. Soon there was a breakfast fit for a king on the table, and my two chaps fell to it as if they hadn't eaten for several days.

When nothing was left and the dishes had been washed and put away, I got down to the business at hand. Both were issued citations for frogging without providing notification to the local game warden. Because of their financial situation, I did not issue citations for frogging on a refuge. After they signed their citations, they asked if it would be possible to pay these off over time, and I said I would ask the clerk of the courts to set up such a program. That seemed to satisfy them. It was obvious they were bound and determined to settle up with society; they just needed some time (they both eventually did pay their fines). Getting out another package of deer meat, I set it out in the kitchen sink to thaw for my family's dinner and then herded my charges out the door and onto the sidewalk next to their pickup.

Then I asked them if either of them had access to a freezer. They said they did with questions in their eyes. There was a communal freezer for the farmhands on the ranch where they were staying, and they could use that. It seemed that even though they were out of work at the moment, the farmer had helped them out a bit by letting them stay in the houses set aside for the workers. "Good," I said. "Follow me."

Down to the Fish and Game storage space we went and inside to my two evidence freezers. Taking two ice chests off the wall, I filled them both up with fillets of striper, salmon, and sturgeon. Then I filled a third one with steaks from tule elk and deer until it was jug-full. Grabbing a heavy cloth sack off the wall because I was now out of ice chests, I filled it with frozen pheasants, ducks, and geese from last year's hunting season and then wrapped the whole outfit up in a small tarp. "All right, lads," I said, "load this stuff up into your pickup and get your tail ends out of my district."

The two men just stood there in amazement. The tall one looked almost as if he were going to cry, and the other one was tearing up.

"Look," I said, "you boys are having a string of bad luck right now. So a little help is all right. Just remember, when you get back on top, help someone else less fortunate and then we can call this gift today even." With that, I grabbed one of the ice chests (full of meat from closed cases that I normally gave away to those less fortunate anyway) and packed it out to their truck. They followed once they had regained their composure, and soon all the food was loaded. I handed a twenty-dollar bill to the one known as Pete and told him it was to buy something for their kids. He just looked at me as if he were going to cry once again. Turning away so as not to embarrass him, I told the tall one, who was named Jamison, to share the money between both families' children. Then I locked up my rental and headed for my truck. The next thing I knew, I was being mobbed by two joyous, crying men thanking me for all I had done to help them. Trying to make light of the moment, I told them that if they were going to frog again to do it in another warden's district. With that, I got back into my truck and bade them farewell with a wave of the hand. As it turned out, both ended up getting jobs within a few months for Yuba County, one as a mechanic and the other as a truck driver. I never saw either frogging again in my district. I was also able to convince Judge Weyand to reduce their fines from his usual $350 to $25 because of their economic plight. They were going to lose their commercial fishing licenses, and I felt that was punishment enough. I had two fewer commercial froggers to worry about and was now down to twelve.

The rest of that summer I stayed busy with the usual snagging, over-limits of fish, spotlighted deer, doves during the closed season, illegally killed pheasants, and the like. However, it was a good year for the frogs, commercial froggers, and … me. I managed to snare four more of the lads frogging where they weren't supposed to be and was feeling good about my little crusade to help the lowly bullfrog. It was getting toward the end of summer, and the frogs had come out of the rice fields and moved back into their old haunts. Driving beside these areas, walking the sloughs, or just listening to the number of hearty *jug-a-rummms* in the evenings told me the froggers had done the deed on my bullfrog populations. Where I used to see or hear hundreds, now seeing two in a day was unusual! There were still a few good places on the east side of my district for frog numbers, and I spent a lot of my time there, hoping to snag another frogger or two before the season ended. But it was disheartening to see the damage done to a highly beneficial but oh so fragile resource. The damn state and its race to gin up a few more bucks in the coffers had damn near ruined a tremendous resource in my county, and most likely in many other parts of the state as well. For that bit of shortsightedness, I found it hard to forgive those folks who were supposedly smarter than the lowly game warden.

One morning I was heading back home after helping Yuba City Warden Bob Hawks on a set-line case in his district. I decided to take the back way so I could run the dirt roads along Butte Creek, checking night fishermen and the like. After checking a couple of black men along a small slough near Butte Creek Farms and sharing my mosquito dope with them, I chanced to hear what sounded like a .22-caliber shot far to the north. All three of us heard it borne on the moisture-laden breeze, and we all stopped as if on cue to listen but heard nothing further. "Looks like you gots your work cut out for you tonight, Misser Game Warden," softly said Wilbur Lawrence, a man I had checked numerous times. Listening to him with one ear and keeping the other tuned for a repetition of the gunshot, I nodded in agreement.

When I finished checking their fishing licenses and fish, I bade the lads good-evening and started slowly working my way north, looking for the mystery shooter. I knew Bob Hawks had a depredation permit out for deer on several of the Butte County farms along Butte Creek, but I sure didn't think any of them would be so foolish as to violate the terms of the permit by using an illegal small-caliber rifle. There were lots of fishermen out along the waterways that Friday night, and I found myself spending a lot more time than I had anticipated checking fishermen and writing citations for various petty violations.

About two hours later I was where I had mentally placed the earlier sound of the shot, but of course by that time the area, if it even really was the area, was empty of humanity. Heading through Warren Davidson's land, I stopped at the south end of the White Mallard Duck Club and got out of my truck to stretch the kinks out of my sweat-soaked back. I got a cold soda out of my ever-present ice chest and, standing beside my truck, took a deep pull from the glass bottle of Pepsi (we still had glass bottles in those days). The only thing that ruined my cool drink was the sensation of the mosquitoes biting through my pant legs—and *a bouncing beam of light off the water on the large slough to the west!* Facing the spot where I had just seen the beam of light bouncing off the water and going high into the air, I saw it again. Sure as shooting, I had a couple of froggers in a boat shining frogs in the slough. This was the same slough in which I had apprehended my second set of commercial froggers. It was sort of my lucky slough, if you will. Who knows? Maybe I will get lucky again, I thought as I left my truck and started my stalk on foot. Finally drawing within forty yards of my frogging lads, I could see two men in a johnboat, with one in the bow frogging and the other in the stern operating the motor. They had a lot of gear in the middle of the boat that I couldn't quite make out, so I got even closer. Once right in their "back yard," I could look down into the boat, and sure enough, there were the representative sacks of live frogs, the trademark of commercial froggers.

Waiting until they got to a place in the levee where I could board their boat if necessary, I stood up and announced my presence. They were at first surprised and then somewhat guarded. I thought I knew why they would be guarded because they hadn't notified me that they would be frogging in my district. If so, and if they were in fact commercial froggers, I had two more notches on my belt! Sure as hell, when I asked for their licenses, they handed me commercial frogging licenses that showed they were both from Sacramento. "Did you boys alert the local warden you were frogging in his district?" I asked.

"Sure did," came a rather strident, self-confident reply.

"Who did you call?" I asked.

"We got ahold of that Hawks fellow," the man named Johnson replied.

"Well, I'll tell you what," I replied. "Why don't you fellows just continue your frogging on down the slough toward where I am parked, and I will walk back to my patrol car and check." I thought I saw a look of something other than supreme confidence fly across Johnson's face, but just for a second.

"Yeah, you do that and we'll meet you there," Johnson said.

Walking back to my truck, all the while keeping an eye on my froggers, I thought I would find out soon enough if they had called Bob. That didn't remove the other problem, that they were frogging in Colusa County. However, it was always nice in a court of law to be able to inform the judge that I had been lied to, especially if Bob had not given his permission. Getting Bob on the radio, I soon discovered that *no one* had called him that evening to get permission to frog in his district! Well, I thought after signing off, these lads were in for a surprise. Little did I realize I would be the one surprised. ...

By now their boat had frogged up to the crossroad on their slough near Butte Creek, and we met not far from my truck. "Gentlemen," I said, "we have a little problem in that Warden Hawks doesn't remember anyone calling him this evening notifying him of frogging activity in Butte County. That really doesn't make any difference, however, because you lads are in Colusa County. I just wanted to check to see if a simple mistake was made, and since that is not the case, I will proceed."

The men just looked at each other as I asked for their driver's licenses. I got out my cite book and told them they were going to be cited for frogging in Colusa County without prior warden notification, and they hardly said a word. That was strange, I thought. Most people would be squalling like smashed cats about now, especially in light of the knowledge of the impending loss of their commercial fishing licenses upon conviction. After I had taken my evidence pictures and started writing out the tickets, I told the lads to start dumping the frogs into the slough from which they had come, and then came the howls. They had about six sacks of frogs, or anywhere from four hundred to six hundred, which represented quite a loss, to say the least. Not having seen them frogging elsewhere, I just assumed all the frogs came from my slough, and that was that.

With a lot of grumbling the froggers started dumping the frogs overboard and tossed their now empty sacks into a fifty-gallon steel barrel that had been cut in half and occupied the center of their boat. Once finished, they sat down in their boat among what looked like a million frogs floating in the water and sitting in the vegetation surrounding them and said nothing. I knew something was wrong because these lads seemed to just want to get their citations and get the hell out of there, but I couldn't put my finger on it. I finished up the citations, had them sign them, and then took a quick look through the boat. Nothing out of the ordinary: lights, batteries, mattress, frog box, gunnysacks, the fifty-gallon drum in the center of the boat holding their spare parts, tools, and an ice chest probably full of something cold to drink.

"OK, lads, you are free to go," I said, and they started to pull their boat up and over the road so they could put it back into Butte Creek and head home. They were struggling to pull such a long, heavy boat up over the road, so I laid down my gear, grabbed hold of the side, and gave a heave as well. When the boat slid over the road and down the other side into the slough, the steep angle caused the ice chest to rapidly slide forward as if it were empty. That was strange, I thought as the men started to get in with hardly a thank-you for my assistance. Oh, well, they are pissed at the turn in the day's events, and so be it, I thought. As I started to turn away, something caught my eye. The bottom of the fifty-gallon drum, in the last of the summer heat and humidity, was *sweating!* What the devil? I thought as I took another look. Sure as God made little green apples, the bottom half of the drum was sweating. "Wait a minute, lads," I sang out as I reached for the side of their boat to make sure they didn't leave before I took one more look.

"What the hell do you want?" snapped Johnson. "Haven't you done enough damage for one day?"

"Maybe not," I said as I stepped into the center of their boat. Reaching over and touching the bottom of the fifty-gallon drum, all the while closely watching the two for any funny business, I was surprised to feel *intense cold.* I straightened up and looked first at one man and then at the other but got only downcast looks in return. Their body language told me something was wrong—*dead wrong!* Grabbing the fifty-gallon drum by the handles cut into the sides, I lifted it up and swung it over the gunwale of the boat, with a lot of difficulty because of its weight, and onto shore. With another quick move, I stepped out of the boat next to the drum. The men looked at me like a couple of trapped rats.

Terry, I said to myself, there is something in that drum they sure don't want you to see. Without a word I began removing articles from the drum. On top were eight wet gunnysacks that had held frogs or lain in the bottom of the boat. Digging further, I discovered tools for the boat and motor, an extra anchor, an extra propeller, then two life preservers jammed into the barrel and, between them and some rags, a broken-down .22-caliber survival rifle like you see advertised in some hunting magazines. Removing it and checking the action, I found one live round in the chamber and five more live rounds in the magazine. Holding it up, I asked the lads, "What is this used for?"

"For snakes," Johnson quickly replied.

"We don't have any venomous snakes in this part of the country," I retorted. Unloading the gun and placing it behind me and out of their reach, I continued digging past another wet gunnysack to a heavy-duty plastic sack. When I opened that plastic sack, I could see a layer of ice. That is why the ice chest was empty, I thought. They had carried the ice cubes in the ice chest until they needed to put the ice in the barrel to preserve something in this heat. Well, well, well, I thought smugly. Maybe I will finally find commercial froggers with a barrelful of cleaned frogs all ready for the market. Shoving my hands down into the ice and grabbing what felt like a piece of meat, I dragged it up out of the ice for a looksee. To my surprise, *I was holding a back strap from a deer!* The look on my face had to be really funny. I was expecting iced-down frog legs for the illegal commercial market, only to find a piece of fresh deer meat. However, the look on my face didn't beat the one on the faces of my two errant commercial froggers with the now very tight sphincters. ... Digging further into the bucket, I discovered more boned deer parts. Now, I thought, that explains the shot I heard hours earlier from the area just south of us. The men had surprised a deer in their spotlight and, thinking they were alone, had killed it, dressed and boned it out, and stuffed it into the plastic bag in the fifty-gallon barrel. Then they had taken the ice from the ice chest (knowing a game warden would always check an ice chest) to preserve it and gone on their way. It seemed likely that they had done this before, or why were they carrying the now empty ice chest full of ice when they went into the field?

"Out of the boat, gentlemen, and spread-eagle down on the levee, please," I coldly said.

"What for?" came the worried reply from the stern man, a fellow called Christian.

"Both of you are now under arrest for the illegal possession of a deer during the closed season," I replied. "Out of the boat, and now."

Both lads obeyed and lay spread-eagled on the bank while I searched and handcuffed them. I then rolled them up into a sitting position and asked, "Is there anything else illegal in the boat?"

"No," replied Johnson, and after a careful search, I found that there wasn't.

I called the Colusa County sheriff's office to request a transport officer, and soon I had Del Garrison on the scene. Del was a bear of a man; he was as gentle as all get-out, but rile him and you might as well have had a she-grizzly protecting her cubs on your hands. Del scooped my lads off the ground like toys, one in each hand, and stuffed them into the backseat of his patrol car with one fluid movement. With a big, typical smile and wave of his bear-paw hand, he headed for the lockup in Colusa. I stowed the boat and motor at a nearby duck club for safekeeping and removed everything that might be stolen if the wrong people came by, placing it in the back of my truck. Then I also headed for the jail to finish the booking process.

After booking my two chaps, I got home just in time to have breakfast with my bride before she went off to drop the kids at a baby-sitter's and to teach school in Williams. "How did your night go?" she asked.

"A rather quiet night," I responded. ...

Her beautiful blue eyes searched mine for more information but found nothing except a happy man, and I got a hug and kiss as she slipped out the door and was gone. I smiled a mile-long smile at my blessings. ...

The next morning Judge Weyand heard the men's pleas in court and found them guilty of possession of an illegal deer and frogging charges. Both lads were fined $500 per offense, or $1,000 total for their night's activities. After their wives showed up and paid their fines, I took the men back to where I had stowed their boat and helped them get it launched into Butte Creek. We unloaded their equipment from my truck, and I never saw those fellows again. I was now down to just six licensed commercial froggers out of the original twenty-six. That ended my year, and come the next spring, I was able to catch four more, leaving only two untouched. By then more men were getting into the business, and I was selected by the Fish and Wildlife Service to become the newest U.S. game management agent in the Sacramento Valley, so I changed agencies and chased the commercial froggers no more.

At the time I am writing this story, many of North America's amphibians are in serious trouble. They are either disappearing at an alarming rate or already gone. For some reason or reasons unknown to science, they are not reproducing or are doing so at such a low rate that they are unable to sustain viable populations. It is not uncommon to find the young missing appendages, mutated, or joined together in unnatural configurations. Many of these amphibians are now appearing on state or federal endangered species lists. That should be alarming to all humankind because amphibians are considered by many to be the first indicators of the health of our environment. They are almost like the canaries in the proverbial coal mines. If the canaries started to show signs of sickness or died, the miners got the hell out of the mines because danger was clearly around them. Today the amphibians may be telling us the same thing. And until we find out what is causing their demise, we had best be cautious.

I am told that California state still allows commercial frogging, but only in limited areas. Those areas where I chased the early commercial froggers in an attempt to protect the resource are now closed to commercial frogging, but talking to game wardens still working in those areas is sadly revealing. To an officer, they all report that in days of old, in the late '60s and early '70s, they had frogs everywhere. Today those same officers, active or retired, report that if they see a few bullfrogs a day of any size, it is considered an event! Very possibly the excessive use of herbicides and pesticides and the overharvest of the frogs made their mark. It is sad that humankind does not really care for or learn from our history. We have had plenty of examples of classic excesses, with the great forests now destroyed, native prairies plowed and eroded, salmon streams barren, bison shaking the ground no more, beaver yet to recover to one-tenth of their original numbers, passenger pigeons gone, and polluted waters and air everywhere. Yet we continue our destructive ways. I sometimes almost doubt the terrible end so prophetically predicted in the Bible because at humankind's current destructive pace, all that will survive will be the bluebottle fly, the cockroach, and the coyote.

I wonder if God plans to bring any of us back as a bullfrog ... ?

8

The World's
Unluckiest Thieves

ONE LATE SUMMER EVENING I was at home having a rare
sit-down dinner with Donna and my children when the
phone rang. The Colusa County sheriff's office was on the line,
and the dispatcher asked if I would go to my patrol vehicle and
contact Warden Chuck Monroe (the Williams, California, warden
and a member of my squad) via our state Fish and Game radio.
Getting up from dinner with a long, I-knew-it-was-too-good-to-
be-true sigh, I went outside and called Chuck. He asked if I would
pick up the county pickup and meet him west of Williams on state
Highway 20, by the old gravel dump. He said he could use some
extra help on a stakeout. Sensing the urgency in his voice, I figured he would tell me what was going on when I got there and let
my many questions drop for the moment. We needed to be cautious over the state radio for security reasons (people listened in
on scanners in those days, as now), so I just gave him an estimated
time of arrival and signed off. I hustled back into my house to put
on a fresh uniform shirt, explained quickly to my long-suffering
bride, grabbed one last bite of her excellent home-cooked, mostly
uneaten dinner off my plate, and headed out the door. Looking
skyward as I always did for any sign from the weather gods, I was
rewarded with a view of a dark front of scudding clouds coming in
from the northwest, the direction from which most of our storms
originated. I also noticed that the air was heavy with moisture,

and the soft wind portended rain. I reminded myself to be sure to carry some raingear for whatever assignment Chuck had in mind.

Chuck and I were each assigned half of Colusa County, which is located in the heart of the Sacramento Valley. He had the southern half, roughly all the area below state Highway 20, and I had the northern half above the highway, about twelve hundred resource-rich square miles. In our earlier days, when I had still been studying wildlife management in college at Humboldt State in Arcata and Chuck had been a young game warden in the area, I used to ride with him for the experience and thrills involved in conservation law enforcement. We were good friends then, as were our wives, and spent many an evening together playing cards or enjoying each other's company over dinner. I went on to become a game warden several years later in 1966 and eventually transferred to Colusa County, where by chance Chuck and I were assigned adjoining districts. Our friendly relations picked up where we had left off, to the point that Chuck's wife baby-sat our first son, Richard, while Donna was teaching nearby at the Williams Elementary School. However, the relationship began to cool almost immediately as we worked side by side and I began to compare work ethics and case production in a county and enforcement district that demanded that everyone pull his full share of the workload. Often it seemed that I was the only lad out and about chasing the knotheads of the county, especially during lousy weather or at night when the critters needed protection the most. For the life of me, I just couldn't figure out why Chuck wasn't out there as well. He realized full well the scope and degree of hunting and poaching pressure in the county, but he just didn't seem to be driven to do the work at the level that needed doing. This was evident when the number of citations issued throughout the year was tallied annually within the Region Two squad. I normally issued at least ten to fifteen general run-of-the-mill citations to his one, and twenty to one in the serious wildlife crimes such as spotlighting, baiting, gross illegal take, and over-limits!

In addition to these differences, there was the history of game wardens in the county. It was a common topic of discussion among many of the county's citizens that some of the wardens who had been assigned to Colusa County before my time had provided less than sterling coverage. In fact, some had been known as lazy, drunks, woman chasers, loudmouths, and the like, which only made the jobs of those wardens who followed more difficult. I felt that if one was paid for a day's work, then a day's work was to be provided. In my opinionated, perhaps self-centered way, I did not feel that Chuck carried his part of the load in a county fraught with opportunities to violate the law. Plain and simply, there was a sub-cultural element in the Sacramento Valley that believed the wildlife resources were there for the taking and that they were just the chaps to do it, especially if the law was nowhere to be seen. In fact, even if the law was "in town," these people took great pride in taking the resources right out from under its very nose—and all too frequently did. Because of those pressures on the resources, I was not a particularly forgiving son of a bitch when it came to the worst bad guys, or those of my own cloth who I felt were not doing their fair share to stop some of these age-old destructive practices.

I worked extremely hard in those days, partly out of my love for the resource, partly because of the excitement of the chase, partly because I had a wife who would let me chase my vision, partly because I was young and "immortal," and partly because my work ethic was such that a long day was a good day. I considered a seven-day workweek of twelve- to sixteen-hour days normal. But when I looked across the county at my counterpart, I did not see the same degree of enthusiasm, or craziness as some were wont to call it, and in the eyes of an immature youth like I was at the time, that was a sign of weakness and sloth. Too many times to count, other officers, landowners, or citizens would ask me for Fish and Game assistance on projects in Chuck's area. I would tactfully inform them that they needed to contact Chuck. If he was not available for the detail, I would gladly provide the needed help, but protocol demanded that they go first to their assigned area warden. The requester would usually say, "OK," in a dejected tone, but they would often tell me that they could never get Chuck to help, they could never find him, he was always too busy, and so forth. Their eyes would seem to say, Yeah, fat chance of getting any help from that quarter. But there wasn't much I could do to help because department policy directed that the area officer was to work his assigned district and that all work requests should go through that person first to avoid wrecks, personally or professionally.

There was no easy way around the real or imagined issue. After several years of real-time exposure to Chuck's actual law enforcement style, it appeared to many of the people of the county, as relayed to me, that he was more interested in hunting, fishing, or goofing off with our patrol captain than in catching people breaking the law. A classic example of my own frustration involved our joint-use patrol boat. Often when I wanted to use the state boat to patrol my thirteen-mile segment of the Sacramento River, I would find it gone, only later to discover that Chuck had apparently been using it as his private fishing boat. This pattern continued when I wanted to use the county patrol truck that had been purchased with Fish and Game fines money for our joint use. I would find it gone and later learn that Chuck had been using it for pheasant or duck hunting with our captain—all under the guise of official business, of course.

I got tired of making excuses for the man and embarrassed at always having to apologize on behalf of the Fish and Game Department for his actions, or lack thereof. Needless to say, after a while a little work-related friction developed between the two of us, and we pretty much went our own ways. I would be damned if I was going to slack off and enjoy myself as he did while the resources burned, so if I wanted to get any work done, I found it best to go my own way. But I had already decided that when he needed help, I would give him the support he needed no matter what my feelings. My philosophy was always that if an officer, *any* officer, called for assistance, he would get it with no questions asked, and any differences we had could be settled later outside the work arena. It just had to be that way or the critters would take an even greater beating in their shrinking world of wildlife.

Cranking up my patrol vehicle, I drove through Colusa to the sheriff's office and got the county pickup. Quickly tossing my

enforcement gear into the front seat, I fired it up and checked
the oil-pressure and fuel gauges. The oil was all right, but whoever had last used the truck had left it with an almost empty gas
tank. Shaking my head, I headed through Colusa toward the town
of Williams. Once there, I topped off the fuel tank in case the
detail turned into a long evening. Looking skyward again, I saw
that it was now pretty black, with heavy clouds to the north and
west. Rain for sure, I thought as I got back into the truck and
headed west on Highway 20 toward the gravel pit where I was to
meet Chuck.

When I arrived, Chuck was there with a reserve deputy Fish
and Game warden named Wayne. Chuck told me he had just received some illegal-kill information from a pair of hunters who
had been hunting deer in the mountains near Cache Creek. They
had come across a freshly killed and gutted tule elk that had been
laid belly down in a dry creek bottom to keep the flies out of the
body cavity. Tule elk were totally protected in California in those
days, and the opportunity to make such a case really got my attention. If the case were made, it would be only the second in the
county to that date. Gutting and laying the elk belly down sure as
hell made it obvious that someone intended to return and reclaim
their illegal prize. Those two hunters who had provided the information, as is typical in such big country, were somewhat vague on
the exact location of the carcass. They thought it was up in the
second canyon, in a dry creek wash, about half a mile to the right
on the side of the mountain near Highway 20, several miles from
the gravel pit. Some directions, I thought. That described just
about every square inch of our mountain districts in the whole
county! This description was even further clouded because we
were in an oak-grassland ecosystem with few landmarks or points
of definition. Also, nightfall was fast approaching, it was now
starting to rain, and the wind was making signs that it was soon
going to blow like a son of a gun.

For game wardens these were small problems, and we went forward with our plans to locate the carcass and capture the elk
killers, whoever they might be. Chuck's plan was to go up on the

mountain, find the elk, and wait for the bad guys at the kill site. I quickly evaluated that plan in light of the unknown terrain, skimpy site directions, time of day, and weather and immediately brought up another scheme. I said, "Chuck, it is starting to get dark, it is going to be raining cats and dogs shortly, and we really don't have a good location on the kill site. Even if we did have a good location, we would have to use our flashlights to find it. That would probably scare away the poachers, and we would end up with a dead elk and that would be about all. Let's just wait at the bottom of the canyon that feeds into the highway from the suspected kill area and wait for these chaps to come to us."

Chuck wanted to stick to his original plan because he thought we couldn't be sure the poachers would come out that way, but I continued to argue my point that the lads wouldn't take the dead four-hundred-pound animal over the top of the mountain because of its weight but would bring it out by going downhill and through the mouth of the common canyon near the highway. If we set up an ambush there, we would let them do the hard work and then reward their efforts by catching them red-handed as they stepped out of the canyon at the edge of Highway 20 and went for their means of transportation. I said, "By setting our plan up that way, we can also concentrate our limited forces to meet whatever number of individuals come off that damn dark mountain. After all, an elk will take at least several lads to transport it through such rough terrain, and by meeting them force with force, we stand a better chance of apprehending all of them instead of capturing just a few if we surprise them at the carcass and they decide to run."

Well, in his haste and probably with a little spirit of competition because we were in his enforcement district, Chuck decided he would go back into the area, look it over, and then get back to me with a final battle plan. I said, "That sounds fine with me. I will sit right here until you return with our plan of action. That way we won't have so many vehicles running back and forth on the highway in the area in question, alerting the lads to our presence." With that, Wayne and Chuck departed, and I sat in the pickup at the gravel pit waiting for their return. Their survey should have taken only twenty minutes, but I waited for over an hour and then, growing impatient, drove down the highway toward the mouth of the canyon to see if I could identify the problem.

As I went up the highway, I met Wayne slowly driving toward me down the now dark road, and the sweep of my headlights showed that Chuck was not in the vehicle. I stopped Wayne and said, "Where the hell is Chuck?"

Wayne said that Chuck had gone up on the mountain to find the bad guys and had instructed Wayne to drive up and down the highway until he returned. It seemed *there were no instructions for me!* Needless to say, I came a bit unglued at Chuck carrying our competition a little too far. What he was doing was patently unsafe and stupid, to say the least.

I bellowed, "Doesn't that damn fool realize hauling out an elk is at least a two-man job? What the hell is he doing taking a risk like that, going one against at least two armed and very determined men? Damn it, doesn't the man realize he has a family to worry about, not to mention his own skin?"

Wayne didn't say much. He was a good local police officer in the town of Williams, and I think he probably also questioned what Chuck was attempting to do but chose to remain silent because Chuck was his friend. Anyway, my mouth was "flying" so much that anything that needed to be said had been, and if there was anything left to say, I guess he was leaving that to me as well. For the life of me, I couldn't see why Chuck didn't follow my plan for the two of us to wait at the bottom of the canyon and just grab those chaps as they came out. It was a natural geographic constriction that all of the three canyons in the area fed into. Plain and simply, the elk killers had to come out at the bottom of one of those canyons, and grabbing them that way would have been a piece of cake. Oh, well—what was done was done.

I told Wayne to follow me and drove off to hide my truck back at the gravel pit. After concealing the county truck, I got in Wayne's vehicle and had him drive me back to the area where the mouth of the canyons emptied out onto the main canyon floor next to Highway 20. Leaving Wayne with instructions to guard the bottom of the canyon from a side road where he could sit in the car and watch and yet be out of sight, I jumped out and started on foot up the now very dark canyon, which was getting wetter every moment.

By now it was raining very hard; it was darker than hell, almost like being inside a dead cow; the wind was blowing like a banshee; and I had no idea where that damn elk was because this area was in Chuck's district. On top of that, I could not use a flashlight for fear of alerting the poachers if they were in the area. Needless to say, I was pissed, not to mention getting soaked clear through. Trying to work my way up through the dense oak brush of that canyon in the dark, with the rain pouring down the front of my shirt, not to mention the back of my neck, with enough volume to make it clear down to my hind end, and the wind blowing at what felt like five hundred miles per hour, was a treat I will long remember. Brush and oak trees loomed at every step, poking me in the face, not to mention hordes of rattlesnakes going every which way trying to get out of the weather. Fortunately, they were more interested in getting someplace dry than in nailing a dingbat struggling through their dark backyard. The more sliding steps I took and the more trees I ran into under the buckets of driving rain, the madder I got over Chuck's stupidity. However, the directions I had, bad as they were, still indicated that I had a ways to go and all of it uphill, so I channeled my energy into that endeavor and put my annoyance on the back burner.

I walked about three-quarters of a mile up the side of the canyon and decided that was as good an area as any to stake out because of the geography I could overview with my adjusting night vision. The spot I picked was pretty much in the middle of the area in question, as near as I could sense in the pitch-black night. With that, I positioned myself at the head of a grassy clearing that was about three hundred yards long and fifty yards wide. I could see 360 degrees around me and move from one side of the clearing to the other with a minimum of effort and noise. Sitting down in the wet mountain grasses with my back against an oak tree, I listened to the night sounds as the darkness passed in waves over the area in concert with the fast-moving clouds and the dim light of an occasional half-moon. The air was heavy with the smells and sounds of the life around me, and it didn't take long to project myself back to primal times through rapidly awakening senses. I was finally at ease with myself and had cooled down enough that I could make a decent decision if the occasion arose. I settled in as well as I could, wet hind end and all.

The rain eventually stopped, but the wind was still blowing and the banks of clouds moved through as if they were in a hurry to get somewhere else. By now I was relaxed and enjoying my feeling of oneness with my surroundings and the night. As my ears and eyes continued to search for anyone above me on the mountain, something made me look up high to the northwest. Way up on the mountain I saw a dim light go on, then quickly flick off. At first I thought it might be Chuck trying to signal me to show his location and indicate that he had the poachers. I stood up and thought of flashing my light on and off so he could see where I was. Then my instincts as a hunter took over and told me to wait and see what was going on before I did something foolish. I stood straining my eyes at the spot where I had seen the light, but to no avail. I waited, focusing hard at that point on the mountain for about half an hour, and then *I saw the light again!* This time it was closer and appeared to have moved down the mountainside in my direction.

The light went out again, and I started taking closer stock of my surroundings. The treeline ended just north of me at a gully that was probably one-half mile long, sloping to the main canyon below, and about thirty yards deep. It was a wide, gradually sloping gully that could easily be crossed. As I continued to examine the lay of the land, the light came on again, and this time it was a whole lot closer than before and in a direct line with my position! I continued to watch the light work its way through the oak trees toward the gully on the north end of the meadow where I was standing. The thought that Chuck might have caught the poachers and was now marching them down the mountain flitted across my mind. However, my "caution light" came on again, and I decided not to expose my position—not just yet, anyway. As the

light continued toward me, I lay belly down in the wet grass to reduce any chance of premature discovery.

The light came to the upper edge of my clearing, paused, then
slowly wound its way down into the ravine and out of sight. I
couldn't hear a sound up to that point. However, in a few moments I heard sounds of grunting and groaning coming from the
ravine as the light crawled over the top of the bank and into view
at the head of my meadow. The light quickly went out, and I
heard what sounded like several people trying to catch their
breath, as one would after moving something heavy. After a few
moments the light came back on, swept the meadow as if looking
for a way out, and then went out again. There was more grunting
and groaning, and in a few moments a huge shape materialized
out of the blackness not twenty-five feet from where I lay concealed in the wet grass. I quietly stood up, my flashlight aimed at
the oncoming mass and my other hand on the comforting cold
steel butt of my pistol, and waited until it was six or eight feet
away. At that point, knowing that escape was impossible if this
proved to be my elk killers, I turned on my flashlight and illuminated two very surprised individuals. They were each holding one
end of a deer carrier (a flat-framed platform with a bicycle wheel
mounted underneath to make transporting the game easier) carrying a skinned and quartered elk, a rifle, and the saws and meat
cleaver they had used to butcher the animal in the field. I quickly
identified myself in a commanding tone, placed them under arrest, ordered them to sit down (which they gladly did out of exhaustion), and checked to make sure there were no more
poachers coming along behind them.

Picture this: here I was at about two A.M. on the side of a massive mountain with two exhausted fellows and one illegal elk.
They could have traveled anywhere on the mountain, but somehow they had walked straight to the only game warden in country
in the dead of night with their illegal game. Talk about unlucky—
these guys didn't have any luck that wasn't bad! The size of the
area was tremendous, yet here they were, almost as if delivered by
Divine Light right to my front step. The odds against it had to be

greater than those against winning the Power Ball Lottery. They had just quartered that elk, wrapped it in game bags, and wheeled it the better part of a mile down a darkened mountain with visions of steaks dancing in their heads. After meeting the local game warden, all they had dancing in their heads were sharp questions about what was going to happen next—and that information wasn't long in coming!

Both men were sullen, quiet, exhausted, and soaking wet. I asked for and received their driver's licenses with a minimum of fuss and noticed some type of badges in their wallets when they opened them. After verifying who they were by their pictures and sticking the licenses in my shirt pocket for safekeeping, I asked, "Where is Chuck, the other game warden?"

The two looked at each other, and the big one said in a surly tone, "Chuck who?" I thought his tone might mean that they had already run into Chuck, knocked him in the head, and left him up on the mountain. Concerned at this prospect, I told the lads, "All right, if that is the way you want it, get back up on your feet, grab the handles on that deer carrier, and let's go." They tiredly rose to their feet, rolled the carrier upright and back onto the wheel, and looked at me for direction. I pointed in the direction I wanted them to head and walked behind them close enough to grab the tail-end fellow if they decided to initiate any funny business, all the while directing their travel downhill with the beam from my flashlight.

We started down the mountain, and boy, we were just "a-foggin'," to say the least. I ran their hind ends off because I was worried that Chuck might be hurt, and I needed to get these boys down the mountain and into Wayne's hands and a pair of handcuffs so I could go back up the mountain and try to find Chuck by backtracking their wheel marks. Moving an elk down a mountain in the dark, at speed, takes a lot of strength. I saw to it that the two fellows on the deer carrier got a lot of "assistance" from me growling at them all the way down. When those poor guys got to the bottom, they were finished physically. Plain and simply, they couldn't go another step no matter how loudly I growled. In fact, one of them was complaining of chest pains and the other couldn't even talk. He just lay on his side in the mud and puked. I noticed that no matter how the poachers had cut it, they would have ended up in the canyon bottom where I had earlier urged Chuck to set up an ambush. But it was Chuck's district, and I guess he knew how to do it better. ... I got my lads up and pushed them to even greater efforts as we wheeled the elk over to the fence along the highway so I could flag Wayne down with my flashlight and get the poachers into his custody.

All of a sudden Chuck stood up from behind some brush at the bottom of the draw where I had originally said we should hide and in a scared voice squeaked out, "Hold it right there! You are all under arrest."

If I hadn't been so tired and relieved at the same time to see him alive and well, I would have reached over and ripped his lips off and fed them to the first magpie I found. Sensing his nervousness at being confronted by three large men in the dark and not wanting him to do something foolish like shooting, I said, "Chuck, just relax; they are already under arrest."

He said, "Oh, I didn't recognize who you were."

Well, damn, it is kind of hard not to recognize me at six foot four and tipping the scales at three hundred pounds, I thought. Maybe he didn't recognize me soaking wet, or with all my hackles still up. ...

We wheeled the elk to the fence, let the two exhausted chaps lie down, and waited for Wayne, who eventually made a pass in his vehicle and was stopped by our waving flashlights. Wayne took me to the county truck, and I brought it back so we could load the elk and all the poachers' gear into it for transport to the evidence locker in Colusa. We escorted both hunters to the hospital for a checkup (the man with chest pains was just exhausted and did not have any signs of a heart attack) and then to the county jail in Colusa, where they were booked for possession of a restricted big-game animal during the closed season.

The following morning the two lads appeared before the local justice of the peace in Williams, pleaded guilty, and were found guilty. They paid $1,000 in fines and forfeited the rifle, the elk carrier, the elk, and all their meat-cutting equipment—not to mention a rather large chunk of their hind ends, I would imagine, when they got home and explained what had happened to their wives. Both of these men were firemen out of Burlingame, California, and they ended up losing their jobs because of their poor judgment in illegally killing a closed-season animal.

After thinking back on the stupidity Chuck had exhibited by going up there alone, I made sure that from then on, whenever I worked in the field where the odds would probably be more than two against one, I used my head instead of my hind end to survive (well, for the most part anyway ...). Whatever I did over the remaining years of my career must have been right because I managed to spend thirty-two years in wildlife law enforcement and come home every night, satisfying the first law of a law enforcement officer.

In this instance we all returned safely, the "elk god" was appeased, and the world's two unluckiest thieves ate macaroni at the jail that night instead of a Cache Creek tule elk steak smothered in good venison gravy in the comfort of their homes.

9

The Mossback and
the Bean Harvester

THE SUN SLOWLY ROSE over the horizon and was greeted
with a thousand square miles of dark cloud remnants from
the furious thunderstorm that had vented itself over the Sacramento Valley the night before. As the sun continued its arch, the
Walt Disney paintbrush seemingly appeared, dipped itself into the
darker layers of the clouds, and then carelessly splashed brilliant
pinks, oranges, yellows, and reds along their edges. Then, with a
flourish, the paintbrush stroked long shafts of sunlight through
the heavens. As the ever-changing crimsons tinged with oranges
ran down the backdrop of this canvas, they outlined the soft
blacks and browns of the darkness surrounding the Sutter Buttes,
still sleeping far below. As the sun climbed higher, the brilliant
colors faded as rapidly as they had formed and then disappeared
into the gray receding clouds, leaving the deep, clear blue of another autumn day in the Sacramento Valley.

Motionless and almost concealed at the edge of a row of oaks
and willows, a pair of brown eyes watched the splendor of the
skies unfold as their owner felt the breezes from the northwest
portending another fall storm. Slowly turning his head and then
moving only his eyes to avoid detection, he carefully surveyed
the milo field before him and the bordering rows of trees farther
to the west along Butte Creek in eastern Colusa County. The
only movement was a cloud of blackbirds numbering in the

thousands lifting up in noisy, joyous undulation over the field. The freshening breeze moved the unharvested rows of milo until the soft, rustling motion of the dampened leaves moved visibly across the field, disappearing along the row of trees bordering the creek. Sweeping that row with his eyes one more time for any movement, he stepped out into the open at the edge of the milo field. Not wasting any time, he ran toward a natural depression in the field and, once there, followed it to the edge of the trees bordering the creek several hundred yards to the west. Having safely crossed the open field, he paused in the covering vegetation along the creek and again carefully studied his surroundings. A startled covey of Valley quail moved out of his way, but all appeared well. Moving to the creek's edge after a careful pause, he took a long-awaited drink.

Concealed and motionless to the south in the row of trees along Butte Creek, a pair of blue eyes, aided by an old pair of navy surplus 7×50 binoculars, watched this drama unfold. An appreciative grin slowly spread across the watcher's damp, sun-bronzed face as he realized he had managed to watch undiscovered.

"Blue eyes" had been there all night in his hiding place, through a driving rain- and thunderstorm, watching two men periodically run a series of illegal drop lines in an attempt to catch more fish than the law of the land allowed. The only reason he was there was that he had discovered a bucket of used spark plugs in the back of a pickup parked farther up Butte Creek while making the rounds to check fishermen and froggers. He knew that old spark plugs were commonly used by people running drop lines—that is, a short fishing line, with a series of baited hooks in the middle portion, which is attached to a stump or root at the water's edge with an old spark plug tied to the other end to act as an anchor. After the anchored end is tossed out into the water, the device quietly fishes unassisted. It is a less-than-sportsmanlike way of catching fish that was illegal in those days in many states, including California, because it allowed serious overharvesting of a fishery. There is no "fair chase" in this method of fishing, only greed and the rapid destruction of a resource.

"Blue eyes" continued watching "brown eyes" as he finished his deep drink and then climbed back up the stream bank to begin a long look back toward the tree row to the east and the protective oxbow from whence he came. Satisfied that there was no danger of discovery, "brown eyes" stepped back out into the open and rapidly headed for the concealing depression in the milo field leading back to his row of trees to the east. Upon reaching the trees and their protective cover, "brown eyes" stopped and looked back to see if his journey had been observed. Still finding no sign that he was being watched, he moved even deeper into cover, stopped, and checked once again. Then he disappeared into the undergrowth the same way he had arrived, in the blink of an eye, like the fabled tigers of India in the works of Rudyard Kipling.

Another smile creased the tired face of "blue eyes" as he realized he had just successfully spied on a private affair without being discovered, even though the two of them had been separated by less than thirty feet of vegetation. Also, that was without a doubt the finest example of a mule deer buck I had ever seen! The animal was in excellent shape, probably tipping the scales at around 350 to 400 pounds, damn near the size of a tule elk. The rack of antlers would put him high in the record books of Boone and Crockett, an organization that acts as official registrar for such wildlife accomplishments. The animal was a beautifully perfect eight-point Western count (eight tines per side), with double brow tines on each side that were at least six inches long. But most spectacular of all were the height and width of the antlers themselves. They extended at least three feet higher than the top of his head and were no less than forty inches across at their widest point. The animal was simply magnificent. He was an old Roman-nosed mossback of many years, to be sure, who had enjoyed the very best of breeding as well as excellent cover and food in his secret, densely vegetated oxbow. Of course, it didn't hurt to have his little refuge standing in the middle of crops of lima beans and milo.

The soft, purring sound of a slowly approaching outboard motor driving the "sports" who were running the illegal drop lines signaled the need to move from the joy I had just experienced back to the project at hand. Two hours later I had apprehended two men from the San Francisco Bay area, along with the thirty-seven different drop lines they had scattered up and down Butte Creek, and written several citations apiece. After a mile-long walk back to my hidden patrol vehicle, I headed home for some dry clothes, a visit with my wife before she went to teach school in Williams, and a warm breakfast.

During my soggy, muddy walk back to the car, my mind kept returning to the magnificence of that morning's moment with the Mossback. Although the Mossback lived just yards into Warden Bob Hawks's patrol district, I made a mental note to keep an eye out for the old fellow and see if I couldn't arrange for him to finish out his life in style instead of at the end of a bullet. I also knew that to discuss the Mossback with anyone would let the cat out of the bag and place his life in further jeopardy. Yep, I said to myself, his secret will remain with me and me alone, period! Though a few Mexican laborers and landowners might chance upon the giant feeding in their fields in the dark of the night, he would be most secure as my personal secret.

However, there was one problem: the Moore brothers. They were the owners of the land that the Mossback called home, and both had reputations for killing lots of large antlered or horned animals year after year. They also had reputations, according to local lore, for running outside the Fish and Game laws if the opportunity presented itself. I had once been in their homes in Yuba City to serve search warrants and had been very impressed with the numbers of *huge* antlered and horned mounts that hung in each of their trophy rooms. In fact, I don't remember any buck hanging on their walls that had less than a thirty-inch spread from tip to tip at the antlers' widest point! You don't consistently get such large bucks in those numbers unless you go past the edge of legality as a matter of course. The big bucks are there in the world of wildlife, but in restricted numbers, and are most commonly found during the closed hunting season on their winter ranges out in the open, or at night in someone's field or orchard. The bottom line is that animals don't live long enough to get that big without becoming very wise or utilizing an angle like my Mossback and his secret little oxbow in which no one would think to look for such a critter.

My thoughts turned to the lay of the land around the Mossback's home. He apparently lived in that very densely vegetated old oxbow from Butte Creek's younger days. That oxbow was at least half a mile long and varied from about a hundred to three hundred yards in width. In it were old oak trees, some at least eight feet wide, tons of poison oak, and every other kind of clothes-tearing vine and thorn plant imaginable. Given those circumstances, I wasn't too concerned about anyone going in there to seek a trophy deer. However, when he came out to drink or feed in the adjacent milo or lima bean fields, that would be a horse of a different color. If anyone saw such a fine trophy animal, it would soon be the talk of the town, and once that word got out it would be just a matter of time before the Mossback was lying on someone's cold garage floor with the light in his eyes and the possibility of passing on his unique genetics long gone.

Pulling into my driveway and sitting in the truck for a long moment, I got an idea that was surefire to allow the old fellow to retire in peace. I would make it a point to live in his circle through frequent visits to everyone who used that area, including the Moore brothers. If I appeared myself often in many nearby places, without mentioning the Mossback, I hoped my presence would cool anyone's ardor for killing *anything* illegally on the lands surrounding the oxbow.

Smiling to myself at such a simple yet effective plan, I went into my house and was greeted by the open arms, smile, and beautiful blue eyes of my bride. Great smells wafted from the kitchen as I gave her my typical bear hug. "Get out of that muddy and fishy-smelling clothing, please," was her first gentle request. She added in a teasing voice, "Breakfast is ready if you are interested." Man, I flew out of my dirty clothing, sped into the shower, and dressed amid the tempting breakfast smells. God never made a finer cook or partner, I mused as I hustled into clean gear and padded softly into the kitchen in my stocking feet. Soon my thoughts of the old Mossback had been replaced by a thick slice of the world's best homemade bread covered with blackberry jam, quickly followed by fried spuds, side pork, three eggs, and a glass of very cold milk. Damn, this woman sure knew her man! As she swung by with more fried side pork (my favorite), I swung out my long arms with the thought of giving her another hug. She deftly sidestepped my extended arms and said with a smile, "I am all dressed for school, and don't you dare to put a wrinkle in my clothes. By the way, don't you have something to do out in your district? You can start on the Beauchamp place. Millie Beauchamp called this morning, and it seems they are having trespass problems again on the west side of their farm. I suggest you get cracking or she will give you a piece of her mind, and rightfully so."

I just grinned. My bride was always the professional business-woman. Shaking my head, I again dove into the breakfast fit for a king, knowing she was right. Millie could be a wildcat if stirred up, and I was sure she would be riled by the time I got there. I could just see her now, giving me hell for taking my time when she and Leonard were having problems on the back side of their farm. I had to chuckle. She was a tiger, but I sure enjoyed working with her on Fish and Game problems. She was one lady who did not mince words when she had something on her mind, and I always liked working with anyone who was frank and to the point. Leonard was a little different. I'm not sure he appreciated game wardens very much in those days, especially after I tore up his farm roads crisscrossing the place chasing some of the outlaws who frequented the ranch. Maybe he was grouchy because I was getting too close to his son Gene, who liked to shoot a "wee bit of the duck." ... Either way, I considered Leonard, Gene, and Millie friends by the time I was promoted and left the Valley for my new duty station in North Dakota.

Many times that year as I made myself visible in the area frequented by my baker's dozen of poaching knotheads, I ran across the old Mossback's track in the soft mud of the milo field where I had first observed him or on the farm roads that ran through the area around the oxbow. I made sure that when the tracks crossed those dirt roads or appeared where humankind might discover them, they were deliberately rubbed out by my Vibram boot soles or tire tracks. About a dozen other times, while working along Butte Creek on foot, I surprised the old fellow drinking or eating and had the chance to observe his magnificence as he retreated to his home in the oxbow. He never sprinted away from me when disturbed but moved liked an old gentleman with the inherent grace of his age. It was almost as if he knew I was not a threat but a friend and that to dash away would be downright inhospitable. He never failed to bring a smile to my usually mosquito-bitten, tired face.

I always seemed to find his large track with the telltale curved-in hoof tips meandering across the soft soil of the Moores' lima bean fields. That wasn't a surprise because the twelve-hundred-acre field seemed to be a favorite nighttime chow hall of all the deer families living in the area. However, tracks in the field like that, in front of God and everybody, were plain and simply dangerous. In those days the state Fish and Game Department allowed farmers who could show that deer depredation was taking place on their crops to spotlight and kill, under permit, the offending animals in their fields. For animals unused to being hunted, much less pursued with the aid of a spotlight at night, such permits provided a killing field of unreal proportions. If the Moores, a wealthy and influential farming family, wanted such permits, the state would issue them posthaste. My thoughts of the possible consequences trailed off unhappily. Night was the one time the old Mossback would feel safe and come out from the cover of his dense jungle home to feed. If he was discovered in the Moores' lima bean fields with a spotlight or the headlights of a bean harvester, he was a goner, especially with that rack of a lifetime—and especially if the Moore brothers were running the spotlight and had anything to say about it. They would like nothing better than to add him to the many trophies already on their walls, even if it meant taking the Mossback under a depredation permit and sneaking his head home (state law stipulated that animals taken under a depredation permit had to be donated to the needy or to public causes). There were then, as there still are now, crooked taxidermists in the Sacramento Valley who for a few pieces of silver would take on an illegal taxidermy job without thinking twice. Damn, I thought; I am going to have to stay on my toes if the old Mossback is to stay upright on his. ...

I never saw the old fellow anymore for the rest of that year, just a few sets of tracks and then nothing. He flat disappeared! Over the next six months I looked closely for any sign of my friend the Mossback. I was beginning to fear the worst, but each time I ignored my misgivings and renewed my efforts to locate the old fellow, or at the very least, the fellow who might have taken him. After all, if he had been killed, most shooters can't keep their mouths shut, which often leads to their downfall. Or maybe the Mossback had moved his home range to another wooded area for some reason. That could happen, I thought, trying to convince myself. Then, knowing how limited the home range is for a member of the deer family, I would again harbor doubts about his survival.

Finally, dying of curiosity, I waited until Old Man Winter had removed much of the vegetative cover that second season and went looking in the last place I had seen the old fellow alive. Walking to the edge of the oxbow early one morning, I paused, almost reluctant to enter, expecting the worst. Then I slowly worked my way into the tangles of blackberry brambles, heavy timber, poison oak, and deep quiet that live in such places. In the damp interior of the jungle the Mossback called home, I paused to get my wind and cool off from the sweat my exertions were beginning to develop. Up to that point I had practiced every trick my dad had taught me about how to stalk, as the Indians had taught him when he was a young man, and I had done quite well. So far that morning in the old oxbow, I had sneaked up on two coveys of Valley quail scratching out a breakfast in the forest litter, one feral cat eating what was left of a muskrat, a pair of wood ducks sleeping on the limb of a large oak not six feet off the ground by a small pool of fetid water, and a sleeping red fox at the edge of an old den in the blackberries. I tried to walk around the fox, but it awoke, winded me, and scampered away as if its tail were on fire. Smiling, I stood and watched it move gracefully and quietly out of sight into the dark underbrush.

Carefully moving through an especially deep tangle of vines and poison oak, I stopped again to catch my breath and figure out which direction I would move next. I had never ventured into one of the Valley's oxbows before, and let me tell you, it was a real learning experience. The ground was literally covered with animal trails, tracks, and sign of every sort. Raccoon, skunk, deer, river otter, mink, wood duck (looking for acorns), rabbit, muskrat, beaver, and bird tracks of every sort and size made up the wildlife soup I observed on the wet earth. Remembering that this area was nothing but a remnant bit of historical geography, I couldn't help but wonder what California looked like during the times of the early Spanish settlers. It had to be nothing short of spectacular in the realm of wildlife, plants, and huge oak trees, I thought.

Stopping to look for another trail that might take me more or less through the middle of this maze, my eyes fastened on what appeared to be a *huge*, unmoving antler rack and deer's head in the tall winter grasses beside several large oak trees. I froze and looked, not believing what I was seeing. I wasn't twenty feet away from my quarry, who appeared to be sleeping. My heart was racing at being so close to the giant and also with the joy of having found the old fellow alive after such a long absence. He certainly was alive and well, I thought, and then I noticed it: he was no longer an eight-point but as pretty a nine-point as I had ever seen. There was no doubt in my mind that this animal, were he to be taken by a sportsman, would rate no lower than third in Boone and Crockett, *if not higher!* He was utterly magnificent and except for the graying muzzle looked the picture of perfect health. God, what a sight for me to behold. Then, as if his instincts had kicked in despite his deep slumber, he opened his eyes and slowly laid his head down in such a way that he flattened himself out on the ground, realizing danger was close at hand. I didn't dare even to breathe and tried to pull in life-giving oxygen in only shallow breaths, but something gave me away, and when it did the Mossback wasted no time. He exploded upward, whirled, and was gone in one mighty, crashing leap! I heard him jump just one more time, and then it was obvious that he quit leaping and began to sneak, easily making his escape. Breathing deeply once again, I felt a smile run clear across my face for that moment of a lifetime—and the fact I had sneaked right up on him and wasn't there to take his life. God, life was really great at that moment.

I walked over to the deer bed he had been using and could tell from its depth and the amount of loose hair that he had been using it for a long time. The deer bed was located right smack-dab in the middle of the best cover in the entire oxbow. Looking the surroundings over more closely, I could see that no matter from which direction someone approached the deer bed, the Mossback could be gone in one jump in any direction before hearing the sing of a rifle bullet or even being viewed by most prying eyes. With a second smile after registering that little bit of information, I quickly left on another game trail and in about thirty minutes emerged from the previously unknown but busy world of the oxbow. With another big smile of accomplishment, I walked across a muddy milo field back to my waiting patrol vehicle, vowing again to keep an eye on the area and be on the lookout for any kind of poaching attempt against the Mossback. The Mossback had just chosen to frequent another part of his home range, and it must have been an area where I was not working since I had not run across his trail. He was alive, and so was I, and for those blessings I was thankful.

One hot, humid July evening after sundown, while patrolling the east side of Butte Creek checking fishermen, I stopped my patrol vehicle by a small drainage ditch to retrieve a cold soda pop from the ice chest in the pickup bed. After giving my Lab, Shadow, a big hug and letting her out to do what she needed to do, I dug out my Pepsi and took a deep drink. Then it hit me. What was that horrible smell? I set my now not-too-interesting soda pop on the tailgate, grabbing my flashlight, and Shadow and I walked down the drainage ditch leading away from Butte Creek some forty yards away. Then I saw it: lying right in the water of the ditch were the gut-pile remains of what appeared to be at least six deer! The piles appeared to move when I illuminated them with my flashlight as a carpet of crawdads slipped away from their dinner back into the protective cover of the water.

Damn, I thought. This degree of poaching has gone on right under your and Bob Hawks's noses, and neither of you even got wind of it (no pun intended)! Closer examination of the gut piles showed that all were from big deer, and all were in varying stages of decay. That told me I more than likely had poachers using a light to work over the deer feeding in the bean fields at night. Since I was not aware of any deer depredation permits being issued in the area, I had nothing more than night hunters on the loose. And it was damn sure obvious they had discovered the numerous deer in the surrounding lima bean fields and were taking advantage of that fact. For the next several months I kept a closer watch in the area but managed to cross trails only with numerous Mexican workers and the Moore brothers checking their bean fields before harvest. Several times I heard shots at night in the area, but by the time I arrived, whoever had done the shooting was long gone and a new gut pile was in the drainage ditch for the crawdad buffet. No matter how hard I worked, the shooters always seemed to give me the slip. It seemed that the only people, other than the Mexicans, whom I consistently met around there were the Moore brothers, and they never had a single critter in any of their vehicles or exhibited any other outward sign of foul play. To make matters worse, I had twice seen the Mossback out at night in the Moore brothers' fields, feeding to his heart's content. Needless to say, this sight gave me not only a tight jaw but a case of the vapors as well.

In those days California allowed a licensed sportsman to take two deer per year. However, one had to be taken along the coast (A tag) and one had to be taken in the interior of the state (B tag). Since my deer season was ongoing in the mountains to the west, I was spending a lot of time in that area and hence had pretty much ignored my Valley floor and everything that usually went on there. One afternoon, tiring of the hot night deer patrols in the mountains, I decided to break the monotony by swapping my patrol work for a night in the valley checking fishermen along the waterways.

Arriving home from the mountains at dusk, I had a nice, quiet dinner with my wife and kids, showered, changed into a clean uniform, and headed out into the Valley. Starting on the north end of my district, I worked my way down Butte Creek, checking fishermen and several commercial frogging operations. 'Long about ten in the evening, I happened to be near the Mossback's territory and thought I would pay his neighborhood a visit. When I got there I was surprised to find that the Moore brothers were running their harvesters and had pretty much harvested the bean fields surrounding the oxbow area. That is good, I thought; now there won't be any more opportunity to surprise the Mossback out in the open. Continuing to work my way down the creek, I was clear at the southern end of my district writing a fisherman a ticket for fishing with more than one pole when I heard two quick, almost simultaneous rifle shots not far to the north. I quickly looked at my watch; it was ten thirty-two P.M. Damn, I thought, that more than likely had to be at a deer, and that won't do. I grabbed my state radio and called my close friend and warden for the neighboring area, Bob Hawks. There was no response. Realizing that if he was not out and about I would have to work the suspicious shooting myself, I quickly finished the citation and left my errant fisherman along the stream bank. I shut down my lights so I wouldn't be seen and drove into the area where I figured I had heard the shots. When I reached a good vantage point I stopped and quietly sat there, watching and listening. All I could see or hear were the Moore brothers running their bean harvesters and the occasional motor boat going up or down Butte Creek behind me.

About an hour after I arrived I noticed that the two bean harvesters in the field next to my hiding place had finished and were heading back toward where the operators had parked their pickups. Frustrated at missing another night-hunting poacher, I started up my patrol truck and, still without any running lights, headed toward them. I wasn't sure why because the operators wouldn't have been able to hear anyone shooting because of the noise the harvesters made, but I wanted to check anyway to see if they had at least seen or heard anything.

It was about midnight when I pulled onto the road leading to the two pickup trucks and the bean harvesters in the field, and my gut instinct told me something just didn't feel right. Stopping, I watched the two men as they cleaned up, washing their hands with water from the drinking containers attached to the bean harvesters. Then they took several drinks of water and stood there for the next few minutes, talking and looking around. Nothing out of the ordinary there, I said to myself, but my instincts still told me something was up, and it wasn't good. Getting into his pickup, one man backed the truck right under the bean harvester's auger boom while the other lad crawled into that harvester and started up the machine. The auger was soon filling the bed of the three-quarter-ton pickup with freshly harvested lima beans. Once finished, the lad in the truck filled with beans threw a few farming items into the pickup bed on top of the beans, and then the two trucks started out of the field. Still nothing unusual, but worth checking anyway, I told myself.

Meeting the two farmers at a wide spot in the road, I turned on my headlights and, for some reason, my red light as well. I got out of my truck and was met by Bob Moore, the older brother of the two, with a great big "Howdy, Terry. What brings you out here to this godforsaken place at this hour?"

Shaking his hand and then that of his younger brother, David, who had gotten out of his truck and approached us, I said, "You fellows hear any shooting in this area within the last couple of hours?"

The brothers just looked at each other and then said in unison, "No, we have been working."

Well, I thought, I didn't ask if you were working; I asked if you heard any shooting. But I let it pass for the moment and asked if they had all their bean harvesting done. They said they did. They seemed a bit more at ease with that response, probably because it was more in line with the truth. I asked again if they were sure they had not heard any shooting and got the same offbeat behavior and uneasy reply.

Then, casually looking down at Bob's pant legs in the light from my flashlight, I noticed what appeared to be several deer hairs hanging around his right knee. Since one might use the knee to help load a heavy animal into the back of a pickup, I was interested.

Without saying anything about my discovery, I took a long, hard look at his hands with my flashlight, especially the area around his fingernails, since anyone gutting an animal can't help but gather blood under his nails. Seeing my intense interest in his hands, Bob nervously asked, "Is anything wrong, Terry?"

"Nah," I said. "Just looking."

"Looking for what?" came the hurried reply. Then, without warning, David suddenly puked at least a gallon off to one side of the road. "What the hell is wrong with you?" asked Bob.

"I don't know; it must have been the tuna-fish sandwiches we had for dinner," replied David. However, his eyes never left mine, nor mine his, as he wiped his mouth.

Noticing they both had heavy rifles in the back-window gun racks of their pickups, which was not unusual in the West, I asked if I could examine the guns and the cabs of their pickups as well.

"Go ahead," said Bob. "I don't know what the hell you are looking for, but we have nothing to hide."

Bob's truck was clean as a hound's tooth (well, as clean as a farmer's pickup can be), but when I walked back to David's truck, I noticed that he appeared uneasy. I said, "Why don't you just sit down and relax, Dave, if you don't feel well. This will just take a minute."

"No, I'm all right, Terry, but can you make it quick? I have to get home."

Turning to face him, I said, "Home for what?"

The quickness of the question caught him by surprise, and he just stood there looking at me without responding. Switching my gaze back to his truck, I noticed that it was filled to the gills with a load of fresh lima beans.

"What are the beans for, Dave?" I asked.

"My rabbits," he responded.

I thought, I never heard of rabbits eating lima beans, but what the hell do I know, I'm just a damn game warden. I noticed he had placed a bunch of farm gear, used oil containers, gas cans, cartons, and the like in the front of the bed on top of the lima beans. Other than that, nothing was out of the ordinary. Turning, I said, "Let me see your hands, Dave."

"What for?" he replied in surprise.

"Let me see your hands," I said again. Dave stuck out his hands, palm side up, for me to look at. "Turn them over, please," I requested. Dave looked over at Bob with an expression like a trapped rat's and then slowly obliged. All around the fingernails on the right hand was what appeared to be dried, caked blood. Realizing what held my interest, Dave quickly put his hands into his pants pockets and looked at me helplessly. I returned to his truck and without one word began removing the farm junk lying on top of the lima beans.

"What are you doing?" he squeaked.

"I'm just looking," I said as I removed the loose farm gear. I didn't find much until I removed an empty, overturned oil box, and there it was! The oil box had been covering what appeared to be a massive deer antler sticking up out of the lima beans. My heart sank.

I slowly turned to Dave, and he blurted out, "It is legal. I killed him fair and square."

"You killed what fair and square?" I asked.

"A buck in the bean field. I shot him right at dusk. After all, Terry, the season is on."

"Let's take a look at him," I said with my heart still in my throat.

Dave jumped up into the back of his pickup, reached down into the pile of beans, and with difficulty lifted up a massive, nine-point antlered head. It was my Mossback, and not only was he deader than all get-out but he was tagged with one of Dave's deer tags as well. I was just sick! I turned to look at Bob, and he quickly looked down at his shoes.

"Let's get him out into the open so I can take a look at him, gentlemen," I said politely, but damn, did I feel empty and angry inside. The two brothers dug the Mossback out of the bean pile with a great deal of effort and laid him out on top. Even in death, this animal was one of God's chosen few. He weighed a good 350 pounds field dressed (just gutted), and his antlers, upon closer review, were even bigger than I had imagined. I turned away from the Mossback to look hard at the two brothers as the roots of my profession kicked in. "Dave," I said, "when did you say you killed this deer?"

"Right at dusk," was his quick but unconvincing reply.

"How did you kill him?" I asked.

"Well, I was working on the harvester and I saw him trot across the field from that there oxbow, so I stopped the harvester, took my rifle, got off the harvester, and shot him," he said, sounding worried and still not too convincing. "Look, Terry, he is all legal like, and I would like to get him home and skinned out so he can cool and not spoil."

I knew instinctively that the Mossback had been taken illegally, but it was going to be an uphill battle to prove it. Thinking back to the serenity of the first time I had spotted him and watched him drink not more than thirty feet from my hiding place, I got very determined to succeed in the chore that lay before me. "Bob, what say you to this?" I said, pointing to the buck.

"Terry, it is like Dave said," he answered, then dropped his eyes to his shoes again.

Without another word and with a great deal of difficulty, I rolled the deer over on the lima beans and noticed that he appeared to have been shot twice: once in the shoulder and once behind the front shoulder. Both wounds would have been killing shots. That puzzled me. Rolling the deer over again, I saw that the shot into the shoulder had not come out the other side. The shot behind the front shoulder, however, had exited the body. Feeling along the shoulder where the bullet should have emerged, I could feel the spent bullet under the skin and by moving the front legs could feel that both shoulders had been broken as the bullet had torn through the flesh and bone of my monster buck. After taking a hit like that through both front shoulders, the animal would have gone down and been unable to walk. Again, why the second shot? Taking out my Buck knife, I cut through the skin on the outside shoulder and dug out the remains of the spent bullet. It was pretty badly smashed up, but the base was intact. Now, I did a lot of reloading in my day and easily recognized from the size of the intact base of the bullet that it was from a .270-caliber rifle. Putting that information in the back of my mind and the bullet into my shirt pocket as possible evidence, I took a look at the other bullet hole, the one behind the shoulder. As near as I could tell, the shot behind the shoulder had smashed a rib going in and another going out. Why shoot the animal twice with two obvious killing shots? I kept asking myself. Taking my knife and cutting back the skin on one side of the exit hole for the behind-the-shoulder hit, I could see little bits of what appeared to be the remains of a silvertip bullet among the bone fragments. Without saying anything about what I had discovered, I turned and asked the two brothers to bring me their rifles, which they did.

Bob's rifle was a .270-caliber Winchester bolt-action, and Dave's was a bolt-action Remington 700 BDL, caliber 30-06. I examined the cartridges remaining in the magazines of their rifles and found that Bob's contained a full magazine of 130-grain Nosler bullets and Dave's contained a magazine, minus one, of 180-grain silvertip bullets! Laying the two rifles on the hood of my pickup, I turned and said, "Gentlemen, your stories one more time, please."

Bob said, "Terry, I just ran the bean harvester and didn't even know Dave had killed the animal. Check my rifle out; it hasn't even been fired in a month."

I walked over to Bob's rifle, pulled the bolt back, and noticed a dark look starting to form on Bob's face. With that, I placed my nose near the chamber and smelled deeply. The fresh smell of burned powder greeted my nostrils! Without a doubt, it *had* been recently fired, but Bob had gambled that I wouldn't smell the chamber. He had lost that roll of the dice, I thought. My eye contact with him said it all, and Bob again lowered his eyes. "Dave," I said, "your turn."

"Terry, it is just as I said earlier. I saw him right at dusk walking across our field, and since our deer season was on and I had my tags, I got out my gun and shot him once behind the left shoulder."

Looking long and hard first at Bob and then at Dave, I gambled and let it all hang out. "First, gentlemen, I was hiding just opposite where you two lads were working in the bean field a good hour before dusk, and I didn't leave the area until at least an hour after dusk," I lied. Legally, since there is no expectation the bad guys will tell you the truth, the courts have ruled that during interrogation

an officer can stretch the truth as well. I chose to use this interrogation technique, and it had a telling effect on my lads, who both
just stood there mute. "Secondly, the animal was shot by each of
you with your own rifle." Bob started to object, but I advised him to
hear me out and not compound this lie any further. The way he
hushed up at my request told me I was on a roll to the brass ring, so
I brought out the big guns, so to speak. Taking the bullet from my
shirt pocket, I held it out and informed them that it was .270 caliber, and once I ran Bob's rifle and the bullet remains through Red
Hunt's forensic lab in Sacramento, I would bet a month's paycheck
and one of Donna's homemade pies (a bet I *never* lose) that the
bullet would match that rifle. Bob hardly breathed in the hot July
air, just stood there unmoving with the sweat literally pouring off
his face. He didn't even swat at the mosquitoes, which was strange,
I thought, in light of their hungry ferocity.

Turning slowly toward Dave for effect, I said, "Dave, you have
silvertip bullets in the magazine of your rifle. That kind of tip has a
tendency to break up into dust and small pieces when they hit
dense bone. There appear to be bits and pieces of the silvertip material scattered throughout the inside of the skin area and bone
chips around the exit hole. I will also bet that the lab can match
up the chemical compounding on your batch of ammunition with
that silvertip material around the exit wound. If the lab does that,
along with matching up the lands [a raised portion of a grooved
surface inside a rifle barrel] and grooves to Bob's .270 bullet, then
that is pretty hard evidence that both of you shot the deer!"

By now, both of the lads were watching me like a rat does a
snake. Good, I thought; you lads are just beginning the long slide
toward a citation for an illegal deer. "Additionally," I said, "either
bullet, placed as they were, would have been a killing shot. That
alone tells me both of you shot at the deer at the same time." I continued, "Now, gentlemen, at about ten-thirty P.M. there were *two*
shots fired, one by each of you, using the dual lights of your bean
harvesters to confuse and illuminate the buck." Again I was reaching, since I hadn't seen anything, but there was no denial from
either man. The long slide continues, I thought. "I watched you

lads pick up and load the animal in Dave's pickup, with you, Bob, using your right knee to help lift the heavy animal up over the tail-gate like a man would bucking a heavy bale of hay." My statement was based on the deer hair I had seen earlier on Bob's knee, and by using that much detail I hoped to push them over the edge away from their stories and gain a confession. "Then the animal was buried under a thousand pounds of fresh lima beans, and out from the lima bean field you lads came. How am I doing so far?"

My question was met with abject silence. I went on, "About midnight we meet here in the road and I discover a buck, surprise, surprise, hidden in Dave's rig. The first thing I notice on you, Bob, appears to be blood on your fingers and deer hair on your pant leg around the right knee, which you used to help boost the animal into Dave's truck. In fact, the deer hair is still there." Bob quickly looked at his fingers and the legs of his pants. Seeing the loose deer hairs, he brushed them off as if they were poisonous snakes, albeit a little too late. Turning to Dave in order not to lose the im-petus of the moment, I said, "And you, Dave—my focusing in on you caused you to puke because you were so scared, not to men-tion the obvious blood on your knuckles and around your finger-nails." Dave got the dry heaves, and I waited until he got control of himself. "Now, gentlemen, as you know I have several advanced degrees in wildlife management and one in wildlife forensics." This was true except that I lacked any training, academic or otherwise, in wildlife forensics. I just slid that in to scare the hell out of my two chaps, and from the looks in their eyes, it did the trick. I fig-ured it was the least I could do for the old Mossback. "Now, let's get down to brass tacks," I said casually.

Taking my meat thermometer from my uniform shirt pocket, I cut a slash into the center of the deer's hip, inserted the ther-mometer to the bone and then withdrew it about one inch, let it sit for a bit, and took a reading. It was so hot it almost burned my fingers. Getting the deer-meat temperature chart furnished by the Fish and Game lab in Sacramento from the visor of my truck, I found that the Mossback's temperature matched a category on the chart for one killed about two and a half hours earlier (which matched the time I had heard the two shots). I let both of the Moores have a look at the thermometer and the meat chart. Nails in the coffin lid, I called it. ... For the icing on the cake, I called them over to watch as I tried a procedure I had just read about in a recent *Journal of Wildlife Management* article (love those biologists). By now both men had eyes the size of dinner plates. I shone my flashlight into the Mossback's eyes and showed the two men that the eyes had barely started to dilate. I said, "Dave, if what you said about shooting the deer at dusk, some six hours ago, was true, the eyes would have already dilated. As you can clearly see, no or very little dilation has taken place." Grabbing the deer's rear hocks, I showed them how they moved freely when flexed. I said, "If you had killed that deer at dusk as you claim, the hocks would already have rigor mortis setting in and would be nowhere near this flexible." By now I had their undivided attention. "When I checked the blood in the animal's body cavity and at the bullet exit points, it is pretty apparent that it hasn't even started to coagulate, which it would have done by now if he had been shot and killed six hours ago. Last but not least, your worry about getting the animal home to skin so you could avoid spoilage in this July heat doesn't hold water when you bury an animal under a ton of heat-retaining lima beans." With that last shot, I just stood there for a moment and looked hard at the lads. Finally I said, "Well?"

"Terry, can I talk to my brother?" asked Bob.

I nodded, and the two of them walked a short distance away to discuss the issue of the large buck still lying in the back of Dave's pickup. I was hoping I had bombarded them with enough fact and fiction that they had been convinced to tell the truth.

In a few moments they returned, and Bob began. "Terry, you are right; we killed the animal illegally. We stopped for dinner, and Dave saw the buck sneaking out of the trees at the edge of the light from his harvester's headlights. I jumped into my bean harvester and turned on its lights, as you probably saw. Then I hit the buck with the beam from the spotlight on my harvester, which anchored him in his tracks. We both quickly got our guns from behind the seats in the harvester and shot the animal. We didn't want him to get away," Bob said lamely.

"He was so damn big that we just couldn't let him go," Dave said as if that justified killing the animal.

Bob added, "We had seen this monster a few nights earlier eating our beans but couldn't get a shot off at that time. Terry, he was just so damned big. You can't let something like that escape."

Looking at them in disgust for a moment, I said, "Well, gentlemen, I am going to have both of you fill out a statement as to what happened, in your own words, please, and I will present that information and what I saw and heard here tonight to the county attorney for prosecutorial consideration."

I got out the paper and pen, and the two men recorded their actions of that night for posterity. When they were finished, I carefully read both statements, in which they clearly stated that they had taken the deer illegally. After that chore was done, the three of us with difficulty loaded the old Mossback into the back of my pickup. I also seized their rifles, putting them into the front seat of my vehicle as evidence in case the lads wanted a trial after all was said and done.

After we parted ways, I took the Mossback to my home for a bit of necessary work. When I got him into my garage, I photographed the deer for evidence and then skinned back part of his neck and, with my meat saw, removed the head. Carefully laying the head on its side on the floor, I took out a measuring tape and measured the outer width of the antlers. They measured 46.5 inches at their widest point. Ah, man, I was just sick. From the looks of the Mossback's body and teeth, he would probably have lasted another three to five years. Imagine what he would have looked like by then! I could just picture the offspring he might have fathered during that period of time and the genes he could have passed on. What a loss! Of course, most animals taken in such circumstances are a loss, but the American people are always the real losers. The animal loses his or her life, but the people lose generations of a quality of life that is gone forever. I was just sick as I took the headless deer to a needy man who worked for the

Pacific Gas and Electric Company and had a very large family. He was understandably excited about getting an elk-sized deer, and he and his oldest son hung the animal from a tree in their front yard and immediately began to skin him. For some reason I didn't have the time to stay and visit, so I returned home.

The Moores didn't even show up in court after I provided the details of the case along with their affidavits to the county attorney in Butte County. He just contacted their attorney, and the two of them arranged a plea bargain. Both men pleaded guilty, and they paid a fine of $500 each and lost their rifles. They were also given three years' probation with no hunting of any big-game animal allowed during that period. The meat, 254 pounds of it cut and wrapped, as reported by my needy family, was put to very good use, and the case was officially closed. Personally, however, it remained open for a few more days. ...

AN INTENSE PAIR OF BLUE EYES scanned the heavens to the northwest for any information to be gleaned from the rapidly gathering black storm clouds. The light breeze was heavy with moisture and foretold the oncoming event. He looked around for any other sign of life but saw only a flock of a thousand or so blackbirds happily undulating over the milo field he had just crossed. Slipping into the dense vegetation of the old oxbow, he followed a time-worn deer trail into the interior. Deep in the oxbow's cover, a covey of quail exploded under the now not-so-careful feet hurrying before the impending storm. After thirty minutes of hard walking in and around the poison oak, blackberries, and other brush, he arrived at an old but well-used deer bed of major proportions. The forest was now silent, as if in expectation, as the man removed a massive deer head and antlers from a large burlap bag and tenderly laid it in the bed as if it were still alive. Stepping back with his hands at his sides, the man uttered some words that even the thrush working in the leaves at his feet could not hear. With moisture welling up in his eyes, feeling older now, the man took one more look at the still magnificent antlered head before he turned and walked away. No one would display that head and antlers in their home or office, he thought; they were the property of the oxbow and all who lived in that micro-environment. Staggering back through the undergrowth, not really seeing it or feeling it clutching at his clothes, the man felt the first drops of the coming storm and redoubled his efforts to gain the shelter of his vehicle.

Safely in the truck, the man listened to the rain as it began to clatter loudly on the metal roof. He looked back at the oxbow as if hoping to see his "friend" emerge one more time, but not surprisingly, he was disappointed. As the rain intensified, his frown turned to a smile. Someone long ago had said that rain is a sign of hope and new life. I hope so, "blue eyes" thought as he drove out of the life of that oxbow forever. *I hope so. ...*

10

"Here Come da Judge"

T HE EARLY-NOVEMBER MORNING AIR flowed in through the open windows of my patrol truck as I sat out of sight in a dense stand of cottonwood trees overseeing probably a hundred thousand noisy, happily feeding ducks on about a thousand acres of Terrill Sartain's harvested rice fields. It was about three A.M., and the many previous sleepless nights were beginning to take their toll as I found my eyelids getting heavier and heavier. It had been quiet for the duration of my stakeout except the occasional car going by on the levee road, the cold buzzing of a few hardy mosquitoes that were still out and about, and the methodical *crump* of zon guns (carbide cannons set to a timer to use exploding gases that produce a loud noise to scare away hungry ducks) in the nearby unharvested rice fields. Intermixed with those sounds were the odd but beautiful fluting calls of thousands of pintail ducks calling to their kinfolk on the ground for a "rice report" as they passed overhead in the dark. The quiet of the morning, coupled with the peace without and within, allowed me to drift back into other lives and times, and being the dreamer I was, it was easy to yield to those impulses.

In the pickup that morning was a man with four ounces of silver on his chest and a cold steel pistol on his right hip who was dedi-cated to the protection of the critters large and small in nature's pantry. I was a state Fish and Game warden assigned to Colusa County, in the heart of the Sacramento Valley, and my presence in the field that morning showed that time of day meant nothing when "nature called." The Sacramento Valley was the ancestral home to millions of migratory waterfowl. It was also home to the last vestiges of the commercial-market hunters, known as "duck draggers" on the West Coast, who killed feeding ducks for those seeking pricey rice-fed-duck dinners in the Valley cities, or to fill their own and their friends' freezers with the fatted duck. Commercial-market hunters were a unique subculture in American history. Market hunting in North America, or the gross killing of wildlife, has been around for many decades. Those who were the best shots, who were inclined to kill for a living, or who simply enjoyed the adventure found in the blood sport of killing found resources beyond their wildest imaginations. They took salmon, passenger pigeons, egrets, cranes, beaver, grizzly bear, bison, antelope, deer, elk, ducks and geese, and just about anything else that produced a payoff, and they never felt a twinge of regret. Markets for these resources comprised both rich and poor, the patrons and residents of the many busy houses of ill repute, railroad crews, restaurants, convict labor camps, miners, road builders, stagecoach stops, logging camps, local families, butcher shops, and more. You name a place with protein-hungry people, and the commercial-market hunters' fare found its way to their tables.

Fur trappers (an early form of commercial-market hunter), when beaver hats were replaced in the market by top hats made from Chinese silk, found themselves out of work. Their abilities to survive in the outback turned many from this earlier trade to that of guiding wagon trains west or slaughtering buffalo for the commercial markets for their tongues, hides, and hump ribs. When the species had been all but destroyed, the animals' bleached bones were picked up off the prairies and used for fertilizer. No matter what the product, all found their way to the many hungry markets. When the buffalo ran out, many market hunters became "wolfers," or predator hunters, and that work carried a portion of this lingering, dying breed of humankind into the twentieth century. However, many of this breed tired of the destruction of wildlife and found themselves turning to law enforcement in a still mostly lawless and deadly land. And many died just as recklessly as they had lived, shot down like the game they killed. At the same time, the market for wild game birds reared its ugly head and the commercial-market hunter thread—or stain—continued to be woven into the American fabric called our national heritage until the 1960s.

Colusa County and the surrounding Sacramento Valley still had their share of millions of migratory waterfowl, numerous markets for the ducks and geese (the Chinese Tong Society, Italian restaurants in the Bay area, Chinatown in San Francisco, local markets in Yuba City, Elks Club private dinners, local people's freezers, bars selling ducks to the not-so-lucky hunters, and gambling houses in Las Vegas and Reno, for example), and shooters for those markets. Hence the need for lads like me, trying to uphold the conservation laws of the land and scrambling to conserve something for those yet to come.

During my tenure as a conservation officer I discovered that commercial-market hunters were like child molesters: they conducted their business when no one was watching (preferably under cover of darkness), did not advertise their exploits except to close friends of their own kind, ran like the wind if discovered, and during the day pretended to be ordinary God-fearing pillars of the community. The waterfowl on the receiving end of their shooting abilities died by the hundreds of thousands in the rice fields, or if not immediately picked up by the shooter crawled off to die in the ditches or tall water grasses in equally gross, *if not greater,* numbers! Many injured birds, too weak to escape once they had hidden, were eaten alive by predators or flew off in the initial fusillade only to tumble from the terrified escaping flocks, falling earthward to die alone. These millions of waterfowl harvested nationally were hardly missed by anyone except a few outnumbered conservation officers, a few concerned citizens, and all of our children today. For those yet to come, who knows if the missing sounds of whistling wings will be felt.

Humankind is such a poor learner from our natural history lessons, I thought. Shifting my body in my heavy coat to preserve more body heat, I slowly started to drift back once again into yesteryear.

What was that? The soft, faraway *crump* of the zon guns in Terrill's unharvested rice fields had given way to another sound, or so I thought. With my mind wandering, I had not been as alert to the sounds around me as I should have been. However, when one makes a living as a law enforcement officer, there is always a part of the mind that never shuts down but remains alert to anything out of place. That far recess of my mind had just told me something was amiss, and I was now alert as any predator as I waited for what was to come. Terrill's zon guns had been going off about every five minutes, and he had four of them surrounding his remaining unharvested rice fields to keep the hungry waterfowl at bay. Several days of recent rains had made the ground too muddy to harvest, so his Hardy Harvesters just sat at the edge of the fields like squat yellow monsters, waiting to eat their way through the fields before the ducks did it for them.

Sitting there now very alert, with my ears straining for any foreign sound, I was aware that it was getting close to the time for the zon gun in the southwest portion of the field to go off. *Crump* went the zon gun, right on time. Nothing unusual there, I thought. The next zon gun to go off was in the northeast quadrant of the rice field. I quietly waited, almost not wanting to breathe for fear of covering any suspicious sound. In a few moments the soft, far-off *crump* came to my ears with nothing following except the soft whirring of wings moving overhead from the Butte Sink to another feeding ground somewhere. The two remaining zon guns went off on schedule, and again I heard nothing more. Changing my focus from that mysterious sound to the multitudes of feeding ducks, I searched for anything out of the ordinary. The noise level of the feeding waterfowl told me all was well, and the overhead pattern of flying ducks seemed as usual both in direction and volume. I relaxed back into my seat, but my eyes and ears continued searching the darkness as I concentrated through one more round of the zon-gun melody. More and more flocks of waterfowl began moving out of the Butte Sink to Terrill's rice fields, and I began to write off my "sixth sense" as a possible false alarm.

I let my mind drift back into an earlier historical era as I re-
called that the Butte Sink was a natural marsh depression that
had held life-giving promise for millions of waterfowl and other
water birds since the earliest annals of time. It has been a natural
landmark and navigation point for hungry, tired waterfowl moving
south in the dance with their genetic makeups and schedules
since before the time of humankind. Located next to the Butte
Sink are the Sutter Buttes, the smallest complete mountain range
in North America, named after John Sutter, a Swiss emigrant,
who settled in the Sacramento Valley on a Spanish land grant in
the early 1800s. John C. Frémont, an early explorer, topographical
engineer, army officer, presidential aspirant, Civil War general,
and more, led a troop of men to the Sutter Buttes during the almost friendly War of the Rebellion against the Spanish in California. In his journals Frémont wrote that he planned to rest his men
in the Sutter Buttes to hide them from the prying eyes of the
Spanish army and its patrols until they had rested from their recent crossing of the Sierra Nevada Mountains. He wrote that "the
roar of the grizzly bear, the din of the feeding waterfowl, the
bugling of the elk and the crashing horns of fighting big horn
sheep" kept his men awake and after three days, he had to move
on so they could get some rest elsewhere. Today all that remained
from that glorious moment in time were the waterfowl and a few
pitiful remnant herds of tule elk. The last California grizzly had
been killed in the 1930s, and the subspecies of California bighorn
sheep were now gone to wherever extinction takes a species.

There it was again! This time there was no mistake, I thought as
I shot forward in the seat of the truck, grabbing the steering wheel
for support. The ducks and I had deadly company in Terrill's far-
flung rice fields! The soft sound of the zon gun had been immediately preceded by the soft, unmistakable, *and illegal* one-shot *thump*
of a shotgun. The recesses of my mind had not shut down as far as
they had earlier, and when this shot occurred my brain "caught"
and "reported" it. I strained to listen for more evidence of an intruder in my world and was soon rewarded with the sounds of
thousands of alarmed ducks flying overhead, returning to the

Butte Sink after a not-so-casual rice dinner. By the very numbers passing overhead, I knew somebody had spooked them and they were wisely getting the hell out of Dodge.

The hunt was on as I quietly stepped out of my darkened patrol truck. Carefully unlimbering my car-seat-stiff, tired frame, I scanned the darkened rice field with my 7×50 binoculars on a hope and prayer. The shooter and yours truly had only about a quarter of a moon to work with, but I had good vision in those days, and my night vision was tops, as my extensive driving around on dirt roads at night without lights attested. I could see thousands of pintail (identifiable by the males' white breasts) moving back and forth in a feeding frenzy to load up on the tan grains of rice scattered about the fields as a result of sloppy harvesting. Everywhere I looked there were ducks moving to and fro in the air, seeking the best place to load up on a "mess of grits." I continued to scan the distant area from which I thought the shots had come in the hope of seeing the silent figure of a shooter picking up his just-killed ducks or stalking more of the feeding waterfowl. But nothing except the soft whir of wings passing overhead and the soft percussion of the zon guns filled the airwaves or met my searching eyes. Half an hour passed. Damn, I knew I hadn't been dreaming that second time, but nothing like the sound of a shotgun again graced my ears.

Retracing the mystery noise in my mind, a trick most game wardens can do, I reexamined the essence of the sound. After running it through my head several times, I guessed from the lightness of the sound and the tenor of the report that the shooter was using a 20-gauge shotgun with low-base shells. If that were really the case, I had an experienced killer on my hands, and the ducks a deadly adversary! Any person using such a small-gauge shotgun and shooting so infrequently was truly a measured killer of the ultimate degree. By shooting a light shotgun he made less noise to echo-locate on; in fact, tracking the sound down was almost an impossibility at night over the many other common sounds. By taking only one shot at a time with a low-base shell (one with less powder, which again translates to less noise), he would be very hard to locate at a distance even if I was looking right at him. Based on the locations of the two sounds I had heard, I also suspected he may have been moving between shots. If that were the case, he had a several-thousand-acre rice field to move around in under the cover of darkness, whereas all I had was the knowledge that he was there. Well, that plus a heap of determination to apprehend such a dedicated son of a gun.

Damn, hunting the human predator is truly a great stimulant, I thought as I continued to scan the area with the pleasant realization that my "motor" was now running at its normal 110 percent regardless of the previous sleepless nights. Every mass of feeding ducks I observed was acting normally. Using my binoculars, I moved the top of the field of view up to the edge of the moon, a trick to gather more light in the ocular. I could still see the fields at the bottom of the glass and, with the extra light, let the peripheral vision work in hope of seeing my silent, stalking killer moving to his next group of feeding waterfowl. Nothing. I next scanned every known roadway into the rice fields foot by foot, looking for any parked vehicle that the killer may have driven in earlier and hidden. Again, nothing. I next reviewed my trip into the area five hours earlier for anything out of place, unknown parked automobiles, anything. Nothing computed there either!

Thump! There it was again, only now the sound was farther north. In fact, it was at least a quarter of a mile from where I had been looking. Hurriedly swinging my glasses to that area, I could see about ten thousand ducks swirling in the air and leaving the ground in black sheetlike masses. I carefully scanned the ground at the point where they were emerging but saw nothing in human form. Again lifting the ocular high to gather in the moonlight, I scanned every levee shadow, looking for the unmistakable form of a shooter outlined in the night or moving about the rice field to pick up dead and dying ducks. Nothing. It was as dead as a hammer out there except for the flying ducks fleeing that rice field like there was no tomorrow.

Damn, this guy is good, I thought. Normally after a shot one would find the shooter or shooters scurrying around to pick up their hard-won gains before the many wounded birds had crawled off into the grassy cover. I watched the area for about another thirty minutes and saw nothing but the last of the waterfowl leaving the area as a reward for all my efforts. Whoever this shooter was, he was very careful, almost coplike, I thought. My thoughts went back to an earlier case in which I had caught several police officers hunting on a national wildlife refuge for hogs in the dark of night, and I considered whether there were any points from that case that might help me. No information came to mind. Cold, stinking frustration was the word of the day. However, in every cloud there is a silver lining: that frustration set my jaw and narrowed my eyes as I told myself this game still had a few innings to go.

Soon the feeding waterfowl were greeted with the false sunrise of another day. As they left the fields they had fed in all night en route to their water-based loafing areas in the Butte Sink, they had to notice a stubborn game warden still hidden and watching. But I saw nothing, so I packed up shop at about eight A.M. and, after slowly driving around the area and seeing nothing unusual, headed southwest to work some of the deep-water duck clubs off San Jose Road. Sleep wasn't an option now because there was just too much on my mind after the recent morning's events. My heading south didn't mean I was relinquishing the battlefield or had lost the desire for a rematch with my shooter. One was forthcoming, you could bet your sweet tail end on that. There was a human out there representative of the highest class of poacher, and just by chance I had been let in on his high-stakes nightshooting game. Now that two were playing with fire, things were going to get interesting or I was going to lose a lot of sleep over the next several weeks. As is usually the case in wildlife law enforcement, it started with the latter.

For the next month my combat with my as yet unseen adversary took on determined proportions. After many fruitless stakeouts on top of all my other duties, much came to light even though I had not caught the poacher. This lad shot my several thousand acres of rice fields only on Friday nights or early Saturday mornings. How he entered and left the fields was still a mystery,

but I was working on it. I suspected it was not by automobile because I left a mark across every farm road leading into the rice
fields, and not once were my marks crossed with fresh tire tracks.
As my frustration and suspicion of a phantom vehicle grew,
I added a little spice to my marking system by using one-inch
mud-colored boards filled with two-inch nails. I always laid my
tire traps after all the normal duck hunters had left the scene and
in the dark to avoid detection. Before daylight and the return of
the rest of the hunting community, I would quietly remove them
and save them for another night.

As my time in the saddle grew, so did my information about my
opponent. This person never shot before ten P.M., always shot a
light shotgun with what sounded like low-base shells, never shot
more than once every thirty minutes or so, seemingly never exposed himself, and left before daylight to avoid discovery. If he was
shooting low-base shells, he was one smart son of a gun who was
very familiar with the habits of the ducks. Bottom line, when you
are that close to feeding waterfowl, you don't need a high-base
shell with lots of power. The ducks are so near that they are easy
to kill with just a light load of shot. Last but not least, the individual had to be local because he knew when the ducks arrived on
this piece of real estate, and he knew the lay of the land very well.
He was also a brave son of a gun because it was known in the
Valley that I spent very few nights anywhere else than in many of
the very fields in which he was treading.

About a week before Christmas the lad stopped shooting my
rice fields and disappeared. He never reappeared for the rest of
duck season, even though I worked the area every chance I could
through January. I checked the local newspapers for any signs of
accidents or illnesses of known violators during this time but
found none. I checked with many of my cohorts, and none of the
regular violators or even any of the old-guard commercial-market
hunters had been incarcerated. I was flat at a loss and began to
think I might have a farmer working out his back door, or maybe
it was old Terrill Sartain, the landowner, himself. In the days of
old, as he had told me during one of our many hunting-related

conversations, he had kept his farm solvent by killing and selling ducks to make ends meet. But I felt the old fellow and I, after many disagreements, had finally reached an understanding. Damn, I thought, blaming Terrill for this latest escapade was rather lame on my part. He was a friend, and I believed he was above this kind of killing at that point in his life. But I still got paid to run out every avenue available, and in this case no one was exempt from my mental gyrations.

Winter left, and with it the millions of migratory waterfowl. I moved on to other problems and managed to while away my summer with nothing more than several hundred cases involving deer spotlighters, set-liners, froggers, salmon snaggers, over-limits of striped bass, littering, one rescue of a sunken boat in the Sacramento River, the taking of quail and pheasants during the closed season, and several trout over-limits in the high country (both in my district and in the Sierras). But the memory of my adversary in the winter duck fields was never far from my mind's cluttered battlefield. I was curious whether my shooter would be back or whether last year's spree had been a onetime event. If a poacher has success in killing and is not disturbed by the long arm of the law, he will usually return to that practice until he is satiated or apprehended. That has been one of "Grotz's Rules" ("Grotz" was what my bride used to call me when I stepped over the line of propriety drawn in her mind) for all time, and I was going to remember it come the fall flights. It really doesn't pay to piss off Mother Nature or one of her guardians, especially the big game warden types, I thought as an anticipatory smile crossed my wind-burned face.

The 1969 waterfowl season in Colusa County began like all the rest: with ten thousand eager hunters, a million pintail who had not been shot at for a year, and only two game wardens for the whole twelve hundred square miles of the county. The odds were just about right, I thought with a grin. I figured I had the bad guys right where I wanted them—they just didn't know it yet. The season progressed as usual, marked with another two hundred citations issued in state and federal courts for wildlife-related violations by the middle of November. During that period the waterfowl population swelled to several million, and the lone game warden on the Colusa side of the district, exhausted from the seven-day weeks and eighteen-hour days since July 1, kept plodding along.

Wildlife dies without making a sound, and the only voice it has is the conservation officer's. If that officer isn't out there kicking ass and squallin' like a banshee, then he or she is just as big a problem as the poacher. ... With that always in the back of their minds, it is no wonder that the officers, with the help of their best friends—their wives or husbands—can go on almost forever. In my case, thank God for the world's best wife! She knew how important it was to me to function at 110 percent and saw to it that any shortcomings in that department were not of her making. It is important for a good game warden to have a good partner standing beside him or her. Donna always did, and let me tell you, a lot of bad guys paid the price because of that woman's strength and dedication—over five thousand such chaps in my thirty-two-year state and federal career.

It was no different this year. I was tired and about half sick and yet had the worst half of the hunting season still to go. Waterfowl work is hard, and many of my fellow officers wouldn't spend much time working duck hunters because of the long days and crappy working conditions. Also, there were a dozen other hunting seasons going on during that same period, so there just wasn't much good help available. The weather was usually the pits, and this was the mud season. I was either stuck in it with my rig up to its axles or lying in it trying to catch someone who needed catching. In between I was trudging through it, day and night, until my legs just burned from the exertion of having to always pull my feet up and out of the sticky adobe mud, mile after long mile. To top everything off, my one-shot shooter was back! Boy, did that realization ever get the juices flowing, regardless of the exhaustion that came from an already long season, acres of mud, and my all but worn-out carcass.

The ducks had moved big time to the east side of Terrill's fields on November 18 that year, and sure as God made little green apples, my adversary from the year before was back in the saddle just two days later. Remembering the previous pattern, I was back in my cottonwood grove that Friday in the hope that he would be there. It wasn't because I didn't have enough to do—quite the contrary! I had plenty going on in a county that on any given shoot day would host three thousand duck hunters. However, I never turned down an opportunity to catch my fellow human, so I guess God acted accordingly. At exactly ten forty-four P.M. he fired his first shot. In a few moments thousands of frightened ducks were streaming from Terrill's fields back to the Butte Sink or the safer adjoining fields in order to resume their feeding. Damn! I had been looking to the south and had not been able to echo-locate the lad, but I was wise to his little game now and waited with a grimness born from the bone-tiredness of an already long season. Exactly forty minutes later another single shot rang out, this time due west of my position in the cottonwoods. The shooter had moved at least a quarter of a mile since his last shot, I thought as I spun my binoculars around to view the area of his last shot. Observing nothing, I thought, Crap, here we go again! This lad is going to be a major problem.

I loaded up my stalking gear and began my stalk in the opposite direction from his last shot, trying to anticipate his line of thinking. My efforts were to no avail. His next shot was across the Colusa-Gridley Highway, three-eighths of a mile north of his last one. It was almost as if he was wired into my thoughts. Sunrise found a very tired game warden beside one of the numerous rice checks in the field, surrounded by ten thousand feeding ducks and none the closer to their assailant.

That afternoon I ran across Jack Downs, the agent in charge for the U.S. Fish and Wildlife Service for Northern California. I shared a dozen citations with him to file in federal court, including several over-limits and untagged-bird citations from the Wallace Lynn Ranch, and mentioned my running battle with "old one-shot." Without a word Jack went to the back of his sedan, opened the trunk, and returned carrying a moderate-sized black metal box. It looked like the kind of heavy-duty case you would use to protect a camera. Opening it, he said, "Tiny, try this on the bastard."

I said, "What is it?"

"A surplus Starlight scope like they are using in Vietnam," he said.

"Damn," I said, my interest running sky high, "how do they work?" As I discovered, they were very simple to operate; you just had to be careful around light sources other than starlight or very weak light. The scope magnified available light by fifty thousand and in essence turned night into a lime-green day.

I thanked Jack, realizing that the battle between "old one-shot" and the world's largest game warden had just taken a turn for the worse for my shooter. I managed a slow grin through a rather chapped, weather-bitten face. Jack took off to attend to another problem in the Chico area, and I returned to my "hoorahs" with the White Mallard Duck Club on the east side. But I was much happier now that I was armed with a device that, if I could get it to work right, was going to catch a son of a bitch who needed some catching.

O'dark hundred the following Friday I was back at my hiding place and holding the high ground. The new secret device lay on the hood of my patrol truck, ready for instant use, and I had a look in my eyes that closely resembled a cat on the prowl and matched the grin on my face. One way or the other, this lad was going to fall if I had my druthers, and the ducks were going to get a little rest from his relentless nighttime pursuit.

Nine minutes after one A.M., my lad let go with his typical single shot. Damn, he was at least half a mile north of me. That didn't surprise me, though, because he always seemed to be wired into my thoughts, so off I went on foot into the rice fields with my newfound "friend" from Vietnam. Those of you reading these lines may be surprised to hear this, but often when you are trying to save a particular wildlife resource, that resource will do its level best to keep you from succeeding in that effort. That night was no exception. Thousands of feeding waterfowl blocked my movements every which way, and in order to avoid scaring them and alerting my prey that there was another predator in the field, I had to move very slowly. Twice more my "friend" shot the ducks, and twice more, as if on cue, he stayed out of sight and out of the range of my new toy. This was not making me very happy, and a determination was building in me that I would find and catch this lad if I did nothing else in my entire career.

Then it happened! Off to the south (thank God for the gift of my wonderful ears) I heard what sounded like an artificial pintail call being softly used. I know that sounds unlikely, but it wouldn't seem so strange if you were a dyed-in-the-wool duck hunter like me. I made extensive use of decoys and the calls when I got my few chances to hunt the duck, and to be frank I was damned good at it—calling, that is. I could charm a mallard out of his socks and a pintail out of his feathers, and by damn, that was a pintail call I had just heard or I weighed only two hundred pounds. (Just for your information, the last time I weighed two hundred pounds was when I was nine days old.) What a smart son of a gun, using a pintail call to bring the birds to him at night: that way he could shoot for the white of their breasts and be assured a group kill every time.

Swinging my Starlight scope in the direction of that sound, I immediately spotted a stockily built fellow standing beside a rice check about two hundred yards away. This man had shot his last duck, as far as I was concerned, and off I moved at a right smart clip, avoiding groups of feeding ducks all the way in order to avoid arousing my target's suspicions. After dog-trotting about one hundred yards, I held up to catch my breath and clicked on my night scope again. There he was, crouched by the same levee and calling in a large flock of swirling ducks who were looking for a place to land and feed. I stood there fascinated as the birds, not realizing they were starting their dance of death, began moving closer to the lad and his excellent pintail call. The ducks swirled around and around him until he was almost lost in the midst of their bodies as they tried to find the "duck" calling them from the darkened field below. Then the lad stood up from his half-crouched position and pulled his right hand way back behind his body while his left hand moved in front of his body. What the hell? The right hand looked like it let go of something, and six ducks fell like rocks while the rest frantically made their escape. There had been no shot fired, I didn't see any telltale sign of a muzzle flash, and he didn't have a gun in his hands—but by God, ducks fell. I saw that clear as hell in the night scope, including their subsequent flopping on the ground.

The lad then commenced to pick up ducks from the field and wring the necks of the cripples. What the hell? I thought again. Then, *thump!* Off to the west about a quarter of a mile away, "old one-shot" made his presence known. Goddamn, what a quandary. Swinging my Starlight scope toward the shooting, I was rewarded with nothing but fleeing ducks, as always. Now I had a problem. I had a night shooter on either side of me and couldn't decide which way to go since I couldn't get both of them, much less even see one of them! I quickly realized that the lad before me, less than a hundred yards away, was a "nest on the ground," so I put my internal crosshairs on his tail end and headed in that direction as quietly as a man my size could move. Watching him all the while with my Starlight scope, I saw that he was carrying a large batch of ducks on a duck strap (a leather device designed to carry ducks) and was now moving off to the west, occasionally calling on his pintail whistle as he went. The rice field was dry, and I was making good time, stalking in twenty-step counts and pausing in between for a rest and a long look-see with the scope.

Each time I stopped I adjusted my line of attack on the lad without the gun, who was carrying something with which to kill ducks, that was for sure. About a thousand ducks passed low over me en route to the lad with the pintail whistle, and I again stopped to watch his actions as he called and waited. The ducks swirled around him as before, and this time I was close enough to see that he had a goddamn *slingshot!* Back went his right arm, and four ducks dropped deader than a hammer. I could not believe it. I wondered how long this lad had been hunting this way. What an ingenious way to stalk and illegally kill ducks at night! This fellow, whoever he was, was a real killing professional, there was no denying that. I had seen a lot of amazing things during my time as a law enforcement officer, but this one had to take the cake—almost. ...

Moving northwest of him, I set up an interception course and waited. It went just like clockwork. In a few moments, betrayed by the crunching of rice stalks under his feet, here he came, lugging one hell of a load of ducks right to me. I couldn't have done better if I had engineered our crossing points: he walked *right to me along the same rice check on which I was standing!* When he was about fifteen feet away I quietly laid down my Starlight scope, and when the crunch of the rice stubble told me he was just inches away, on went my five-cell flashlight, right in his face. The lad was totally stunned and let out a surprised *"Hey-hey-hey!"*

I grabbed him by his jacket and told him in a tone meant to be obeyed, "Game warden; you are under arrest!" Then I quickly turned off my flashlight so as not to warn "old one-shot" of my presence in his private killing field. Once I had my pintail-call-blowing culprit under control (he wet his pants, I scared him so badly), I relaxed my grip and told him to sit in terms he clearly understood. His bottom and the ducks he was carrying hit the damp ground with a *whomp*, and he never wiggled after that.

The lad turned out to be one of a group of men I had met working at a rice drier in Butte City. He was kin to a long line of market hunters living in that neighborhood and the Princeton area. Several older men in his clan had been identified in the old book about commercial-market hunters titled *Hunting the Lawless*, by Hugh Worster (a U.S. game management agent in the '40s and '50s), and it looked as if David were following in their footsteps. I had apprehended David Forney several times before, once for late shooting (about one hour late) near the town of Willows and another time for a rather sizable over-limit of geese, but I had lost sight of him since then in the work-filled Valley. On that night we left the field of battle, I carrying with difficulty the thirty-nine pintail he had killed with a homemade slingshot and he carrying the realization that he was in trouble again. I thought, I guess a guy never learns not to poach once it gets into his blood. Maybe for some people it is almost in their genes.

Back at my truck I examined his slingshot more closely. It was made with four sections of surgical tubing (two to a side of the yoke), with a wide, homemade metal yoke and a large leather sacklike pouch tied with wire at the end of the tubing for holding lead shot. He carried a small bag at his waist containing about three pounds of number 4 lead shot. I surmised that David would load the slingshot pouch with lead, call in the ducks until they were just a few feet away, and kill them just as cleanly as if he had shot them with a shotgun, only with no sound.

I asked David how long he had been doing this, and he just smiled and said, "Since I was a boy after watching all my uncles getting caught after night shooting in the rice fields in the '40s and '50s because the sound of their shotguns gave them away." Well, at least he was honest with me.

Thump went the sound of "old one-shot," who was still in the field as I loaded David and the ducks into my vehicle for transport to his vehicle, hidden in the trees to the southwest. A quick look at Dave showed that he did not hear the shot because he was lost in worry about what was to come in the Colusa Justice Court. Good, I thought. I didn't want anyone to know that shooter was still at large. It didn't take much in the close-knit Valley communities for the word to get out that the game wardens were on your tail. This shooter was mine, and I needed no other odds heaped on his side before we connected. Looking into the dark of the night toward where I had heard the shot, I promised myself that I would come again when there were just the two of us and my Starlight scope. I drove out of my hiding place down a small levee and out of sight of the rice field before I turned on my headlights.

I felt nothing would be accomplished by booking David in the Colusa County Jail, so I just took him back to where he had hidden his pickup. I wanted to see where he had hidden his truck so next time I would have a place to hide—or to check out to see who else might be there before I began my night's work in the rice fields. David's pickup was parked in some heavy brush and trees with brush thrown over the top so no one would notice it in its weedy hiding place. While David uncovered his truck, I wrote him citations for taking migratory waterfowl before legal hours and possession of an over-limit of ducks: twenty-nine over the limit. (David forfeited bail and ended up paying $500 for the early hunting and $500 for the over-limit in the Colusa County Justice Court two weeks later.) I returned his slingshot with a warning that to return to that judicial district for a like offense would probably land him in jail for six months. I never saw or heard of David in the field hunting waterfowl again, but I did see him around the town of Colusa, and we remain friends to this day.

When I slid into my usual hiding place the following Friday, it was misting rain and Terrill's fields were full of feeding waterfowl. I tried out my Starlight scope and found that its abilities were somewhat impaired by the weather, but if the rain didn't get any heavier I was still in business. Rolling down my windows, I snuggled into my heavy hunting coat while visions of one-shot night shooters danced in my head. ... This time I had a good gut feeling about my chances and kept my motors idling at the usual 110 percent. *Thump!* There was my friend, right on schedule at one thirty-three A.M. and only about three-eighths of a mile directly east of me.

This time I was off to the races and tried a new technique. Getting a mental picture of where this shooter had just shot, I took off at a dog trot, scope in one hand and unused flashlight in the other. I stopped when I had covered about two-thirds of the distance in order to gather some wind and collect my thoughts. Travel had been a little difficult owing to several flocks of feeding ducks and rutted terrain, but I managed to avoid spooking the birds as I slid into some tall rice grass next to a rice check. I knew the lad would have to pick up his ducks after shooting, and now that I was closer I might see something that would help me catch him. Because it was raining lightly, I figured he would feel safer (after all, what game warden would be stupid enough to work on a night like this?) and might drop his guard and expose his position. Peering up over the rice check, I laid down my flashlight and turned on my scope. Nothing but ducks flying around in dozens of small bunches, looking for a place to land among their kind. Damn, he had to be there, I thought as I looked in the direction of the last shot. I scanned the entire area for about 40 minutes, eventually swinging 360 degrees but seeing only flying ducks and the fuzz of rain in my Starlight scope.

Thump, not more than one hundred yards to the north this time, followed by the soft roar of the rain-soaked wingbeats of at least fifteen thousand feeding ducks frantically taking to the air. I held my scope at the point of alarm identified by the cloud of escaping ducks, and then *there he was!* Beside a rice check, standing totally motionless, was the figure of a small man from the shoulders up. He stood there for about ten minutes, and then the Starlight scope picked up the light of a penlight directed at the ground before him as he began to walk out into the rice field. When I removed the scope, even my sharp eyes could not make out the beam from his small penlight. Boy, this guy is good, I thought. Seeing that he was busy picking up his latest kills, I moved in a direction where I could head him off if he continued north. To throw him off, I even let my mind tell me I was going south. No, I am not superstitious, just careful when I am that close to the object of my attention. Especially after taking two years to get there ...

Dog-trotting at a slower pace, I had just stepped over my second rice check with a big, long step when *crash!* down I went, face first into the rice-paddy mud, and I do mean hard. My right leg hurt like hell because it had landed on some sort of metal contraption. Goddamn it, I shouted internally over the pain. Lord, don't let me get this close and lose it over a piece of farm equipment carelessly left in the field, I thought as I rolled over and got up on m good knee. Fortunately my flashlight and Starlight scope had landed at my fingertips, and I quickly retrieved them. Feeling back to the crash point with my hands, I was amazed to find what appeared to be a bicycle lying beside the rice check with two canvas saddlebags tied over the bar between the seat and the handlebars. One bag was clear full of freshly killed ducks, but the other was empty. Thank God, I told myself as my hands continued to explore the object in the dark. If I had landed on the hard metal parts of the bike instead of falling partly on the full bag of ducks, there was no telling what damage I might have done to my leg and knee. As I have often said, God loves little children, fools, and game wardens.

My right knee had smashed through the spokes of the front wheel after my left foot had hooked the rear wheel, damaging the machine to such an extent that no one would be using it for a while unless he was a member of the Keystone Cops. Then it dawned on me: this bike belonged to my shooter. That devil! He had been using a bicycle all along to get to and from the field of his dreams. Once in the rice fields he would carefully push the bike to a central position among the feeding waterfowl and ditch it. He would then stalk his ducks, pull his shots, and bring them back to the bike once he had killed too many to carry. When the saddle-bags were full, he would wheel the ducks out of the field and to his car, wherever that was hidden.

Quickly getting over the shock and pain in my right knee, I turned on the Starlight scope and began to look around for my shooter. He was nowhere to be found! *Damn,* I said to myself in frustration, how can that be? I kept looking wildly from side to side, thinking he must have heard me meeting the bike in the dark and then made good his escape, figuring the jig was up. But after what seemed an eon, there he was! He was walking along a rice check carrying a large load of ducks as if he owned the place. My knee hurt like hell, but it was feeling better already after I found my man in the scope again. He was still thirty-five or so yards away but appeared to be making his way toward his bicycle cache and, unknown to him, one very happy but sore-legged catch dog.

The lad was only a few feet away when I turned off my Starlight scope and laid it down to get ready with my flashlight. He was carrying a substantial number of ducks and stopped several times to rest. I figured this was his last load, given the time of morning and the fact that one saddlebag was already full. I waited until I could hear the *squeech* of his rubber boots on the rice stubble and smell the odor of tobacco on him before I rose from my kneeling position and turned on my flashlight. He couldn't have been more than two feet away and was so surprised that he continued walking right into me, hide, feathers, and all!

"State Fish and Game warden; hold it right there!" I commanded. I had him in an instant with my left hand as I felt him tighten up and start to throw the ducks at me in preparation for running. Dropping my flashlight (leaving it on to illuminate the area), I sank

my right hand into his shoulder where the neck joined the body and hissed, "Don't try it unless you want to die this morning in this goddamned stinking rice field." His body was still taut in my hand, but I sensed resignation starting to well up in him and loosened my grip somewhat as he cried out in pain at the grip I had in the meat around his collarbone. "Sit down" was my next command, which he slowly did, whereupon in one fluid motion I grabbed his shotgun, jerked it from his hand, and unloaded it. Picking up the flashlight and shining it into his eyes, I realized I had seen his face somewhere before. Damn, where? I asked myself. As we both got our breath, he from exertion and I after the adrenaline rush, I realized who he was. The one-shot shooter was none other than a judge from an adjacent county whom I had appeared before several times! I could not believe it. This bastard had been a hanging judge on the few cases I had had before him, and yet here he was doing the same damn thing other bad guys were doing.

"Judge?" I asked, still in shock and not believing what I was seeing. "Is that you?" I have found over the years that a conservation officer will ask dumb-ass questions like that when he or she is really surprised. *And surprised I was!*

"Screw you," was his polite judicial reply.

I just could not believe my eyes; yet this had to be the chap I had been chasing for some time. Regaining my composure, I did what I had been sworn to do with a certain degree of relish, sore leg and all. "Judge, you are under arrest for possessing an over-limit of ducks and the illegal night shooting of the same. Roll over on the ground, Your Honor; I am going to handcuff you before we head in to the local jail."

I got the coldest look for a moment, but then he did as I directed, and the deed was done.

Looking over my evidence, I found that he had been carrying a Winchester Model 12 20-gauge shotgun. In addition, the judge was carrying only 20-gauge low-base shells, size number 8 lead shot. He had a total of thirty ducks on a large homemade duck strap, mostly pintail drakes, plus, as I soon discovered, another twenty-one mallards, pintail, and wigeon in the saddlebag on his bike.

The judge was a pro, and there was no telling how many ducks he had taken in this manner, but it had to be plenty over the years, I thought. "How long you been doing this, Judge?" I asked.

"None of your goddamn business," he replied.

Rolling him over on his side, I had him dig out his wallet, then helped him to his feet and had him place it in the saddlebag full of ducks still attached to his bike so that if he somehow got away I would still have a solid identification. With that, I said, "OK, Your Honor, we are heading for my truck." I grabbed his stringer of ducks with one hand and the saddlebag full of ducks with the other, and he walked out of the field while I struggled with the load of evidence.

Once we reached my truck, I seat-belted him in and then drove back out to the field on the nearest farm road to pick up his smashed bike and the shotgun. Then off to the Colusa County Jail we went, he with a scowl and I with a hitch in my giddy-up from the bicycle collision that was more than offset by the smile on my Robert Redford–like face.

I didn't let on to the booking officer who my prisoner was, and the booking proceeded normally. The judge never appeared in court but was allowed by Colusa Justice Court Judge Weyand to forfeit his bail, which ran to $950 for his morning's work. A few weeks later the judge came by my place and with hardly a hi, 'bye, or kiss-my-last-part-over-the-fence greeting picked up his shotgun, bike, and saddlebag and left. My one-shot judge was defeated in the next election, and I never again ran across the man while working as a state game warden or federal agent in the Sacramento Valley. I continued to work in and around the area where I had caught him, but it was as if the earth had swallowed him up. However, I doubt that I stopped the man from doing what he did in the early-morning hours in the rice fields. I suppose he just moved over to Butte County and continued where he had left off, even after being so rudely surprised that morning by a man who ruined his bike and the seat of his pants when he rose up out of the rice field and grabbed him by the "stacking swivel." ...

I eventually found out that his method of operation in Colusa County had been to drive his pickup to Terrill Sartain's duck club parking lot near Butte Creek and leave it there among all the rest of the hunters' vehicles. It would be late at night and the rest of the duck club members would be asleep when he would take out the bike, ride it down the levee road until he found a mess of feeding ducks, and then wheel it out into that field and leave it in a place where he could find it later in the morning as he left the field with his loads of ducks. He would then quietly work his way into and around the feeding ducks, shoot them until he had killed what he wanted, load them on his bike, and wheel them back to his truck. I had never thought of this strategy because I was so focused on finding a motor vehicle that I had never looked for bicycle tracks. They were there, as I later discovered; I was just too damn dumb to look around me for *all* the signs. He was a pretty clever chap with an outstanding game plan, until a clumsy game warden literally stumbled into it—or was it through it?

You never know what will happen when dealing with members of the judicial cloth in my profession. They represent the good, bad, and ugly segments of our society, just like anyone else. Fortunately there are enough of the good ones that folks like me can get our jobs done and continue to have hope. I never held court in a rice field in the wee hours of the morning, but if I did, that was one time when I would happily have said, "All rise—here come da judge."

11

The Rubber Chicken

L EAVING MY HOME AT DAYLIGHT, I paused to drink in the cool of the morning and thanked the good Lord for another fine day. It was fall, one of my favorite times of the year, and even better, the duck and pheasant hunting seasons were in full swing. Hunters both good and bad would be out there trying to kill the elusive fliers as they fled for their lives, hoping not to end up on the dinner table. What better time to have the local game warden eyeballing the hunters as they pulled their triggers than this fine day? Also, because this was Colusa County with its many wildlife treasures, there would be a number of real outlaws out there, local as well as visiting, killing everything eatable in quantities greater than legally allowed or morally acceptable. That class of outlaw would be my special object of attention today, I decided, and with that I stepped off the porch and headed for my patrol vehicle. I hadn't gone two steps when reality quickly rained down upon me with the realization that I wasn't built like a cheetah. Given those limitations, I would take *anyone* crossing the line who came within arm's length and be just as happy. You betcha! *But a big boy or two would be nice. ...*

The reason why flashed across my mind. Today's society has somehow forgotten that governments can pass all the conservation laws they want, but if those laws aren't enforced, *and well*, then grab your hind end and hope for the best because the critters are going to pay the price. The American people have a grim history and deadly track record in their wildlife dance of death, leading in

some instances to the black hole of extinction. I won't bother listing the many hundreds of examples, though the passenger pigeon
quickly comes to mind. However, it doesn't have to be that way.
Enter the lowly (in some people's eyes) game warden, who is often
the only voice for the critters. Since they can't vocalize their objections to their raw treatment by humankind, wildlife officers can
and do. The wildlife we still enjoy today exists because of the
numerous unsung men and women who over the years since the
late 1700s have given their best, and sometimes their all, so others
can appreciate this natural link to our national heritage.

Before I got to my truck I was brought up short once again and
paused in midstride. I was suddenly overcome by a very strong gut
feeling letting me know that something special was on the menu
today. It wasn't a feeling of dread but a sense I had experienced
many times during my short tenure as a wildlife officer, and one I
would experience many more times over the next thirty years. It
told me I was about to catch a special culprit. In times past my instincts had guided me to the poacher's pot of gold, and I knew
that before this day was done I would have my hands on the
"golden guilders" once again. Damn, I thought. What a great way
for a game warden to start his day. I finished my walk to my patrol
vehicle with a little more zip in my step and an even bigger grin.

The engine of my muddy patrol truck roared to life, and after
checking the gauges I headed down Eighth Street, which was still
puddled with rain from last night's storm. I rolled down my window so I could smell the cold, clean air and hear leaves crunching
under my tires as I watched last night's leaves dropped by the wind
dancing off the hood of my truck. Taking another moment to
thank the good Lord for my senses, I asked Him to let me be a
good catch dog this fine day. Now, I expect some readers will say
one is not supposed to pray for such things: prayer is for something
very special, not the mundane. Well, it's obvious you have never
been an outnumbered, outgunned game warden buried up to his
eyes in outlaws. Many times a wish and a prayer are all we have.

Crossing the Sacramento River and turning north on the River
Road, I noticed a few late-season fishermen in their boats, but

none aroused the primal hunting instinct. After continuing north for about a mile, I turned down a muddy road leading to the west side of Butte Creek. As I bounced over and through the muddy, rain-filled potholes, I couldn't help but notice that the sky was as blue as my bride's beautiful eyes. Blue sky, or "bluebird weather," meant catching real duck-shooting outlaws would be difficult because the birds would be flying higher and less inclined to land among old decoy sets because by this time in the season they had been shot at so often. Quickly eliminating the notion of working the deep-water duck club shooters that morning, I figured unless I came across a gathering of snow geese and hunters in the fields, I would channel my efforts toward the pheasant hunters. That thought drew a smile of anticipation across my wind-burned face as I scurried deeper into the outback en route to several good hunting areas.

Working pheasant hunters was always a pleasure because there were lots of them pursuing the elusive table fare, and many times they ended up breaking the law more ways from Sunday than I would have thought possible. Hence, chasing and catching those hunting the wily pheasant gave me many surprising real-life moments. Before the day was done I would have several new memories, and one in particular. ...

Finally reaching Butte Creek and a fork in the road, I turned and drove north after opening and going through a locked gate. Driving slowly with my windows down, I cautiously headed deeper into the hunting area, looking and listening for anything out of place. Normally I would have been out and about at "o'dark thirty" that morning, but after working on waterfowl night shooters the previous evening and late into the morning, I had decided to get a few hours' rest before I hit the road again. Those three hours of sleep had felt really good, but it felt even better to be back out on the prowl.

Soon I came out of a dense stand of swamp and timber into the open agricultural areas. Rice and milo fields abounded around me as I continued down the muddy road, heavily traveled by that morning's hunters. Many of the harvested areas had been flooded and were occupied by large numbers of coots, snipe, and water-fowl, with pheasants ducking in and out of the roadside cover in front of my patrol truck. That morning was exceptionally beautiful, but that hunting instinct was still hanging with me like an anchor on a line, slightly dampening my simple joy in my surroundings. Swinging around a turn in the muddy road, I saw a lone man walking fifty yards away, hunting pheasants in the tall grasses beside a feeder canal that ran into Warren Davidson's Butte Sink duck club. I quietly stopped the truck before he saw me, took out my binoculars, and gave him a once-over. He appeared to have a very full game bag, based on the bulge I could plainly see in the back of his hunting jacket. I waited until he was pretty much out in the open so he couldn't hide any of his game if he was in the wrong before I drove up to him. When he recognized the Great Seal of California on the door, I noticed a slight look of dismay crossing his face, but only slight, mind you. I got out of the truck and walked toward the hunter as he kept heading my way on the ditch bank as if nothing were out of the ordinary.

At that moment I flushed a rooster pheasant at my feet that had been sneaking ahead of the hunter through the tall grasses on the ditch bank. He cackled his displeasure at being discovered, rose into the air, and thundered out of sight, dropping into a nearby stand of trees and brush. My hunter raised his shotgun to shoot the pheasant and then for some reason, after a split second of swinging after the bird, lowered the weapon. That was strange, I thought. The bird was in range and a clean kill if the man wanted to shoot. I kept that bit of troubling knowledge at the back of my mind as we kept working toward each other until finally I greeted him with, "Good morning; state Fish and Game warden. How is the pheasant hunting this fine morning?"

"It's all right," he grumbled.

Ignoring his sour demeanor, I said, "If you don't mind, sir, I would like to check your shotgun for a plug and check your hunting license and game bag."

"What difference would it make if I didn't want you to check it?" came the unexpectedly surly reply. "You are going to check it anyway." Those harsh words on such a nice morning, plus the way he had avoided killing the pheasant at close range, put me on high alert in a heartbeat. This chap appeared to have gotten out on the wrong side of bed that morning—and if his current disposition meant anything, he had probably slept on a hard concrete floor!

"Well, sir," I replied, "I am sorry to disturb your morning's shoot, but I will be as quick as I can and let you get on with your hunting just as soon as possible."

He just grunted as he extracted the shells from his shotgun and handed it to me. I quickly checked the now empty magazine of his Model 11 Remington auto-loader and found it to be unplugged, or capable of holding more than three shells. I gave my grouch a look, and he snarled, "Yeah, I know it is unplugged and in violation of the law."

Now I was really on my best enforcement toes. Apparently I had a bad fellow who not only didn't care but appeared to have been in a similar situation before. Carefully laying his shotgun on the hood of my vehicle, I asked to check his game bag. Now that I was closer to him, I could see several tails of rooster pheasants sticking out the sides. The limit was two rooster pheasants per day, and it surely appeared that this shooter had a few more than that. Soon six male and two female pheasants were lying at my feet, putting my chap four over the limit on roosters along with two closed-season females. With that revelation lying before us, he just stared at me as I looked at him.

Man, I thought, this fellow is something else. How little did I know what an understatement that would turn out to be! "May I check your hunting license, sir, and while you are at it, would you please hand me your driver's license as well?"

The man sullenly handed me both items and then stood there as if he were waiting for the other shoe to drop. Looking at the hunting license, which was in order, I learned that the man standing was one Anthony "Tony" Figone from Oakland, California. He was a middle-aged man of medium height and build. Then it dawned on me! I had just finished reading a book called *Hunting the Lawless* by U.S. Game Management Agent Hugh Worcester. In the 1940s and early 1950s Hugh had worked many of the same areas that I was working in the late 1960s. His book was published in 1955 and was a detailed historical record of the old-time market hunters in the days of hordes of ducks, extensive night shooting, and the common use of "Long Toms" (shotguns possessing magazine extenders used to increase the shell capacity, sometimes to fifteen rounds). When I read that book I discovered that during my short time working the valley as a game warden I had already cited five of the same men Hugh had caught in the 1940s and '50s. And standing here in front of me with an unplugged shotgun, an over-limit of roosters, and a pair of closed-season hens was probably my sixth, who had been arrested as a young man for buying and selling ducks in the San Francisco–Oakland Bay areas!

"Mr. Figone, you aren't the 'Figone' in the book *Hunting the Lawless,* are you?"

Tony looked at me for a second and then said, "Yeah; just write the ticket, asshole."

Boy, was I tickled! It was always nice to catch outlaws, especially *real* outlaws, and it now appeared that I had started my day with an exceptional catch. I issued Mr. Figone a citation for possession of an over-limit of rooster pheasants, illegal possession of two hens, and possession of an unplugged shotgun while hunting game birds. I then seized the pheasants, and we parted ways, Tony with a hitch in his giddy-up and I with a damn big smile. Catching my sixth person from that book of outlaws from the days of yesteryear really made my day. Tony later paid $50 for the unplugged shotgun, $200 for the hens, and $250 for the over-limit of roosters. All in all, I paid for the day's gas and oil before I got out of the gate, as I used to say.

As I drove away I heard two shotguns interrupting life to the northeast with their telltale *thump-thump.* Swinging the nose of the truck and my own proboscis in that direction, I headed south and east of Warren Davidson's stilted clubhouse on another dirt road to investigate. High overhead in the direction from which I had just heard the shots, I could see a dozen or so pintail and mallards pulling for the heavens as if scared to death. Stopped behind a grassy levee for cover, I located two lads in a blind surrounded by water and waterfowl's sirens, decoys, after a few moments of "stalking" with my binoculars. With the air full of pintail looking for some big water in which to rest after being scared up from a neighboring duck club, it was just a matter of time before these lads ran "afowl" of the law, so I stayed in my place of concealment. Ten minutes later a large flock of mallards from the north, dogged by an equally large group of pintail coming from the east, responded to the siren's call and tumbled into that zone of no return. When the mallards were in range, the two lads in the blind stood up with their shotguns, to the horror of the lead mallards swinging into the decoy set, and commenced their deadly but not yet illegal business.

Dive brakes went on, flaps went down, and the mallards made a frantic effort to regain speed and distance from the men suddenly standing up in the blind. The speedy greyhounds of the air, the pintail coming in behind the mallards, overshot in their efforts to overtake their "friends" and flew into the mallards as the leading ducks were frantically trying to put distance between themselves and the men below. The result was a great mass of ducks directly in front of the guns at a distance of only thirty yards! The predictable happened, and the shooting quickly became illegal. Numerous shots poured leaden death into the center of the colliding flocks, with devastating results. Down tumbled broken and wounded bodies by the score as the Winchesters did their intended work. The limit was eight ducks per hunter in those days, and these lads had stepped across that threshold and into my world: thirty-seven ducks over the limit, to be exact. Through my binoculars I saw their looks of genuine surprise at the appearance of the great ball of ducks, then greed as they looked hurriedly around to see if anyone but Mother Nature had seen the deed. The coast apparently being clear, they quickly walked out into their duck pond, picking up the floating dead and snuffing out the lives of the wounded with a quick neck-wringing action. They hurriedly produced a giant decoy bag from the blind and placed a few decoys from the pond in the bottom of the bag to provide the needed cover. Then they laid a layer of ducks on top of the decoys, then another layer of decoys all around the dead ducks to finish filling the bag and hide their ill-gotten gains. They put the remainder of the ducks, the legal bag of sixteen, across the bench seat of a small boat they were using as a "sled" to drag their gear out to the blind. Happy with their morning's shoot, the two men, one pulling the small boat, began the walk to their vehicle, which was hidden in a nearby grove of trees. As they walked the hundred yards to their car through the flooded rice field, they kept looking all around to make sure no one had seen the shooting twenty minutes earlier. Fortunately, the right kind of someone had. ...

I let the lads trudge out through the rice field to their vehicle, then moved from my hiding place to meet them moments later as a happily oblivious game warden requesting a routine game check. A brief discussion of the day's hunt ensued with no revelation of my knowledge and no admission on their part of the illegal deed. I dutifully checked their licenses, plugs, duck stamps (part of the license system), and the birds placed in plain view on their tailgate for the not-too-wary public servant to observe, count, and then, they hoped, go away. Having gone through those motions, I asked the lads if they had any other birds, and they predictably announced that they had not. Their innocent faces would have made their mothers proud. More small talk ensued as they continued loading their vehicle with their hunting gear. I let them load the large decoy bag full of illegal ducks as if nothing was out of the ordinary. Then in a loud voice and with eyebrows arched for effect, I said, "Wait, did you hear that?"

The hunters looked at me with questioning expressions and responded simultaneously, "Hear what?"

I said, "The wet sound of rustling mallard and pintail feathers."

I got the goddamnedest looks, but my statement was calculated to have a profound effect on the lads regarding a game warden's "magical" powers. Their looks of disbelief showed that I had struck a killing blow! Hell, there was no way I could have heard feathers rustling in a noisy bag full of clattering plastic decoys, much less told the ducks' species from the sound. But from the looks on their faces, they thought I could, and at that moment that was exactly the point I wanted to make!

I said, "Gentlemen, I think I need to look in that decoy sack. I'm sure that is where the sound came from."

They just looked at me in utter surprise, and I can't say I blamed them. One of the men, with a look as if someone just bitten his hind end, removed the decoy bag from the back of the pickup and laid it on the ground in front of me as if it contained some sort of radioactive material. Suffice to say, I discovered the bodies of my "feathered friends" and avenged them administratively, not to mention psychologically.

When the paperwork for these violators was finished, I loaded the seized ducks in the back of my truck and headed back down the muddy road. I guess those lads learned a lesson that fine day on *just how good a game warden's ears could be*. I had several opportunities over the following years to let these local businessmen in on my secret, but I never chose to do so. This lesson was best left for future generations to hear about around the campfire so it could be learned by the many. We went on to become friends, and I often did business in their stores, but even under their constant questioning I never told them how I had really discovered their over-bag. With the writing of this tale, I guess the "duck" is out of the bag. I am sure one or both of these gentlemen will read this book and discover my secret. Only they will know who did what, but they will recognize themselves in this story. Oh well, that can be another tale told around the campfires to their now middle-aged children and their grandchildren as well.

Damn, what a good way to start my day. Those men paid $450 each for their mistake, and it turned out to be a great lesson in life, especially when they brought their children to duck hunt with them several years later. As for Tony, I suspect that he was like a coyote: if he got the opportunity to kill outside the law, he would take it. After all, he hadn't learned a lesson from Hugh some eighteen years earlier.

As I left my latest adventure, it was apparent that I had not yet completed what fate had ordained for me to accomplish. I still felt the instinct from earlier that morning. Even after three pretty good cases, my gut feeling was telling me there was more to do.

Heading north on a farm road, hub-deep in mud, I happened onto the south end of Sartain's land and observed a group of twenty-three hunters north and west of the White Mallard Duck Club. Strung out in a long line, they appeared to be making a drive for pheasants across a large harvested rice field. Settling into a copse of trees and brush, making sure my vehicle was out of sight, I got out the spotting scope and started to do what a game warden does best—sitting, watching, and being patient.

Sure as shootin', as I looked over my latest group of hunters, my gut instinct told me I was on to something. First of all, the men appeared to be Italians, and my firm belief was that the Italian community's motto generally was "If it flies, it dies." I also believed that many of the Italian people had trouble in the counting department when it came to the numbers of birds in the game bags. This feeling was validated when I saw several hen pheasants, which were totally protected, rise into the air only to quickly fall to the gun of one of the lads. In a second he was on them, and they went into his game bag in a flash. He got back in line and the twenty-three shooters continued their drive as if nothing unusual had happened. It seemed that just as soon as a rooster rose from cover anywhere in front of this group, a cloud of feathers became his legacy and testimony to their firing accuracy. Damn, I couldn't wait until these lads were close enough for me to sally forth and work the game warden's magic once again. With the way they were shooting and the numbers of birds that were falling, there just had to be tremendous over-limits at hand!

The hunters slowly worked their way from the north end of the rice field to the south, where a twenty-foot-high earthen dike confronted them. When they gathered at the southern end of the field near the base of the dike, the air was filled with the beautiful sound of Italian being spoken freely and happily. It was obvious that they had just had the pheasant hunt of a lifetime and wanted to share the tale of their good fortune.

Well, I said to myself, I will end that happy chatter. Someone is going to pay for that pair of hen pheasants, and maybe just a few over-limits of roosters as well, before the sun sets this fine day. Over the top I went like my countrymen in the battle of the Somme with strains of Wagner ringing loudly in my ears, with the image of overlooking the brood clustered below like a Cooper's hawk flying over a covey of quail! *Die Walküre* was ringing in my ears as I made my unannounced, magnificent entrance down the back side of the levee. The beautiful language that had filled the air moments before was replaced with silence. That didn't surprise me. They had a secret, maybe many, that they hoped I wouldn't be sharing. Well, we will see about that, I thundered to myself.

Elegantly approaching this bevy of sportsmen, I announced my presence as a state Fish and Game warden and said I wanted to check their guns for plugs and examine their birds and hunting licenses. I was immediately surrounded by these folks, all talking at once and all wanting to help the game warden do his job. That is the type of behavior that quickly tells a game warden something is wrong with the folks he is checking. *I have them!* I thought as the familiar strains of Wagner filled my ears again. As I checked the numerous birds, licenses, and guns that were eagerly thrust forward, I noticed that not a hunter had exceeded the limit. There is something wrong with this picture, I thought. What the hell is going on with this bunch? However, I noticed one fellow constantly moving in the confusion to the rear of the group. From his clothing, I recognized him as the one who had shot the two hen pheasants. Since he was the obvious "dirty" one, he was soon to be the apple of my eye. Keeping a casual eye on him to make sure he didn't discard the goods while I was checking his hunting buddies, I continued to be surprised at the lack of violations among his partners.

When I finished with the rest of the sportsmen, I asked if I had missed anyone since it was such a big group, and they all said no. Turning my gaze like a laser upon the lad who had kept moving to the rear of the group, I said coldly, "What about you?" He instantly froze and then hesitantly said that I had already checked him. With my gaze firmly fixed upon my prey, I said, "I haven't checked you at all. Come here, please." Now the conquering music was so loud in my ears that I couldn't figure out why my Italian friends hadn't heard it as well. ... Maybe they just didn't appreciate the *brass* of Wagner.

There was total silence now, which told me I had a "kill" in the offing. The shooter of the hen pheasants slowly approached, all the while casually keeping his left side away from me, a sure sign that the illegality was concealed on that side. I checked his gun and license, saving the bulge in his coat for last, then asked if he had any pheasants. He said no. Reaching around him and patting the obvious bulge in his hunting coat, I said, "What about this?" Panic flashed across his eyes for a moment, but he caught himself rapidly and said that the bulge was just his lunch. Seeing a pheasant foot sticking out of his game bag, I reached over, grabbed it, pulled out a freshly killed hen pheasant, and said, "What about this?" Silence ... Reaching further into the game bag, I felt another pair of bird feet and pulled out the other freshly killed hen pheasant. By now you could have heard a small mouse fart in a large bag of cotton. Looking him in the eyes, I said, "Are there any more?"

He said in resignation, "No, but you can look if you would like to." The game bag was now flat, so I figured he was telling the truth. I told the shooter I was going to issue him a citation for taking and possessing two protected game birds. His citation later came to $200. As I walked away from the group, I noticed that the burning that had manifested itself since early that morning was now gone. I couldn't figure out why I hadn't made more pheasant over-limits, but it appeared that this bunch could count. The rest of the day proved uneventful except for the enduring strains of Wagner heard only by the world's greatest game warden of all. ...

When I walked out on my porch early the next morning, all was good. I thanked the Lord for another day, checked the sky for any sign of inclement weather, and noticed the aromatic smell of someone burning wet leaves in the neighborhood. *Then I noticed it!* There was a strange feeling similar to yesterday's, that instinct of something unusual to come. By damn, I just couldn't put my finger on it. It was almost as if half a kill rather than a full kill was in the wind. Keeping that gut feeling in mind, I loaded my gear and tired frame into the patrol truck. The engine roared to life in expectation of another day's adventures, and as the leaves crunched under the wheels and last night's leaves danced off the hood, I pulled out once again en route to the east side of my district.

The muddy road to Butte Creek didn't produce the covey of quail I had seen the day before but did produce a rooster pheasant in all his fall splendor, slipping across the road and into some dense cover. As I drove north along Butte Creek the plaintive, croaking calls of sandhill cranes greeted me from a milo field where they were feeding by the thousands. Totally protected in California in those days, they had a lot to be thankfully croaking over: a clear sky for flying, no one shooting at them, a noisy crowd of their kind on the ground, and an unharvested milo field for easy pickings. Yes, in the world of the cranes, life was good. Thousands of hungry mallards and Pacific white-fronted geese added their din to an already hectic sky as I drove toward the north end of the area, which I had targeted for the day's work. The duck clubs I passed were strangely quiet as the birds traded back and forth just out of range of the guns, the siren duck calls, and the good-looking decoy sets.

Moving into the harvested rice fields farther to the north, I heard several shots to the west and angled my truck in that direction for a look-see. I noticed several sportsmen with dogs in a large rice field, hunting the rice checks for pheasants, but nothing seemed to warrant a closer look, so I moved on. That instinct was still hanging at the outside edge of my awareness. *Then it happened!* In a rice field to the northeast, I saw what looked like my Italian gang of twenty-three from the day before, shooting up a storm at the pheasants and Lord only knew what else. That was too good to be true, and off I went on an intercept course. I had missed all of them in the over-limit chase the day before—maybe today was my day! Surely they would drop their guard and shoot over-limits, figuring they would not be checked by the game warden two days in a row. With a hunter's grin of anticipation, I headed for my hidey-hole alongside the levee. Dropping into the same spot where I had hidden the day before, I again set up the spotting scope and commenced to watch the "sons of Old Italy" as they hunted the wily pheasant. They were moving in my direction and if they continued on their present course would pass about a hundred yards to the west. I planned to drive right to them across the levee road and trap them at the end of the field. Presently the lads were in range, and although I hadn't seen any illegality, the gut feeling was getting stronger—not to be ignored.

Then it was time! Down the levee and out into the flock of shooters I drove as they watched me in apparent consternation. Stepping out of my vehicle to the recurring strains of Wagner, I sauntered over to my Italians, who were rapidly bunching up like a school of king salmon in the face of a pod of killer whales. Damn, it was too good to be true, I thought. The chap I had pinched for the two hen pheasants the day before was clearly moving to the back of the pack as he had done the day before. You could bet your bottom dollar I would keep my eyes on him. Being the good guy I was, I informed the lads that I wouldn't check their guns or their licenses because I had done that yesterday. However, I did want to check their birds. With an eye on my suspect, who by now had clearly moved to the back of the pack, I commenced to check their day's kill. The hunters had done quite well, and it took a little while to check all of their game bags. No one had anything other than what was allowed by law, and they seemed pleased that they had gotten by the game warden grim reaper one more time.

Finishing with everyone but my suspect, who kept moving to the rear as I checked all his buddies, I asked, "Did I check everyone?"

They all replied, almost in unison, "Yes," just like the day before.

Looking at my unchecked fellow in the rear, I said, "What about you?"

The lad very calmly said he had been checked while his eyes never left mine. He was like a trapped rat, I thought. His voice displayed some emotion, and my heart raced with the knowledge that I was about to nab this chap for a second time in two days. Hot dog, life could be good!

Looking him right in the eyes, I said, "I haven't checked you. Why don't you get your tail end over here?"

He hesitated but finally walked slowly over to me. His buddies parted to let the lad through, but for some reason, instead of scattering to the four winds as they had done yesterday when I zeroed in on him, they all kept close to the action. That is kind of strange, I thought; usually they scatter like quail or jump all over the arresting officer when one of their own is about to be run to ground for a violation. Not today. They were all acting out of the ordinary for a gang of Italian hunters. Keeping that notion at the back of my all-knowing and all-seeing mind, I watched the lad's approach. He carefully kept his left side away from me as he had the day before, and the rest of the pack was as silent as the Roman Colosseum today as the drama unfolded before their eyes. As the fellow approached, my eyes quickly picked up a telltale bulge in his hunting vest and a blood spot that had soaked clear through the side of the game bag.

I said, "What is that bulge in your game bag?"

Without looking me in the eyes (a sure sign of guilt), he said, "My lunch."

I said, "Sure it is." I turned him slightly, reached into his game bag, felt a set of legs and feet, and lifted the bird out. Looking him right in the eyes with my canned "you are dead" gaze, I held the bird at arm's length and said in a commanding voice, "Yeah, well, what the hell is this, then?"

Instant pandemonium! Every Italian was either on the ground or bent over laughing his heart out. What the hell? I thought. The laughter didn't abate, and then I looked at what I was proudly waving in the air for all the world and God to see. My eyes almost fell out of my thickheaded skull. *It was a goddamned rubber chicken.*

The strains of Wagner were quenched by the increasing volume of Verdi as the realization that I had been set up by a bunch of fun-loving guys dawned on me. Damn, did I look appropriate, all the mass and might of my Teutonic magnificence holding a goofy rubber chicken high in the air! As it began to sink in, I realized I had been had to the nth degree. My scowl slowly changed to a "gotcha" grin, and I added my laughter until tears came to my eyes.

A great laugh was had by all, albeit at my expense, and right-fully so, I might add. ... Once things settled down, I put an official evidence tag on the rubber chicken and allowed my picture to be taken by the hunters as a memento of the day they had pulled the wool—or should it be feathers—over the game warden's eyes. Their actions surely were warranted. After all, I had been roaring around with great self-importance and a big head of steam—or perhaps like a chicken with its head cut off! Sometimes God has a unique way of using Mother Nature's sword, and today was cer-tainly one of those days.

As I drove away down the muddy road and the hunting party disappeared from view, I noticed that the strange feeling of things to come was now absent. In its place was a calmness that spoke of the gentler associations of my many dealings with the human race. God is good, and so are a great many of the people He created. We just have to take the time to appreciate that fact, especially those of us carrying the authority and the gun in the forefront at all times. Otherwise we may find ourselves eating a lot of crow—or should I say rubber chicken?

It is amazing what you can learn during the fall of the year, when the leaves are dropping to the ground, a snap is in the air, the sky is that intense blue, the smell of burning stubble fields is in the air, and the clarion call of waterfowl graces your ears. I suppose even the feeling of the legs of a rubber chicken being removed from a hunter's game bag qualified as an autumn experience as another life lesson was well earned and learned.

12

The Survival Instructor

THE CALIFORNIA DEPARTMENT of Fish and Game, where I was employed as a warden for four and a half years in two duty stations in the 1960s, was always big on keeping its officers current by presenting various types of training on a regular basis. To their credit, the department leaders realized that ignoring this need might subject the state and its workers to adverse legal consequences. As a result, it was not uncommon for game wardens to be subjected on a monthly basis to some kind of training designed to enhance our skills, reduce the prospect of liability, and increase our chances of survival. I remember being trained in crowd control, first aid, the operation of snowmachines, firearms proficiency, fire safety, safety around aircraft, pursuit driving, watercraft safety, search and seizure, and rules of evidence, among other things. The opportunities to learn seemed endless in those days.

For the most part the training was good quality and well intended. But the old-timers always grumbled long and loudly about being taken off the job to get more "dadburned" training. They felt that this newfangled regimen was a waste of their time, and they attended such "tomfoolery" only because they had to. A great many of our officers were World War II and Korean War veterans who had seen just about everything and just wanted to get on with their lives without what they saw as the constant interruptions of training assignments. When they had come to work for Fish and Game in the late 1940s and early 1950s, there had been little or no training given or required. In fact, most of them had had to furnish their own cars and weapons. It seemed that when they had become wardens, they had simply been given a badge, a code book, and a citation book and told to "go get them." I guess I could see why they grumbled so much. They probably longed for the freedom of the "good old days," just as I do today. After all, they had performed the tasks of the profession without any training, so why should they have to go through it this late in the game? However, I ate the damn stuff up because I was a rookie and dumber than a post. Realizing its possible value to my success as an officer, I was happy to get as much help in the form of training as I could. Plus, it gave me a chance to mingle with older squad members, listen to their wildlife law enforcement war stories, and in the process glean a few tips of the trade from those more sage and seasoned than I. Those training assignments also had a hidden value because they brought a lot of us together so that officers got to mingle and renew old friendships and catch up on each other's news. So like it or not, training opportunities were mostly beneficial to us hardheads.

One afternoon I opened my official mail and found a letter assigning my regional law enforcement squad to another training assignment. This time we would be located in the Nevada City area in the western foothills of the Sierra Nevada Mountains. The squad was to gather at a bible camp, whose name I have long forgotten, on a Tuesday evening and spend the following two days being trained in field survival and firearms proficiency. It sounded good to me, especially the part about firearms. In those days I was a crack shot with my .44 magnum and always enjoyed the afternoons I spent shooting competitively with my squad mates. I figured I could always stand to learn more about how to survive as a law enforcement officer, and I figured this survival class might be a training opportunity in street survival. Man, was I off base. ...

As I hammered up along the mountain roads on my way to the bible camp that Tuesday afternoon, I let my mind wander through the pages of California gold rush history passing before my eyes. Small piles of rock along a streambed told of the miners hard at work to get at the paydirt and gravel beneath the large rocks but above the bedrock. Small pine and incense cedar trees, all of the same age, told me a mining town was nearby that in the mining days had cut down all the trees for miles around for mine timbers and firewood. Because this deforestation had occurred about 120 years earlier, the forest was still growing and the trees were all about the same height. Then the bright orange and softer reds of several hillsides with even smaller pine trees reclaiming a toehold on the almost sterile soil told of the huge "monitors" with their powerful streams of water directed at the hillsides during the gold rush heyday, eating up huge chunks of land and destroying the waterways and fisheries below in the miners' frantic quest for the yellow metal. I passed many small remnants of mining camps as I continued through the gold country and its many larger, sleepy towns with rich historical names such as Downieville, Rough and Ready, Poker Flat, Dutch John, and Hang Town, adding spice to an already exciting trip.

Stopping at the only stoplight in the town of Downieville, I let my eyes wander over the storefronts of old buildings on both sides of the street, stone buildings from long ago with eight-foot-high windows and long iron shutters to protect them against the spread of fire, the nemesis of many a town a hundred-plus years ago. I knew that if I went inside I would be greeted with the view of dark-stained wooden floors that rolled unevenly across the building, high pressed-tin ceilings, and a smell that still spoke of stale cigar smoke deeply ingrained in the wood. A dreamer like me could still sense the strains of excitement and disappointment involving the signs of "color" discovered on the claims so many years ago. Or the arrival of the latest mud-wagon stage bearing mail from loved ones in faraway places. Or the arrival of freight wagons and cursing teamsters bringing flour, fresh onions, potatoes, canned sardines, or barrels of whiskey.

With the changing of the light, I mentally rolled back to my modern-day world and began to follow the letter's directions to the nearby bible camp. When I arrived at the place that would be my home for the next day or so, I stepped out of my patrol truck, stretched my tired frame, and slowly looked around. It was like most camps I had visited, either as a kid or as a state employee.

This one was surrounded by a forest of ponderosa pine trees a hundred or so feet high, with many single-level wooden bunk-houses scattered about. A small lake and a .22-caliber shooting range lay off to the west. In the center of the wooden sprawl was a house of worship and another large building I took to be the mess hall. A hearty "Terry, over here!" from Clyde Shehorn, the Blairs-den warden, brought me back to the work at hand. After a firm handshake and a quick, genuine smile from beneath an 1850s wal-rus mustache from one of the finest human beings and wildlife professionals in the country, I got down to the business of register-ing and locating an unoccupied bunk on which to throw my sleep-ing bag. I spent the rest of the afternoon and evening with old friends, many bottles of good whiskey, and numerous tales and jokes from times past. As the evening got long in the tooth, the group began to drift away to the bunks and the noisy talk and laughter were replaced with the soft, velvet dark typical of a night in the Sierra Nevada Mountains.

The next morning found me and the rest of my squad standing in line in the mess hall waiting for a typical tight-budget bible camp breakfast: two eggs, two hard-as-a-bullet strips of bacon so thin I could see through them, and two pieces of burned toast. That was it except for coffee, milk, and a small glass of watery orange juice. I found that each bite had a tendency to vaporize before it even hit my stomach. No wonder Jesus appeared so thin in all the pictures and icons, I thought. Since there were no offers of seconds, I re-treated to my truck, a good game warden's ever-ready larder, and partook of a feast of sardines, crackers, cheese, apples, and two cans of apple juice. Looking around the parking lot, I noticed sev-eral others visiting their mobile larders for the goodies they too had stocked for just such emergencies. Grinning at my compatriots, I slid two large chunks of homemade venison jerky into my uniform shirt pocket and was set for what the day was to bring. You laugh! At six foot four and topping the scales somewhere around 320, I would have been a mere shadow of myself after a few days on that bible camp fare. Since Jesus wasn't there with his loaves and fishes, I did unto myself before others did me in. ...

When we gathered back at the mess hall, the captain told all his officers to meet at the small rifle range by the lake. He also informed us that the district's wildlife biologists would be going through this training with us. That news created quite a stir, to say the least. In those days in California, plain and simply, the game wardens hated the wildlife biologists and the wildlife biologists hated the game wardens. The game wardens felt that the biologists gave away the shop with their liberal bag limits, doe hunts, and long seasons, and the biologists felt that the game wardens were a bunch of whiskey-drinking, skirt-chasing, uneducated louts who didn't know a good game management plan from a bag of popcorn. So that joint participation announcement set the stage for the commencement of grumbling from many of the more senior lads. In addition, the captain announced that the training to take place that morning was wilderness survival training, not the "street" survival we had thought would occur. Boy, that set the lads a-buzzin' and chirping big time! There wasn't a game warden in the room who considered himself (we didn't have women in the force in those days) anything less than a Jim Bridger, Kit Carson, Hugh Glass, and Joe Meek all rolled up into one bundle of fighting, surviving fury. When the open grumbling and bellyaching hit triple forte, the captain waved his hand over the heated assemblage, requesting quiet. "Gentlemen, the training is going to be given by one of the Strategic Air Command's finest survival training instructors. I think once you hear him and see what he has to offer, you will see that every one of you will benefit from this information and will find that it may help you survive an unplanned wilderness stay or accident someday."

The grumbling was still there but what could one expect from such a bunch of know-it-alls? I knew what was going through everyone's mind (except those doorknobs like me) regarding a survival instructor trying to teach us something we thought we did on a daily basis. To make matters worse, we had to sit beside those hated biologists, who at best had only half a brain and were hippie wimps in bad need of a shave, a bath, and a decent pair of shoes!

Needless to say, Captain Leamon had an unhappy crew gathered behind him like a gaggle of wing-clipped geese as he led the way out to the bleachers by the shooting range. Not wanting to sit near the hated biologists, almost all of us wardens took seats in the top of the bleachers and let the biologists sit in the bottom rows. Soon about forty wardens and biologists had filled the small bleacher area and were waiting for the arrival of the vaunted instructor. I could already sense that some of the older wardens, if they got their head and the bit in their teeth, would give this Air Force guy a real run for his money.

We didn't have long to wait. Without any fanfare, a mountain of a man hobbled out in his Air Force work uniform and took a position directly in front of the center of the bleachers. He stood there without a word, studying us as we stared at him. He had to be at least six foot nine, even slouching, and weighed at least 385 if he was an ounce. The stripes on his sleeves identified him as the highest-class sergeant in the Air Force, and he appeared to have served about three hundred years in the military given the number of length-of-service stripes! He carried a cocked and locked Colt .45 ACP on his right side and a rather large Bowie knife on his other hip. His pants were tucked into a highly polished pair of black jump boots, and he wore no hat. His face showed many prominent scars, including one showing that his nose had been sliced almost in half. He continued to stare at us with a pair of flat, coal-black, gunfighterlike eyes, shaded by the furriest set of eyebrows I had ever seen. No two ways about it, this man had our undivided attention, and I do mean every man jack of us in those bleachers that fine, hot day!

"Good morning, gentlemen," came a deep, resonant bass voice. A heavy smoker, I thought until I looked more closely at his throat and saw what appeared to be an old knife wound running from one side to the other below his Adam's apple. Damn, I thought; this lad has been there and lucky to get back, from the look of all those wounds and scars.

There were a few halfhearted "good mornings" from the crowd, but most just stared at this larger-than-life apparition. All of a sudden we weren't as tough as we had somehow thought. ...

The voice boomed again: "Gentlemen, I am Chief Master Sergeant Renaldo Hernandez from Stead Air Force Base, which for those of you lost in a geographic funk is located just outside Reno, Nevada."

Some of you may say, "There isn't any Stead Air Force Base just outside Reno." You would be correct because it was shut down in a round of base closings years ago, sometime in the '60s, I believe. However, the base at that time had one claim to fame: its Strategic Air Command (SAC) survival training center and prisoner-of-war (POW) camp. The SAC would train its air crews in methods of survival in case they had to bail out or were forced down over hostile territory. Then, after weeks of training, the SAC would dump the lads out over the semiarid eastern slope of the Sierra Nevada Mountains and make them try out their skills as they attempted to live for two weeks off the bounty of Mother Nature. Meanwhile, Stead aircraft and ground patrols would comb the backcountry, trying to "capture" the air crews. If captured, they were interned in the then supersecret POW camp at Stead Air Force Base, where they would be treated no differently than if they had been captured by, say, the Russians. In short, this training program was as close to the real McCoy as they could make it, even down to the beatings and brainwashings that routinely took place. The purpose was to avoid a repeat of the huge numbers of men who had broken under POW treatment in Korea. Those who were caught repeated the survival training and escape process all over again. Those who survived moved on within the SAC training system.

The survival instructor continued, "I have been in the Air Force for over thirty-five years. I have tried to retire, but the Air Force will not let me out until they find a replacement for me. At the rate they are going, I will be here for another five years or until I die." Without taking his coal-black eyes off us, he took an ugly, twisted black cigar out of his shirt pocket, unwrapped it, and looked long and hard at it. There wasn't a sound from his awestruck audience, and every eye in the place was on that ugly cigar. I recognized it immediately as one of those very strong Toscanni devils that only *real* men and Italian fishermen smoke. In fact, I smoked that same kind of cigar during the summer and fall in the Sacramento Valley because its smoke would kill mosquitoes at twenty feet! They are one of the deadliest cigars I ever came across, and not many folks smoke them because they are so damned strong.

Without a word, the instructor popped the entire cigar into his mouth and began to slowly and methodically chew it like a regular mouthful of mild chewing tobacco, all the while eyeballing us for any reaction. Not a soul moved, including the battle-hardened veterans. This is one tough son of a gun, I thought as I observed some of my comrades looking like they might gag at this display. I knew I would listen to anyone tough enough to eat a Toscanni cigar and not die on the spot. There was no way I could do what he was doing without puking up everything inside my abdominal cavity. And in those days I chewed as well. I'm sure my compatriots were thinking the same thing.

"Let me give you a little background on what I do for a living, gentlemen," came the deep voice. "I train many of the nation's SAC fighter and bomber pilots and crews in the art of survival. Some of those chaps will get shot down in foreign lands, and not all will make it home. That is to be expected. Some will be killed in the crash or during the moments when they are being shot down. Some will die at the end of the parachute fall or in the hands of the enemy. Others will die of starvation or end up giving themselves up because they didn't listen to me. Others will survive because they paid attention and did as I told them. That is why I am here with you today—not because you will be shot down over some foreign land but because you make a living in the back-country and may find yourself in need of survival skills at some point in time. You may fall from a horse or injure yourself using a snowmachine and have to survive for a while before help arrives. You may get stuck in the backcountry, trapped in a winter storm, or busted up traversing a piece of rough country on foot patrol and need to hold on and hole up until help arrives." By now, anyone who wasn't paying rapt attention was a damned fool. He hadn't missed a scenario that every one of us had been in at one time or another, and every man was now there for himself. "So today I will teach you some of the basic survival skills and hope you will listen as my troops do. Whether you do or not is your call. However, I understand that the first rule of law enforcement is to come home every night." He let those words sink in and then said, "Listen to me and follow my teachings and you will come home every night."

Pausing, and looking off to one side, he let out a stream of tobacco juice that totally covered an unfortunate stinkbug that just happened to be crawling across the concrete pad where he was standing. It didn't take long for the nicotine to do its job, and the beetle rolled over, waved its legs in the air for a few moments, and then died. Forty sets of eyes watched that little drama, and no one moved; in fact, most of us found ourselves hardly daring to breathe for fear of being singled out by this giant. The instructor reached over, picked up the dead beetle, placed it beside his feet, and then began his instruction as if nothing out of the ordinary had happened. However, forty sets of eyes were still on that damn bug, wondering why it was next to those size 15 feet holding up the man mountain before us.

"Gentlemen, I was a crew member on a B-25 in the South Pacific during World War II." I couldn't believe it. A B-25 is a twin-engine medium bomber, not much bigger than the man in front of me. How the hell he had gotten inside that plane was a marvel to me! "My plane was shot down, and I was the only survivor, breaking both of my legs when I landed in the treetops of New Guinea after parachuting out. I remained in the jungle for two weeks in that condition, slowly crawling inch by bloody inch toward the Australian lines, before I was rescued. Know what saved me?" None of us moved because obviously we didn't have the foggiest idea what had saved him in some fetid jungle more than twenty years earlier. "A stinking Asian buffalo killed by an artillery shell that had been dead for about two weeks before I got there. Yes, I ate the damn rotten thing, maggots and all, and survived, and you can do the same thing if you just do what has to be done." He paused to let those words sink in and then said, almost as an afterthought, "You know, that meat was so rotten from the hot jungle sun that it was green in color and had the consistency of Jell-O about to set. I was glad because my face had gotten messed up by the flak that had hit the plane, and it made it easier to eat with what I had left of a broken jaw. In fact, gentlemen, I just sucked it off the bones and was damned glad to have it."

By now several of the hated biologists with lighter-than-air stomachs had dismissed themselves and were walking away at a rather brisk pace. The rotten-water-buffalo story had plain and simply done them in. The instructor watched them walk away and shook his huge, furry head. All the game wardens, tough as they were, just grinned and watched in glee.

"In case some of you don't believe what I have to say, take a look at these." He pulled his pant legs from his boots and lifted them up to about the knees. I don't think I ever saw a worse set of legs in my life. They were of many ugly colors, purple predominating, with immense holes where huge chunks of flesh appeared to have rotted off. Then there were the terrible scars from the damage to his legs as he had crawled to safety from behind the Japanese lines, and from the subsequent operations to repair what was left. Another biologist in the front row, seeing the legs close up, just got up and without a word left the bleacher area, and shortly afterward the bible camp. Damn, it was tough just surviving the man's presentation, I thought. I wondered what his survival lectures were going to be like. Another hour of this chap and I would be the only man left!

"Now, gentlemen, let's get down to the business at hand." For the next several hours the survival instructor talked about how to set snares with fish line to catch rabbits and other small creatures. How to build woven willow fish traps and, with the aid of a rock dam, run fish into them so one could have something to eat, even if it had to be eaten raw. How to identify certain plants—which ones to eat and which had medicinal qualities. What those medicinal properties were. How to alert those hunting you from the air if they were friendly and how to survive in everything from snow caves to the front seat of our vehicles during snowstorms. He instructed us in how to build fires without matches using flint, steel, wooden sticks, and pieces of glass and the sun. He also told us how to care for minor and major wounds and how to forestall dangers such as infection.

As he droned on, the warm midmorning sun began to take its toll, and many in the audience began to drift off. After all, most of us hadn't slept worth a damn in those small wooden bunks the night before. In fact, most of us were fairly tall, and our feet had hung out over the ends of the bunks most of the night. The survival instructor seemed to sense that he was losing his audience, but he was unable to bring some of us back from la-la land. He droned on, and those of us who could tried to stay with him.

Then Warden Bill Frazier, a friend of mine, noticed a small blue-bellied lizard running along the shooting-range backstop about ten feet behind the instructor. Bill poked me in the ribs to get my attention and showed me the lizard. It was catching flies, so like a dingbat I watched the lizard instead of listening to the instructor. Fascinated with the lizard's antics, I pointed it out to another warden beside me, and soon about a dozen of us were leaning to one side, looking around the instructor, watching the lizard procure a breakfast that had to be better than ours and ignoring the steady droning of the survival instructor.

The instructor, mindful that he was losing his audience to the warmth of the sun and the lizard's own survival tactics, turned and looked hard at his competition. He turned back toward us for a moment, then reached up behind his neck and in a whirling flash pulled a dirk from a neck holster, spun, and in the blink of an eye and one blurred throwing motion pinned the lizard to the wooden backstop with the knife! He had moved so quickly and unexpectedly that it caught everyone unawares. About half of us jumped at the quick movement, and the rest just sat there slack-jawed as we watched the lizard wriggling on the tip of the knife.

Without a word, the survival instructor walked to the lizard and withdrew his knife from the backstop with the lizard squirming on the tip of the blade as we watched, now alert, wide-eyed, and transfixed. Without a word the sergeant withdrew the dirk from the lizard, wiped the blade between his fingers, and put it back into the holster behind his neck and under his shirt collar. Holding the dying lizard in his left hand, he reached with his other hand into his right-hand pants pocket, withdrew a small pocketknife, and opened it, droning on all the while about keeping our knives very sharp because we might be out in the bush for a long time and a very sharp knife would give us a better chance to survive.

A flash of sunlight glinted off the blade as he held the lizard up high by its head for all to see. Then, taking the tip of the small knife, he started at the lizard's vent and with one quick upward thrust opened the critter from stem to stern. Then, with the tip of this obviously very sharp knife, he flicked out the intestines, held the lizard up again, and then opened his mouth and dropped the whole animal down his throat. He didn't chew once, just swallowed the whole damn critter in less time than it takes to talk about it.

Jesus, about a third of the folks still in the stands bailed out and headed for somewhere other than here. It was plain that a lot of those lads would rather die than try to survive on what Mother Nature had to offer from the bottom of her larder. I will admit that I would rather have a hamburger than a lizard, but to each his own. Without missing a beat and ignoring the loss of part of his audience as if they had never existed, the survival instructor told us that the lizard tickled going down, but in a few moments the acids of his stomach would kick in and the movement would cease.

By now there were about twenty-five of us left, all wide awake and intently listening to this lizard-eating giant. He went on to inform us that most of the things out there in the wild were eatable and a good source of protein, and if we wanted to survive, we would eat what was set before us by Mother Nature and keep going. Then he picked up the tobacco-spit-covered stinkbug he had killed earlier, cleaned the dirt off, and gently but deliberately placed the dead bug directly between his molars. *Crunch* went the bug, and I could hear it plainly clear up where I sat. "You place large beetles on your molars because they still may have a bite left in them," he said in a matter-of-fact tone. With a noticeable swallow, down it went to the lizard's happy hunting ground. Damn, I thought, no wonder this guy is so large; he eats everything in his range of view. Off the bleachers went another three guys. That iron man looked at his shrinking assemblage with a hint of disgust. Oh

Lord, let me tell you, there wasn't a man jack among us who was not now totally glued to what the instructor was saying and doing.

The instructor took a three-pound coffee can out of his rucksack and walked back to stand before the group. He tipped it slightly so we could look inside and showed us about two pounds of maggots, alive and wiggling in the bottom of the can. By now every one of us in the stands had a bad case of the "big eye"! He held a large lit candle to the bottom of the can until we could hear the maggots popping like popcorn. After a few moments of "cooking," the instructor turned to us and said that maggots were a super source of protein because they concentrated the energy from their food source, and that if we were in the backwoods in a bad sort of way, they were the way to go. He walked along the front row of the bleachers, holding out the can and asking everyone to reach in, grab a handful, and try. Everyone demurred until he got to a biologist and old-time government trapper named Jack Foster, who was sitting on the end of the bench. Good old Jack, without a moment's hesitation, reached into the can, took out a handful of maggots, and popped the lot into his gaping maw. The maggots squirted through Jack's stubby fingers and fell down the front of his shirt and onto the ground. However, a large number made it into his open mouth. The rest of the biologists, except Jack, fled the bleachers, leaving all the game wardens perched on the top with their "big eye" and, I'm sure, a few rolling stomachs. The instructor asked how the maggots tasted. Jack said, "Not bad. In fact, quite pleasant." The survival instructor offered the can to Jack again, and without a moment's hesitation he put his hand back in, took out another handful of maggots, and stuffed them into his mouth. It was as if a bomb had gone off under the wardens as they bailed out of the bleachers. The man who had been sitting next to me broadcast-puked perfectly into Warden Bud Reynolds's holster as Bud left the performance as well. I sat there in disbelief. Old Jack Foster was a tough man and had been known as such by my family for over fifty years. I conceded that he was one biologist who was one hell of a lot tougher than any game warden I knew, myself included! I looked around and saw that there were just four of us wardens left in the bleachers, including my captain, who was a beautiful shade of yellow.

"Sergeant," he said, "maybe we'd better pick this up tomorrow after the men have a night to settle down."

The sergeant just chuckled. "Maybe that was just a little too graphic for the class of students here today, but I enjoyed it just the same," he said with a large grin as his paw of a hand went into the can for a handful of maggots, which he promptly shoveled into his maw of a mouth. Brushing loose maggots off the front of his shirt, he grinned and chewed with obvious relish. That cleared out the captain and the rest of us in short order! Jack and I were the last to leave, with Jack grumbling about how the maggots gave him a stinking breath.

We spent the rest of the afternoon qualifying on the pistol range, and just about everyone shot ten to twenty points under their previous best scores. Guess what? It got even better the very next day.

The next morning I rose early and beat it over to the mess hall, figuring that if I got there early enough I might be able to con the cooks into giving me an extra share of grits. I found four other wardens heading for the chow line with the same thought in mind. Four female camp counselors slid into the chow line just ahead of me, and I quietly joined the queue behind them. Then I heard heavy footsteps behind me, and it was as if the lights in the building had gone out. Turning, I saw the sergeant major standing directly behind me with a pleasant smile on his face. I stuck out my hand and said, "Good morning, Sergeant." He took my hand, which is a damn good-sized one itself, and buried it in his powerful paw as he returned my greeting. The thing I remember about that handshake, other than the sheer power of his grip, was that his fingers were above my wrist during the shake!

The chow line began to move, and we moved with it without a lot of fanfare. We got the usual piss-anty amount of food, and all I could think of was another trip to my pickup for survival rations of sardines, crackers, and cheese. We early arrivals picked out a large table, sat down, introduced ourselves all around, and began to eat. I had just put some jam on my toast from a collection of condiments in the middle of the table when I noticed out of the corner of my eye that the survival instructor appeared to be looking intently at me. Looking up, I saw that he was actually looking at the condiments in the middle of the table. I looked to see what caught his eye but saw only several kinds of jams, a sugar bowl, mustard, salt, pepper, and ketchup. Nothing out of the ordinary, but the sergeant sure thought so. After a moment everyone at the table stopped eating and began to look at the condiments and watch the sergeant as well. Finally the sergeant slowly moved his food tray from in front of him and began to slowly move his beefy right hand toward the jam. By now the entire table was frozen as we watched the drama being played out. A very large bluebottle fly was happily enjoying a breakfast from the lip of the jam jar until, with a lightning move that bespoke a mongoose rather than a man his size, the sergeant's hand flew forward and neatly snapped it up, touching nothing but the fly. None of us said a word or even moved as we watched the sergeant bring his hand up to his ear and listen to see if he had the fly. A big grin on his scarred face told the observers that he had his quarry.

Slowly, to the accompaniment of our noticeably loudly beating hearts, he stuck his index finger and thumb into his paw, careful not to lose his prey, and extracted one very live blowfly. Without looking at his audience, he carefully removed the wings, tossed his head back, and gulped the fly down like there was no tomorrow. The four female counselors screamed in unison and fled the table in a heartbeat. My four game warden buddies, with a little more reserve than the ladies, stood up and walked away in disgust, leaving me quietly alone with the sergeant. I probably would have gone with them except that I was in shock. The sergeant said, "I take off their wings because if you don't, they tickle on the way down. Besides, the wings hold no food value."

Then the sergeant stood up and, with a huge grin on his face, scooped up the abandoned breakfast trays from the eight diners who had fled and scraped their contents onto his plate. With a flourish, he sat his massive frame back down at the table and, seeing me just staring at him, said with a big grin, "I get more food that way." Without another word, we finished our breakfasts.

After input from many of the squad, the captain decided that we game wardens had had enough survival training and canceled the rest of the day's training in that arena. I was disappointed. Having studied under various wildlife instructors in college, I was used to blood, guts, parasites, and the like. I wouldn't have enjoyed eating some of the things the instructor had eaten, but I understood his reasoning and didn't have a problem once I got it past my nose.

Many years have passed since that survival class, and in that period I have eaten shark, raccoon, beaver, muskrat, bobcat, mountain lion, crab and crawdad guts, tripe, coyote, eyes from sheep while a guest in Indonesia, monkey, spider, alligator, and much more. None of it killed me, and I came to realize that such foods were nothing more than another good life experience. However, I always kept my patrol vehicles well stocked after that survival training experience so I never had to resort to eating anything that didn't come out of a can, a bag, or a cast-iron skillet over a roaring fire.

I imagine the survival instructor is retired or dead now, and the survival concept once preached at Stead Air Force Base is long gone or even more advanced. I truly hope that before he died the sergeant had a chance to launch into a platter of home-fried chicken; heavily seasoned mashed potatoes mixed with sour cream, cream cheese, and a cube of butter and smothered with good chicken gravy; a platter of fresh-cooked peas; biscuits so light you had to eat them to keep them from drifting off into the air; and a fresh blueberry pie with a crust like my bride routinely makes. If he had that kind of feast before him, he wouldn't have to trap flies off jam jars. Then again ...

13

Screwups

L AW ENFORCEMENT, especially conservation law enforcement, is one of the most unique and eventful professions in
the world. Anything and everything can and will happen, for better or worse, if you give it just half a chance. Over my thirty-two
years in the profession, watching myself as well as others, I have
seen innumerable wrecks, funny events, unreal situations, unusual
happenings, and glorious sprays of luck, frequently intermixed
with the smell of skunk, many times as a direct result of screwups.
The key to survival in this world of wildlife, particularly in the law
enforcement arena, is to learn from such mistakes and grin at
those sometimes deadly turns of events as you try not to make the
same wrong turns twice.

Equally important is being able to laugh at yourself over such
wrecks, all the while making sure your buddies don't find out.
There is nothing quite as funny as laughing at your compatriots'
mistakes while hiding your own.

Last but not least, you need to thank your lucky stars (if you are
into that) or your guardian angels (a theory I subscribe to) as you
keep going in the hope of eventual rewarding success against the
forces of nature and humankind hell-bent on destruction—usually of the resource but sometimes of you!

Now, most officers wouldn't like to put into print the little fun-
nies and pratfalls that happen as we stomp along in the backwaters
of our conservation law enforcement careers. But now that I am
getting older and less worried about saving face, I am ready to share

a few of my milder screwups. Don't be surprised if you see parallels to your own life, regardless of what profession you are cruising around in. God made it that way. It is called the spice of life.

A Rainy Opening Day of Pheasant Season

FOR THREE STRAIGHT DAYS in the Sacramento Valley of California, it had rained hard and without letup, the kind of rain that comes straight down so vigorously that it stings your prematurely balding head if you don't wear a hat. Usually rain is welcome to a game warden because it makes a lot of life more active, especially anadromous fish and big game—and the outlaws too. But working with only a two-wheel-drive pickup in a county almost totally made up of adobe mud was pure hell. I had a two-wheel-drive because the powers to be chose not to purchase four-wheel-drive vehicles in those days for the wardens located in the flatlands, in part because they cost $3,200, or $1,000 more than a two-wheel-drive. The old timers running the outfit felt that they hadn't needed four-wheel-drive vehicles when they were out and about in the flatlands, so why should the young whippersnappers? It was more an issue of simple economy than common sense, and our success at helping the critters be damned.

The adobe soil was great for the rice that covered that part of the country come spring, but it sure was hell on game wardens come the fall and winter rains when we were negotiating muddy roads to chase the bad guys happily using their four-wheel-drives. No matter where I went in my two-wheel-drive, after one turn of the rear wheels in the adobe mud, I might as well have had racing slicks for tires. Then the mud and rice straw from the fields would build up under the front wheel wells until I could hardly steer. As if that was not enough, whenever I stepped outside, in four steps my boots would become loaded with gobs of sticky mud, giving me a twenty-pound weight on each foot before I had gone more than a few yards—especially since I had a set of size 14 EEE brogans!

Last but certainly not least, wet weather made for a poor pheasant opener because the pheasants would go to dense cover to remain dry. Their natural waterproofing system was not the best in the avian world, nor was the density of their feather tracts, so to the deep cover they would head to try to avoid a damn good soaking. If soaked they became chilled, and then when they flew it was like a box of rocks. Rain just wasn't their box of biscuits.

Now for a game warden, that kind of weather and pheasant behavior was tantamount to disaster. Game wardens like everyone to obey the wildlife laws, but to be frank, humans are a lot like coyotes and will often take more game than the law allows. In Colusa County, which is located in the heart of the Valley, the pheasant opener was a big annual fall hunting event, kind of like dove hunting to the chaps in the southeastern United States. However, because of the heavy rains that had occurred over the previous three days, I knew the kill would be way down, and with it the number of over-limit citations I had hoped to write. Still, I was young and full of piss and vinegar, and a little rain was a small challenge to a fellow who had the world by the tail with a downhill pull.

Dawn on the opening day found me on the east side of my district, high up on a muddy secondary Sacramento River flood levee, quietly overlooking a thousand acres of freshly harvested rice fields. Getting to my hiding place had been a trick because once I left the pavement, only the luck of the Irish allowed me to stay in the center of the muddy road as I slipped and slid to my hidey-hole. It took every bit of my driving skill and a new set of rear snow tires to slowly travel the muddy levee road. It soon dawned on me that without the previously made ruts in the road to guide my tires, I would long since have slid off the road and down the side of the levee. However, with my driving skills, stubbornness, and abject use of my two guardian angels, I was soon safely hidden in a spot where I could watch vast areas normally hunted by the great American sportsman in his pursuit of the wily pheasant.

During my routine patrols over the past two weeks I had seen numerous pheasants in these large rice fields. Every road I had driven was always full of running pheasants, and at daylight I could hear at least a dozen roosters crowing in the area at any one time. In addition, the fields were a natural hideout for them because the dikes were loaded with weedy cover, a pheasant's paradise. I knew these fields would ultimately produce many pheasants for the gunner, rain or no rain—and possibly a few citations for the local game warden. Man, I couldn't wait for the day's events to begin!

Sitting in the dark in my pickup, feeling the wind gently rocking the vehicle and hearing the pelting rain on the roof, made shivers of anticipation run up and down my back. To heck with the rain and the mud, I thought as I gathered my winter coat up around the cold back of my neck. That was just part of the game warden's life and to be considered only a minor irritant. Pheasant hunting season was here, and I was part of that great coming-of-age phenomenon once again! I could feel my grin of anticipation slowly starting to stretch from ear to ear. With that came another blast of wind and the soft pelting sound of the rain on the metal cab. It was good to be alive—and soon in the middle of wildlife itself.

Daylight came late that morning owing to the overcast skies, and, expecting that weather-related delay, I patiently waited. I had observed the headlights of five vehicles driving to the edge of the rice fields and knew I would soon have a passel of clients to observe. About half an hour after legal shooting hours began, it got light enough to shoot, and I grinned widely as I observed seventeen hunters emerging from the five vehicles now parked at the edge of the main rice field. Even with the rain, if these lads could shoot, they should get some great hunting, I thought. I felt even better as I watched three of the lads release four hunting dogs from the back of a Chevy Suburban. It was apparent that these hunters were downright serious about their pheasant hunting because if anything would kick the birds out of their deep, wet cover, it would be the dogs. That meant the men would have an even better hunt than if they just walked the fields. Damn, I thought, with the limit at only two rooster pheasants per day, someone surely would screw up, and guess what would happen in that event? I reached for my binoculars and continued my wait.

The rain had slacked off to a large degree as it got lighter, and I began to feel that maybe God would be my copilot that day after all. The lads got the dogs untangled and let them do their thing of sniffing everything in sight and leaving little packages behind from last night's Purina dog chow. After a joyful roll or two in the wet rice stubble they were ready for the business at hand. The hunters spread out in a long line, obviously based on experience from previous pheasant outings, and commenced to slowly walk across the wet rice fields with their dogs casting back and forth in front of them. *Boom, boom* went two faraway shots as a pair of hunters successfully dropped a rooster each not more than twenty yards from where they had parked. The dogs raced to pick up the fallen birds and in so doing flushed a hen and another rooster, both of which also fell to the gun of a single hunter on the outside of the line. Now my day was really getting with it! Hens were protected by state law, and it was illegal to take them anytime. The fellow who had just shot both birds was a large man, six feet plus and carrying a large potbelly on his big, rawboned frame that was evident even from this distance through the binoculars. They were still too far away to identify which person was doing the shooting by their facial features. But it was easy to identify the shooters by their clothing, which I duly noted in my notebook as I watched the gang shoot its way across the muddy but productive rice fields. I knew they would hunt right up to the bottom of the levee where I was sitting, and then I would have but a short jaunt down the side of the muddy levee and right to them. Damn, my setup couldn't have been any better, I thought. I had the high ground, behind cover and in the pickup staying dry while the lads hunted oblivious to my presence in a light, misting rain. With a violation already in the net, life was great and getting better.

The shooters continued to hunt across the rice field, killing a dozen or more rooster pheasants before they had gone halfway. I noticed that my big guy, the one with a potbelly like mine, had killed two more roosters, which put him in violation not only for killing a hen but for taking an over-limit of roosters. He seemed to be the only one who had any opportunity to violate, and he took advantage of every chance that presented itself. Good, I thought; this chap is looking at a rather substantial fine as it stands and still has half a field to go. With a little more luck, he could really go

into the crapper. … On they came, shooting and slipping and sliding in the muddy field. By the time they got near where I sat in
hiding, they had killed six more roosters, and my main man had
now taken a total of six roosters along with the hen. He was one
hell of a shot because every time something got up in front of him,
he killed it straightaway. He was looking at a fine of at least $400
dollars for the over-limit of roosters and at least $100 for the hen,
or $500 total, and in those days that was big money. As for the rest
of his hunting party, they stayed to the legal straight and narrow
and didn't do anything outside the law as far as I could ascertain.

Then the identity of my illegal shooter dawned on me as I got a
closer look at his face through my binoculars. The man I had been
savoring as a violator was none other than a very big (no pun intended) cowboy movie star! Damn, I couldn't believe my eyes as I
squinted through my binoculars. It was him all right! I had heard
that this fellow was a game violator but had never run across his
trail before. I also knew he was a friend of Terrill Sartain's who
often hunted on Terrill's farm, and that meant Terrill would be
close at hand. Scanning the group once more, I finally located
Terrill hunting as a member of the party off to the side away from
my cowboy as if setting the pace. I made a mental note to be sure
to get on top of the situation before Terrill got involved. Otherwise there would be a shouting match between the two of us, with
me trying to do my job and Terrill trying to protect his guests.

Terrill, God rest his soul, was one hell of a man. He had been a
farmer during hardscrabble times and was a good one, tough as a
horseshoe nail and not prone to be a wimp in any aspect of his life.
During our many talks about historical times, he used to tell me
about his commercial-market hunting days, not in a lot of detail,
mind you, but in terms I understood all too plainly. Terrill told me
that during the Depression he had shot and killed ducks to sell in
the marketplaces of San Francisco in order to make payments on
his properties. "Terry," he used to say, "without the ducks to pay
the way, I would have lost the ranch. I wasn't going to let that
happen, and laws and game wardens be damned." We used to
have our real go-arounds, but he frequently supported me in what

I was trying to do in the field of conservation. I bet many of the people of Colusa County would arch their eyebrows to hear that, but it was true. With Terrill's help I started many conservation programs, especially during the times when the land was flooded and the resident game birds had nowhere to go except up on the barren levees. We fed a lot of starving birds and got the roads closed off on his lands so they would have a dry place to stand until the floodwaters receded. He could be a hard case when he wanted, but he was the type of man that helped weld this country into what it is today.

Swinging my binoculars back to the cowboy, I took one more hard look. Sure as hell, I had a man who had been one of my favorite movie stars since I was a kid in my sights for several intentional wildlife violations. Oh, well, regardless of his fame he is going to have to pay the piper for his straight-shooting indiscretions, I grimly thought.

When the lads hove into range at the end of the rice field next to the levee, I got out of my vehicle and, slipping and sliding down the side of the muddy levee, met them at the bottom of the rice field. Terrill recognized me and started toward the cowboy as if to remove a few roosters from his game bag and claim them as his own, since he seldom killed any for himself. "Terrill," I said, "don't muddy the water any further than it is."

Terrill realized that I already knew what had transpired. "But Terry," he sputtered, and then stopped as I raised my hand.

"Terrill," I said, "let's not embarrass each other."

With that, Terrill slowed his walk and rejoined the main crowd of hunters. All the men were cordial, and as I worked my way through the crowd, checking their hunting licenses and game, I noticed that the movie star kept up a jovial chatter with those around him and seemed untroubled by the fact that his game bag held some items destined to get him into trouble with the Fish and Game Department. Finally getting to him, I asked to check his license and gear as I had done with the others, ignoring who he was.

"You got me, sonny," he proclaimed loudly, with his famous trademark grin and high-pitched laugh.

"I know," I said. "I have been watching you since you left your vehicle, which included killing the hen and four roosters over the limit."

He gave me another trademark grin and handed me his license. Then he began to dig out the illegal birds from his game bag, keeping a legal limit of two roosters for himself.

"I am sorry, sir," I said, "but you shot an over-limit of pheasants, and as such the law requires me to take all of the birds to show the court that you did in fact take an over-limit."

"OK," he said. "You are the law, and a damned big one at that, I must admit. I figured I was large, but you take the prize in that category in this rice field." He laughed as he handed me the two remaining birds. While we were talking, not much was said by his friends, which usually meant a bunch not too happy with the world. Oh, well, I thought; I have the goods obtained by direct observation, and if they care to try me on for size in the local court, so be it. However, I turned out to be wrong about the reason for their behavior, and I realized later that they were silent out of embarrassment for their famous friend.

After I had issued citations for taking a closed-season species and for taking an over-limit of pheasants, I bade a cordial goodbye to all and then told my movie star that his pheasant hunting was over for the day because he had already more than limited out. He could hunt the following day, but his pheasant hunting was over for that one. He gave me a big grin and wave of his ham-like hand and said, "That is all right, sonny; I will beat the brush for my friends if that is OK."

I said that was fine and then slid and crawled back up the steep levee bank to my patrol vehicle with my evidence birds in one hand and two hot movie-star citations in the other. Boy, talk about excited! I not only had several good cases but had caught a very well-known person from the film world. I couldn't wait to get back to civilization and share the secret with my wife to show what a good—no, *great*—catch dog I was. Stepping into my patrol truck, I tried to kick the great globs of sticky adobe mud off my feet. Damn, what a mess, I thought as I noticed that my uniform pants also had mud on the insides of my legs all the way up to my knees. Hearing a lot of shooting in a rice field about half a mile away, I hurriedly started up my truck and gently tried to nurse it down the muddy levee.

Varoooom, went the engine, racing to about four thousand rpm's when my muddy, sticky feet mistakenly jammed the foot throttle to the floor. With a lurch, the truck shot forward and promptly started to swing its rear end toward the edge of the levee road. Before I could get the truck back under control, it slid sideways out of the guiding ruts and off the edge of the levee road. I was stuck, and good. Without four-wheel-drive to help nurse me back up onto the road, there was no way I was going anywhere for the rest of the day. Damn, I thought, this will ruin my day's work because now I am going to have to get a wrecker out here to get me unstuck. That ought to be easy since everyone hunting today is probably stuck in the mud and calling for help as well. Damn, was I miffed! I was also embarrassed beyond all get-out. Not sixty feet away stood the group of hunters the "big stuff" game warden had just checked. Now the "big wheel" game warden, like an idiot, had gunned his vehicle's engine and gotten stuck. Brother, was my face red. It didn't make any difference that the heavy, sticky mud on my boots had caused my damn mishap. What the hunters standing below me had just seen was a dingbat gunning his engine and spinning his wheels instead of easing the vehicle out onto the road and slowly working his way down the levee.

Getting out without looking at the men below me in the field so they wouldn't see my crimson face, I grabbed the shovel from the tool box and began to try to shovel my way out. The shovel didn't do anything except stick to the mud, and it readily became apparent that it was going to do me no good. Then I heard the sucking sounds of people walking toward me in the mud. I turned and saw the entire group of hunters from the rice field coming my way, led by the movie star. "Come on, boys," he boomed out in his high-pitched, squeaky voice, "let's give this man a shove so he can be off and pinch some more of those violating, pheasant-killin' sonsabitches!"

I couldn't believe what I was hearing! The man I had just glee-fully pinched was in good spirit helping me get my vehicle unstuck so I could go forth and pinch some more hunters needing my kind of attention. Boy, did I ever feel small. Moments earlier I had been gloating about the citations I had issued to this man, and now, without being asked, he was helping me get on the way so I could continue my work.

The gang of hunters made short work of pushing me back up on the road with the brute force of seventeen sets of hands. With a wave of my hand I was off and moving, this time carefully, down the road toward my next adventure as the lads went over the levee to another field farther north to continue their pheasant hunt.

For the rest of the day I thought about the man's generous act after being cited and my rather unprofessional attitude of wanting to gloat over having caught Mr. Movie Star. No matter how you cut it, I had to look pretty damn stupid to those lads as I spun off the road into the deeper mud. The movie star is dead now, but I have never forgotten his friendly gesture. After all those years and a whole lot more maturity, I have come to realize that my guardian angels had something to do with that lead-footed screwup and an attitude that needed a little Christian adjustment. ... As I said earlier—the spice of life.

Snow Camp

TURNING OFF THE MAIN ROAD onto an old dirt road, I drove past an abandoned farmhouse and hooked up with a road that eventually led to a place high on the ridgetop called Snow Camp. It had been the site of an old logging camp just after the turn of the century as the lumberjacks took down the giant redwoods and now was a favorite resort for spotlighters, or deer shiners. After the big redwoods had been removed, that part of Humboldt County had quickly returned to Douglas fir and a million other forms of plants, making it a super buffet for the little species of Columbian black-tailed deer that inhabited the area. It didn't take long for the out-of-work members of the logging and lumbering communities to realize that it was a tremendous deer-killing area, and a remote one. Bottom line, if one wanted a quick, illegal kill with a minimum of legal interference, it was just the spot. It didn't take us game wardens long to realize the same, so the area became a giant cat-and-mouse arena. Hence my trip into the Snow Camp area for a stakeout in a likely spot in the hope of apprehending a spotlighter that damp and dark evening that seems like yesterday instead of yesteryear.

I stopped to switch on the cutoff switches so my lights would remain off even if I hit the brakes or turn signals by mistake. Then I just sat there with the windows down, letting my eyes adjust to the inky blackness one finds in a climax stand of Douglas fir. After about twenty minutes I started moving slowly up the dirt road toward the top of the ridge in general and Snow Camp in particular. As I moved higher I began to emerge from the dense conifers into more varied forested vegetation, with every kind of shrub and brush known to a temperate rain forest. I soon became aware of a quarter moon hanging high in the sky. Just the right amount of illumination for a game warden to run the backcountry dirt roads at a pretty good clip without needing headlights, I thought. It was always kind of exciting to drive without lights, especially when you ran from the quarter-moon light illuminating the road into a dark stand of conifers. You really had to be on your toes then, or you would end up on the business end of an old redwood stump. Up and up I went, in and out of the bunches of trees and brush to the woodland prairie. Several times I had to brake abruptly when a deer feeding along the roadside, surprised by the sound of the patrol car's tires on the gravel, bolted out in front of me to better flee down the ready escape path of the road. It was a great night to be alive, and I thanked the Good Lord above for His many blessings as I slid into a small bunch of fir trees at a vantage point that allowed me a full 360-degree view of the landscape below. Shutting off the engine, I sat quietly as my vehicle cooled down, clanking and clunking. In about thirty minutes all was quiet, and I began to enjoy the cool, damp air as it flowed through all the windows I had previously rolled down so I could hear anything like a shot from a distance.

After an hour or so of silence, complete except for the occasional hoot of a great horned owl or the sound of a frightened deer fleeing through the undergrowth after it came too close and realized a motor vehicle was sitting nearby, I noticed fog from the nearby ocean beginning to roll into the valleys below. Realizing that it was getting very late, and knowing that the spotlighters would probably not be out this evening because they would think the mountains were also covered with fog, I prepared to leave. However, I decided I would slowly patrol a few other old logging side roads on my way back to my house in Eureka.

Starting the patrol car, I nosed it out onto a dirt road that had once been part of a narrow-gauge railroad bed used to haul logs. It was quite narrow but more than sufficient for one car, or two if the drivers were careful. Since my eyes had adapted beautifully to the reduced light, I could see quite well and drove about twenty miles per hour without lights. I surprised deer at nearly every turn in the road, and it was an experience I will long remember, especially because my night vision is so poor now as I continue the aging process.

Coming out of the darkness of a large copse of trees, I sped into a moonlit opening and then entered a long railroad cut into a small hill that was probably thirty to forty feet high. The cut left plenty of room for the passage of a vehicle but banked steeply upward on both sides right at the edge of the road. As I entered the cut, I was surprised to see a large black bear, about 350 to 400 pounds, ambling down the middle of the road. The bear, hearing the approach of the car, panicked and began to pour on steam as he tore down the road before me. I will never forget my view of that bear rolling from side to side, loaded with the fat of a good summer, back legs moving rapidly forward and reaching past his front legs as he steamed down the road to get out of the way of the onrushing mechanical noise behind him. Letting the devil take over, I sped up until I was right behind the bear and could hear him through the open windows bawling his objections. We were in the middle of the steep cut, and I got the wise idea of turning on my siren and really giving the bear a lift. Realizing that the bear couldn't go anywhere except straight down the road and that the intensity of the sound of the siren would be amplified in the cut, I figured I would see what the top end of a black bear's speed really was. Since I was already going twenty, I thought my siren boost would probably send the bear into the fifty-mile-an-hour range and give me a good laugh. I was sure wrong on that account—almost dead wrong. ...

On went the siren, and its howl, amplified by the narrow cut, set up such a noise that I bet I tumbled even God out of bed that morning. The bear, absolutely scared out of its wits, turned and tore right up the steep bank instead of going straight down the road, as I had expected. My speed carried me about even with the madly scrambling bear, not six feet away, so I hit the siren once more for good measure. Damn, all hell broke loose! The bear literally jumped sideways off the steep bank and right onto the hood of my patrol car! *Crash* went the impact as the forward movement of the car carried the bear back into the windshield. *Smash* went the objecting windshield into my face and lap. Instantly I felt a warm wetness all over my face and shoulders, causing me to fear that I was bleeding like a stuck hog from all the flying glass. In addition, the back of the bear, which was howling mad at that point, was only the thickness of a badly cracked front windshield away from the business part of my body! I reached for my sidearm, thinking I was going to have a visitor join me in the front seat of my patrol car at any moment, and smashed my foot down on the brakes, *hard*. With the sudden impact of the brakes, the bear flew off the hood of my car and rolled head over teakettle down the road for about twenty yards before more or less regaining his composure and speeding off into the forest on the other side of the cut. The car slid to a stop as I bailed out to get out from under the badly broken windshield, now mostly lying in my lap. High on my list was the need to assess my personal damage because I was wet all over from a warm liquid, probably my own blood. I could still hear the bear growling as he sped away when I grabbed my flashlight from under the seat to look myself over for damage. I was wet all right, but it wasn't blood. Damn, whatever it was, it stunk to high heaven. That would teach me to wake up God, I thought. Then I realized what the mystery liquid was. When the bear had fallen onto the hood of the car, he probably figured the metal monster had him and in sheer terror let go with a gallon or so of urine and liquid dump, which was just enough to coat me and the front seat of the car for the next ten years. Brother, did I have an aroma, and it sure as hell would not be a best-seller on any Paris perfume market. ... Looking at my injured machine, I found that I no longer had a front windshield. It was in the front seat of my patrol vehicle and was of no use to anyone in its present state. I also noticed that my hood contained a fair-sized crater. The weight of the bear had fair to middlin' messed it up pretty good. Finally getting the hood unlatched, I found that the bear's landing had popped off my air cleaner, but otherwise the damage was more extensive to my pride and ego than to the car. I picking up the short end of a log and hammered out the hood until it looked respectable, reattached the air cleaner, threw the windshield into the trunk, and started back off the mountain. As a result of my screwup I found that I was a whole lot wiser in the black bear department, short one windshield, and long on a glorious smell (to another bear, that is).

I made it home all right and the next day had my windshield replaced. A friend of mine made the hood look as nice as a hood can look after a bear hits it, and a $4 investment in a handful of car deodorizers masked the smell enough that I at least could continue using my car. The only bad thing was that for several weeks afterward, when I approached people to check licenses and the like, they looked at me strangely, as if I smelled—even more so when the outside temperature warmed up. ... Sensing that at some point I would have to explain my screwup to my game warden buddies, I got my story down and planned a face-saving defense. I figured that in response to their questions I would just say, "Sometimes you eat the bear and sometimes he eats you." That drew many funny looks, but until this day that screwup never made it past my somewhat vainglorious, foolish self. However, I bet that bear had one heck of a story to tell his cubs. ... Then again, maybe he felt he had screwed up as well and neglected, like me, to tell anyone.

Set Liners One, Game Warden Zero

THE MOSQUITOES BUZZED MADLY around my prone body, trying to decide if they should try to eat me there or save me for the next several seasons. Fortunately, the gallons of Off I had sprayed on myself hours before were holding, and thank God for that. Keeping the biting bugs at bay allowed me to continue watching the two individuals across Butte Creek from my hiding place as they ran their illegal thirty-hook set line, periodically removing fish, cleaning debris off the lines, and rebaiting hooks. It had been a busy evening for my two chaps as they caught a pile of warm-water game fish, including one catfish weighing about ten pounds. At their current rate of success they would soon be over the limit on several warm-water game fish species. I had been watching these fishermen since sundown after checking them at their fish camp near the Colusa-Gridley highway and finding them legal but very nervous. I drove away after this field inspection to give them a false sense of security, crossing over Butte Creek and parking my patrol car in a brushy area where it would not be easily discovered. Then I walked the mile or so back to their fishing camp, coming in from the opposite side of the creek to where they were camped. For the next six hours I had silently, if a guy my size can run silently, dog-trotted up and down Butte Creek, somewhat behind my fishermen in their motorboat, watching them run seven different bank-to-bank set lines. Each set line was anchored on roots of trees growing along the creek, and each line carried thirty hooks spaced at regular intervals, which I easily counted through my binoculars as the men checked them.

When my outlaws tended the lines every hour on the hour, they would drift over the deeply submerged center of the line in the middle of the creek in their small boat, then motor back upstream just below the line. Slowly moving their boat to the far bank, they would grab the set line with a boat hook, raise it out of the water, and then pull themselves by hand, using the heavy mainline, across the creek to the opposite bank, cleaning off debris, baiting hooks, and removing fish. They repeated the process on every line, and each time I lay just feet away in the brush on the far bank, recording the events for a court of law down the road if necessary.

In those days it was a $100 fine for running set lines and an additional $10 per hook. As you can see, with seven set lines, each carrying thirty hooks, these lads were in for a long haul walletwise in the local court of law. Also, the fishing had been so good that the lads were fast approaching over-limits of catfish and crappie, cases I had yet to make in my career as a game warden. Sensing that with a little patience I could snag these lads for the set lines as well as over-limits of two species, I got greedy and went for the brass ring. ... Screwup number one.

At about four-thirty in the morning the lads had twenty-two catfish over the limit and thirteen crappie over the limit. I had watched them go back to their camp and fillet out all the fish just as fast as they could, hiding sacked-up fillets in the empty spare-tire well of their old station wagon. On the return trip downstream to check their lines, they dumped all the guts and skin into the creek for the crawdads to do away with. Boy, I thought, if there ever was a case involving criminal intent, this was the one. These lads were real poaching professionals. I had visions of them forfeiting the boat and motor as well as their financial hind ends before this fishing trip was over. All I could do was lie on the riverbank and congratulate myself for being such a clever fellow ... (uh, mistake number two).

Getting up when they weren't looking, I hiked down to the set line farthest down the creek and figured that when they came to tend it one more time and were on my side of the bank, I would grab the lad in the bow of the boat as he reached for the line. After all, I had an airtight daisy of a case, and it was no use letting them continue to break the law. Enough was enough! However, when the hour came for them to tend the line, no one appeared. I gave it another fifteen minutes and then sneaked slowly up the bank to see what was keeping them. I found the creek empty of my fishermen and their boat, so I kept walking. As I neared their camp I could see that they had loaded their boat on top of the station wagon and were in the process of fixing breakfast and breaking camp. Damn, I thought. Nothing like pulling out and letting the lines fish until they fell apart. That was pretty cruel to the fish hanging on the lines until they starved to death, but it was also damn smart. If the game warden had caught on to the illegal fishing scheme, he more than likely would be waiting alongside a line to grab the illegal fishermen. By quitting in the middle of their fishing, they would probably foil the sometimes greedy waiting fish cop and allow for a clean getaway. Well, not if I had anything to do with it. True, they were almost loaded up and I had a good country mile to run through the brush to my vehicle, but even a game warden my size could move when the price was right. ...

Moving silently away from their camp into the bush, I split for my truck like there was no tomorrow. Poison oak be damned, down through the overgrown gullies and draws I sped (uh, mistake number three). Brush tore at my clothing, and I plowed unknowingly through numerous patches of poison oak in the waning predawn darkness, all the while sweating like a pig. Open sweat pores and poison oak don't mix very well, as I was soon to rediscover. By the time I reached my vehicle I was soaked with sweat and covered with mud after a couple of grapevines had tripped up my churning feet and caused several terrific nose-into-the-dirt crashes. But the sun was just starting to come up, and I figured my lads probably hadn't yet left. Hoping they were still eating breakfast, I kept up the hustle. I jumped into the patrol truck, spun the engine to life, and tore out of the field and onto the Colusa-Gridley highway. I had no more than headed their way when I saw my culprits a mile to the west, pulling out of their fishing area along Butte Creek and heading toward Colusa. Putting the pedal to the metal, I quickly caught up to my chaps and then followed them for about a mile.

Both men were apparently tired from their night of fishing because at first they didn't notice my vehicle close behind them. They kept tooling on down the road, and then the driver happened to look in his rearview mirror. He saw me sitting there on their bumper and damn near drove off the road in surprise. As he looked at me in the mirror I mouthed the words "set line" and shook my head, indicating a no-no. He immediately turned to his partner, and I could see him say something that really shook the other fellow up. Then his partner turned in the front seat and looked back at me through the rear window. Taking my right hand off the steering wheel, I gave him an arrogant little wave with just the bent tips of my fingers. Even from that distance it was obvious that my little gesture turned the man ashen. It was also plain from the looks on their faces that they knew I knew about their little poaching escapade. Being such a bright lad and so full of myself, knowing they were just seconds away from apprehension, I didn't even take the time to memorize their license-plate number. There were so many by that point that I have forgotten what number that mistake was. ...

With my little bit of psychological warfare over, I turned on my red light to pull them over. Now the face in the mirror and the face in the passenger seat looked as if someone had just bitten a chunk off their rear ends. However, they wouldn't stop! They just turned around and kept their eyes on the road ahead, pretending not to know I had my red light on them. That is even better, I thought. If they want to behave like horses' hind ends, they've come to the right corral and found just the right fellow to slap a brand on their last parts over the fence. Reaching over to the siren switch, I figured that if they didn't want to stop for the red light, they surely would run out of excuses if they heard the siren. If they still didn't pull over, I would file additional charges for failing to yield to an emergency vehicle. I was beginning to really enjoy what lay ahead for these two hardheaded old-time poachers.

Flipping up the switch for the siren, I was astonished to find that the truck motor instantly died and billows of white smoke rolled out from under the hood. *What the hell?* I thought. It turned out that when I flipped the siren switch, a recently frayed wire shorted out my battery and everything else electrical, not to mention starting a small fire. My truck rolled to a slow stop, and through the space where my hood joined the rest of the front end I could see flames happily dancing around inside. Bailing out and grabbing a fire extinguisher from under the seat, I popped the hood, in the process burning all the hair off my arms from the backdraft, and put out an electrical fire that had consumed the better part of the top of my battery and a ton of wires.

After the emergency of getting the fire out, I remembered my two set-liners. Quickly turning, I looked down the Colusa-Gridley highway. They were nowhere to be seen! They had just driven off like there was no tomorrow or game wardens, and there I sat, dead truck, dead radio, totally frustrated, and covered all over with the oil from the leaves of poison oak. I had gotten greedy hoping to catch the lads with a series of violations, and now all I had to show for it was a dead truck and a dead-tired and sweaty-smelling carcass. I had screwed up by overextending my abilities, not to mention not taking better care of my truck or taking down the culprit's license plate numbers. I never saw those lads again in the remaining years I spent in the Valley, though I looked long and hard for their miserable carcasses. However, I did get something out of the deal other than a good lesson in life—a beautiful case of poison oak! Needless to say, I never again made the mistake of poor vehicle maintenance or overextension of my abilities caused by greed. ... Well, not often anyway, or during any circumstances to which I would admit.

The Washtub

IT WAS NOVEMBER in the heart of the Sacramento Valley of California, and because of the recent rains and winter winds the duck and goose hunting was excellent. I was working the back side of the Jess Cave Duck Club in an effort to catch the members baiting (illegally placing feed in the form of wheat, corn, and the like in the water to entice waterfowl to come to the guns, or "putting out the candy," as Jess Cave called it) or shooting over-limits, and I had been partially successful. One shooter had stayed late on the deep-water duck club, and his slow (to avoid gaining the game warden's attention, I suppose) but methodical shooting had caught my ear and interest. Since I didn't have a boat with me that morning, I was relegated to the shore near where the club members moored their own boats when they finished hunting.

I was lying in the tall weeds next to the boat dock waiting for my duck-hunting "friend" to return when I heard a shot off to the east that didn't sound like someone duck hunting nearby (shots over water and over ground sound different). Crawling out of my hiding place by the boat dock, I chanced to see a fellow through my binoculars, fifty yards away by a dry, heavily weeded ditch, putting a tan handful of critter into his game bag. The object resembled a protected hen pheasant, so I sneaked down a row of trees toward him for a look-see. The shooter was so interested in his hunting that he didn't hear or see me until I introduced myself from about six feet behind him. Damn, you talk about a jump—that lad just about set a new world's record for a vertical leap. I knew my man still duck hunting in the marsh would probably come out soon, so once my current shooter got control of himself I got right to the point. Being in uniform, I skipped the identification and said, "I would like to see what you just shot back there a few moments ago." The man, still amazed that I had crept right up on him without being seen or heard, just stood there in shock. I repeated my question, whereupon the fellow reached into his game bag and pulled out a hen pheasant.

A few minutes later, with my evidence pheasant in hand and a freshly filled-out citation in my cite book for the illegal possession of a protected game species, I was dog-trotting back to await my duck hunter. I arrived none too soon—I could hear his outboard motor coming my way. Without any wasted time, I dove into cover and quickly set up to meet him. A lone shooter, not the particular club member I had hoped for and suspected, motored up to the boat dock and tied up. From my hiding place I could see a limit of drake mallards and pintail all proudly laid out on the boat seat in front of him. Looking into the bottom of the boat, I saw only hunting gear and a few loose decoys. But with the hunting as good as it was and the reputation of this club for violating the Fish and Game laws, I figured there were more ducks in the boat than the ones I could see. I waited until the fellow stepped out of the boat and had his back turned to me as he messed with his gear and lifted the shaft of the outboard motor out of the water. Then I quietly walked up behind him and just stood there until he turned. Damn, today was a day of vertical leaps.

"Where the hell did you come from?" he blurted out once he got back to earth.

I always enjoyed sneaking up on people, so I just grinned and said, "Good morning; state Fish and Game warden. May I check your license, gun, and ducks, please?"

"Yes, you may," came his reply, "but how the hell did a man your size sneak up on me without making a sound?"

I lied, "They teach us to sneak up on people at the academy."

He just looked at me for a moment and then handed me his shotgun, which I checked to see if it contained a plug in the magazine, restricting his shell capacity to only three total. It was legal, so I checked his hunting license and duck stamp. They too were legal. I noticed that he was unusually quiet and somewhat nervous, but when I checked his ducks I found him to be within the legal limit allowed for that year. Feeling strongly that something was wrong and that there should be more ducks than those laid before me, I just looked at him.

"What?" he said.

Knowing that the duck club was behind locked gates and inaccessible to outsiders except by foot, I figured a member killing an over-limit would feel very secure and would probably bring out his illegal birds rather than leaving them behind in the duck blind. Looking the shooter directly in the eyes, I asked, "Are there any more birds killed this morning that I need to look at?"

The lad said, "No," but he looked away from my stare.

Aha, I thought; this person just stepped into the twilight zone by lying to me, and now the fun begins. I looked over the bottom of the boat once more, and finding nothing more interesting than a few fresh-looking hen mallard feathers, I looked back at the lad while he looked at me. In fact, he looked at me kind of the way a small frog would look at a large, hungry water snake. There was only one place left where this lad could hide any ducks, so I told him, "Drop your chest-highs, please."

"What?" came his surprised retort.

"Drop your chest-highs, please. I would like to see if you might be hiding any birds in there."

The lad just looked at me and said, "You must be crazy! I told you I don't have any more ducks."

"I know what you said, but your eyes tell me differently. Please drop your chest-highs so I can check and see if you are hiding any ducks inside them."

The man kept looking at me but then, slowly, as if he really did not want to be there, undid his suspenders and rolled his chest-highs down. Well, bless my buttons, out dropped five green-winged teal and a hen mallard! That put the lad precisely six ducks over the limit and made a nice collar for the state of California. I made him roll the waders all the way down after the additional ducks were revealed, but he wasn't carrying any more illegal game.

Since the sounds of shooting were still going on around me and I wanted to get after some of those folks, I quickly cited the shooter for a possession over-limit of ducks, seized all his ducks, picked up the hen pheasant from my previous citation, and headed on foot toward my vehicle, which was parked about half a mile away. I was feeling pretty good about my day so far, so I stepped out pretty lively, jogging all the way so I could get on with the business at hand.

When I got to the truck I tagged the birds with evidence tags, drew their entrails, and placed them in a locked utility box in the back for safekeeping. After taking a drink of water and washing the entrail juices off my hands, I decided I would work some of the other duck clubs along Lurline Road and see if my luck was still holding. Heading that way, I drove slowly so I could watch what was going on around me while I traveled toward the collection of duck club buildings. Just as I passed the main boathouse of Jess Cave's duck club, I noticed a man cleaning ducks in the canal. Realizing that he hadn't seen me, I stopped and quickly backed up until I arrived at the turnoff leading to the Cave Duck Club. Swinging into the parking lot next to the boathouse, I bailed out in plain view of the man. He spotted me just as I recognized him as Harry Dart, an infamous (according to the local folks) wildlife poacher. Harry put down the duck he was picking as if it were a hot potato and watched me stride up the walkway to the boathouse. I walked over to where he sat in an old wooden chair in front of a huge zinc washtub filled to overflowing with fresh duck feathers.

"Morning, Harry," I said.

"Morning, butthole," came his caustic reply. As you could probably guess, we were not the best of friends, being at opposite ends of the law and given the fact that I had cited him twice before. Before him on the boat-dock floor were seven unpicked ducks and one partially picked. The limit in those days was eight. But to a sharp-thinking and keen-eyed game warden, half a picked pintail did not a full washtub of feathers make. ... Without a word I quickly looked around the inside of the boathouse, all the while keeping an eye on Harry because he had a reputation for erupting easily and starting a physical stir.

I didn't find any other ducks in the boathouse, so my eyes focused on the washtub. That was where any others had to be, I thought, all covered up with that pile of feathers. Harry was a killer, and today the birds were flying thicker than all get-out. He obviously had been hunting on the Jess Cave Duck Club, and in those days that was one hell of a duck-killing place to be. Surely he hadn't stayed within the limit, especially since he didn't even know I was in the country. With an arrogant all-knowing, all-seeing grin, I walked over to the washtub and stood there as Harry sat easily in his wooden chair and picked his duck, watching me.

"What is in the washtub full of feathers, Harry?" I asked.

"Check for yourself," came the challenging reply.

That was all it took! I knew the extra ducks were hidden beneath all those feathers. "Don't mind if I do," I smartly replied. With a got-you-now grin, I plunged both of my arms up to the biceps in what I thought was a tub full of feathers and hidden unpicked ducks. Jesus, did I get a surprise! My fingers hit the bottom of the tub only to find it full of very warm, rotting duck and goose guts, greenish-black liquid ooze, and a zillion madly wriggling maggots! I pulled my hands and arms out of the tub and was greeted with the sight of duck guts, slime, and maggots falling off my discolored shirtsleeves. You talk about stink! Realizing that I had just screwed up and made a hind end of myself in front of one of my main adversaries, I didn't miss a beat: "I would like to check your hunting license if I may."

Harry, also without missing a beat, dug into his shirt pocket and handed me his license before he realized that my hands were still dripping with green-and-yellow slime. I checked his license, leaving a little of my smelly calling card on it, then returned it to him and thanked him politely. Then I walked over to the edge of the boat dock and calmly washed as much of the remaining slime and maggots off my sleeves and hands as I could. Still stinking like my worst possible nightmare, I thanked him again, tucked my tail between my legs, and ambled off with as much dignity as I could muster. Once in my truck I tried not to touch anything I didn't have to and headed for home, which was about four miles away. "Dad, you smell" was the greeting I got from my two small sons as I got out of the truck. Ignoring them, I removed my fetid uniform shirt in the garage, washed off in the outside sink, stripped off all my clothes, and went grumbling inside. "Phew," said my wife as I headed into the shower without responding to her damn observation either.

Feeling better after the shower and a change of clothes, I sat at my kitchen table and drank a strong cup of hot tea. The quiet of that moment gave me a chance to reflect on the morning and my chance meeting with Harry. I had approached him with blood in my eye, figuring him to be in violation just because of his reputation. I hadn't given him any quarter, so I got a comeuppance that was more than due. I grinned over my latest lesson in life, namely, treat everyone as you would like to be treated. That was one screwup I tried never to repeat—and I never again stuck my hands and arms into a tub without knowing what lay beneath the surface.

A Sackful of Frogs

MOVING NORTH UP FOUR MILE ROAD just east of Maxwell, California, at about one in the morning, I spied a light at the public fishing area on the north end of Delevan National Wildlife

Refuge. I had been checking fishermen, who were after both fish and frogs, all night in the July heat and rice field humidity and had little to show for my efforts but a million mosquito bites and salt-encrusted, sweat-soaked clothing. In those days we didn't have air-conditioning to go along with our wonderfully hot, sticky vinyl seat covers.

I was just about to turn for home and a few hours of much-needed sleep when I spotted the light on the refuge and decided to hold sleep off for the moment. I wheeled my state patrol vehicle onto the public access road and headed for the light. I had been running without lights on the back roads and levees most of the evening and was doing so now. However, I slowed my speed to a crawl so my tires wouldn't make so much noise on the gravel road and drove to within forty yards of the light. Quietly parking my vehicle, I let my dog, Shadow, out of the back of the truck, and the two of us silently walked up to the edge of the light. Using my binoculars, I spotted two old black men cleaning some fish and frogs at the edge of one of the many sloughs on that end of the public fishing area, but nothing more of interest. Swinging my binoculars in a 360-degree sweep, I spotted their old De Soto sedan sitting at the edge of an access road with an eight-foot homemade wooden rowboat tied down on top. No one else appeared to be in the picture, so I quietly moved to within ten feet of the two unsuspecting fishermen, watching their actions and listening to their conversation for a few moments. They were happily talking about their good luck at the fishing hole that evening, but not much else came forth, so I left my hiding place and quietly walked up to the men.

"Good morning, gentlemen, state Fish and Game warden," I announced.

"Whoa," yelled one lad in surprise as he stepped into the shallow water before him in surprise.

The other man jumped up from cleaning a bullfrog and whirled around. "Who did you say you was?" he asked in a worried tone.

"State game warden, gentlemen," I replied. "How you folks doing?"

"Better now that we knows who you is," said the first fisherman as he walked out of the water and up onto the bank, water pouring out of his low-cut street shoes.

"It appears you fellows had some pretty good luck," I said.

"Yes, sir, Mr. Game Warden, we limited out on catfish and bullfrogs," came the happy reply.

"Well, gentlemen, if you don't mind, I would like to check your fishing licenses and catch if I may," I replied. Making Shadow sit, I walked into the soft light from their Coleman lantern to check their licenses and game. For the past month I had checked quite a few night fishermen, but none had had more than just a few frogs or fish, much less full limits. That was probably because of the heat of summer and the critters being off their feed in the somewhat deoxygenated water. It seemed strange that these fellows had caught limits, so I kept that thought in the back of my mind as I checked their fishing licenses, limits of catfish (twenty-five in those days) and frogs (also twenty-five in those days), and two gunnysacks of carp (no limit because it was a nongame fish). "Where did you fellows catch so many fish and frogs?" I asked.

The tall, skinny man said, "We caught the fish just below the refuge dam right over there on the 2047 Canal and the frogs in all the small ditches and canals on this here refuge public fishing area."

I knew that was a lie because the area was just about fished out by the many fishermen who frequented the refuge area. My interest level went up, and I examined them more closely. They appeared nervous, as people are wont to do when they have something illegal to hide, and eye contact was minimal. Figuring it might just be my dominating size or some cultural issue I wasn't aware of, I gave them the benefit of the doubt. I asked if I might check the contents of their vehicle as well. I received an instant affirmative reply, and the three of us and the dog walked over to their old De Soto. A thorough check revealed nothing out of the ordinary except a lot of trash scattered about inside, typical for a fishing vehicle. I knew something was wrong because of the fine limits of game fish and frogs they had, not to mention the growling of my gut instinct. Yet they seemed to be cleaner than my dog's food bowl after she had eaten. If any of you readers owns a black Labrador, you know what I mean about a clean bowl. ...

Taking their driver's licenses, I called the Colusa County sheriff's office and asked for a check on my lads and the license plate of the car. They came back clean of any wants. Damn, I knew something was wrong, but I couldn't put my finger on it. My gut instinct was howling almost to the point of being physical, but I was still drawing a blank.

"Can we go now, Mister Game Warden?" came a somewhat nervous query.

Before I answered their question, I took a long, hard look at the men and said, "Are you fellows sure you don't have any more fish or frogs?"

There was a little hesitation, but the tall one, with water still seeping out of his low-cut shoes, said, "This is all we have, Mister Game Warden."

I looked hard at them once more before I finally said, "Yeah, have at it, gentlemen; be on your way."

They hurriedly loaded up the rest of their gear, threw the fish and frogs into the car's trunk, cranked up their old tanker, and lumbered down the refuge road and out onto Four Mile Road. I heard them heading north, grinding their gears as they slid the car into second. I just stood there and for the life of me couldn't figure out what was wrong. Taking my flashlight, I walked back to where they had cleaned their fish. Nothing out of the ordinary here, I thought. The quantity of fish and frog guts seemed to match their limits (for some reason they hadn't cleaned the carp). I was starting to turn away when I noticed a small piece of intestine draped over a bush at the edge of my flashlight field, about twenty feet to my right by another feeder canal. Walking over to that bush, I discovered a very fresh gut and skin pile and after a quick count found that it represented at least seventy more frogs! Damn, I knew it, I thought, swearing up a blue streak as the dog and I made a beeline for my patrol truck. As I ran, I said to myself, Terry, where the hell did the lads have those extra frogs? I checked the car with a fine-tooth comb, and it was clean as all get-out. Not coming up with an answer, I jumped into my patrol truck as Shadow leaped into the back, gunned the engine, and roared down the refuge road toward Four Mile Road. Where did those lads hide the extra frogs? I kept asking myself over and over. *The boat,* the damn *boat!* I had failed to check the inside of the boat that was fastened to the top of their car, bottom side down. *The goddamned boat*—they had to be there, I mouthed as I slid through the turn from the refuge road out onto Four Mile Road, going north.

Then it hit me as I locked the brakes and slid forty feet to a stop on the gravel road, hearing the resonating *bonk* as the dog slid across the pickup bed and headfirst into the back of the cab. Don't go north, Terry, I told myself. Those lads were from Oakland, and to get there they had to go south on I-5, the local north-south interstate. They turned north on Four Mile to throw you off and almost did, I thought. I did a full-power, wheels-spinning turn in the road and headed south at high speed on Four Mile Road until I arrived at the Colusa-Maxwell highway. Sliding through the stop sign in a hard right turn, I headed for Maxwell and the north-south interstate. I didn't know the old pickup had it in her, but she did, and in a matter of moments I was sitting just off the interstate, watching the early-morning traffic go by. I hadn't been there five minutes when *surprise, surprise,* an old De Soto sedan with a wooden boat tied to the top came lumbering southbound down the interstate. I let the lads pass me and pulled them over in short order. Getting out of my truck, I walked over to the driver and said, "Good morning again."

"What is the problem, Mister Game Warden?" he replied.

"I forgot to check your boat when you gave me permission to check your car. I assume the permission to check your boat was included as well?" I said.

There was a long pause as the men looked at each other, and then the driver said, "Well, yeah, I guess so."

I had the men get out of the car and stand in front of it while I stepped up onto the bumper by the trunk and looked into the boat. Lying in the bottom of the boat were two black heavy-duty plastic bags! Quickly grabbing one, I pulled it to me, untied the opening, and looked in. Lo and behold, there were thirty-nine skinned and gutted bull frogs in the sack. Keep in mind that some people eat the whole bullfrog, not just the legs. The other sack had the same contents in similar numbers. Stepping down off the old De Soto with my two black plastic sacks of screwup reward, I said, "Gentlemen, I need to see the both of you for a moment."

The men walked over to me, and I could tell by the looks on their faces that they knew they were had. "Mister Game Warden, we can explain," said the man who had been the passenger. They told me they had been invited onto a duck club that was draining its ponds in order to dry out the soil and get in to mechanically control their bullrush (a rapidly growing waterway-choking plant commonly found in the Sacramento Valley on deep-water duck clubs). During the draining all the fish and frogs in the duck club ponds had been concentrated into the deep end of one large pond, making pretty easy pickings. Because of the July heat and deoxygenated water, all the fish, with nowhere else to go, would have died within hours. It was a different story for the frogs, however. They were fairly mobile and could hotfoot it over to any adjoining duck pond. Drainage of duck ponds was a fairly common occurrence in those days in the county, and more than once I observed an exodus of frogs moving from one site to a more suitable one. The two fishermen, it seemed, never having seen such a bounty of fish and frogs, got carried away and hauled away more than the state's limits allowed. If they had contacted me in advance, I probably would have given them permission to take all the fish they wanted so I wouldn't lose so much of the resource. However, because of the subterfuge, lies, over-limits, and all, the lads had strayed across the line and would have to pay the piper. Seizing all the frogs (their fish, even though caught by hand, were legal), I issued the appropriate citations and let them get on down the road.

Having such a mess of frogs, I took them to the Colusa County Jail and, after photographing the evidence, released the whole mess to the jail cooks (which the county attorney allowed) so they could feed the prisoners and save the county a little tax money. As I walked out into the light of another day, I was pleased that I had caught my fishermen. I had screwed up royally by not doing a complete search of a crime scene, but it had turned out well for one tired game warden, screwup notwithstanding. ...

I later went to the judge and requested that the fine for the frog over-limits, which would normally have been $425 for each man, be reduced to $100 because of the circumstances—that is, the circumstance that the highly trained and motivated game warden had to make two tries to unravel the mystery of the frogs in the boat. I guess I figured God had cut me some slack in my search, so turnabout was fair play. ...

Take a German out of a Tank ...

I WAS WORKING on the east side of my district one December morning when my state Fish and Game radio crackled to life. The voice on the other end was none other than my good friend and fellow game warden from Yuba City, Bob Hawks. Bob was a short, stocky lad of California Indian descent and was as fine a game warden and friend as anyone who ever took a dump between a pair of boots. I could tell from his tone that he was stressed as he asked where I was. I told him, and he asked if I could head his way and give him a call back on the radio when I got to the Yolo Bypass (a spot that allowed the floodwaters of the Sacramento River an overflow relief point). I didn't have anything better to do because it was bluebird weather and the duck hunters were having a slow shooting day, and Bob usually didn't ask for assistance unless he really needed it, so I headed south.

Once on the Yolo Bypass I called him again on the state radio. Bob responded and then asked that I switch from using the radio towers, which everyone and his brother could listen to, and go to the shorter-range car-to-car frequency. I switched over to the car-to-car frequency and asked what he needed. Bob came back with some rather fiery language, which was typical of his natural temper when something had his goat. Through the blue haze coming over my radio I got the message that he was stuck on Sutter National Wildlife Refuge in his one-wheel-drive Chevy sedan patrol car.

Evidently Bob had been trying to zip along a mud road out in the middle of the refuge to check up on a mess of snow geese recently killed by fowl cholera when the Mud God reached up and got him. And it sounded as if the Mud God had eaten his Chevy right up to the axles. Chuckling to myself as if I had never been stuck myself, I drove out to the refuge, hooked Bob's vehicle up to mine, and pulled him out. Once he was free we stopped alongside each other while Bob again filled the air with blue haze describing his miserable one-wheel-drive patrol car and the powers that be who had ordered such a piece of crap. I let him vent until he slowed a bit, then said, "Well, that is what happens when you take an Indian off his horse. He will get stuck every time." *Boy*, did that set him off, and only our close friendship kept me from being shot between the eyes with the 9-mm pistol he carried as a service weapon. Laughing at Bob's run of bad luck, I bade him good-day, left him to stew in his juices over being stuck, or unhorsed, if you will, and returned to my own patrol district to see what trouble I could stir up.

A month or so later I was driving early in the morning on the east side of my district on a muddy road that was a shortcut toward the White Mallard Duck Club. About halfway along it I was confronted with a mud hole about fifty feet long running dead center across the middle of the road. It appeared that quite a few other vehicles had crossed it, so without a second thought I gunned my two-wheel-drive Chevy pickup and splashed into the mud hole. It was deeper than I thought, so I poured the power to my gutless pickup and slammed from side to side in the ruts as I made my way across. Mud flew up over my hood and covered the windshield, but I kept hammering along. Finally, as I approached the end of the mud hole with what little was now left of my forward momentum, I saw that there I had to climb over about a one-foot-high lip to get back up onto the dry road.

Wham, the front wheels of the pickup hit the muddy lip and bounced up onto the dry road, but the impact jammed the floats in the carburetor and the damn engine died. With the loss of power, my pickup rolled back into the mud hole before I could apply the brakes, and there I sat, stuck like a hog in a wallow. Damn, was I hot. Restarting the pickup, I tried to get free of the mud hole, but to no avail. Realizing I was there for the duration unless I got help, I called the Colusa County sheriff's office for assistance. They got Joe Willow of the Willow Towing Service out of bed, gave him directions, and sent him to rescue the mud-trapped game warden. Joe arrived about half an hour later and pulled me backward out of my mud hole, to the accompaniment of a lot of swearing about my gutless pickup. I went back to work but spent the rest of the morning in another part of my district, far from the offending mud hole.

The next morning, about three o'clock, I was working on the east side again. I was moving along the same muddy road where I had gotten stuck the morning before when I stopped to relieve myself and heard a clear, distinct rifle shot to the north! Putting everything back where it belonged and jumping into my pickup, I quietly moved in the direction of the shot with my eyes sweeping the area ahead for the telltale signs of a spotlight in use. There were lots of deer in this area, including some real monster bucks, and I figured someone had just illegally helped himself to Mother Nature's pantry. Then I saw the pencil-thin, blue-white stream of a powerful spotlight before me, about three-eighths of a mile away. The beam was sweeping a long row of trees when it stopped and held still for several moments. *Boom* went the sound of a heavy rifle, and then the light went out. Soon I saw the sight of flashlights moving along the tree row, obviously held by two individuals looking for the deer just spotlighted and killed. *Hot damn,* I thought, these lads are *mine*—they just don't know it yet!

I was speeding without lights down the muddy road toward the lads, whose vehicle and activities were now hidden behind a Sacramento River flood levee, when it hit me: Terry, that damn muddy set of ruts is before you, and you will have to get across that spot in order to have any chance of catching those lads! I knew the lads would quickly load that deer, speed off to a place of safety, and then gut and clean their hard-won gains. Because of the distance I would have to travel on other roads to get there, there was no way I could reach their location in time to grab them before they got out of the area with the illegal critter. That meant only one thing: I would have to run the Mud God gauntlet that was rapidly approaching. Taking a chance that the lads behind the levee would not see me, I turned on my parking lights and floored the gas pedal as I approached the mud hole. The pickup gained speed, and we were literally flying. I hit that mud hole going at least a thousand miles per hour. *Whoom*, said the objecting mud and water as I hydroplaned over the slop. Water and mud flew clear over the top of the cab and landed in the back of the truck, changing my black Lab, who was lurching around in the bed of the truck, to a brown one. Careening from side to side with such force that everything inside my truck that wasn't tied down went airborne, I flew across the mud hole and fast approached the lip at the end. *Wham* went the front tires as they hit the lip and up onto the road I went. Well, almost. The impact of the front end hitting the edge of the mud hole again jammed the floats shut in the carburetor, which quickly killed the engine. Just as slick as cow slobbers and before I could jam on the brakes, the pickup rolled back into the mud hole, sticking me as tight as a tick! I quickly restarted the engine and spun the rear wheels in an attempt to get free. All I did was dig myself a deeper hole.

About that time I saw the headlights of the spotlighting vehicle flashing high into the dark of the night as it started to drive up onto the levee, and I quickly turned out my lights. Without a thought, the poachers' vehicle rolled down the levee and out of sight, and they never even knew I was in the country. Since they could drive out on any one of eight different roads going to four different towns, I didn't even call the sheriff's office for a cutoff. By the time they arrived my spotlighters would be long gone, so there was no hope. I just sat there and fumed *big time!*

Finally, after gaining control of my raging temper over the piece-of-crap two-wheel-drive pickup and my inability to do my job, I called the Colusa County sheriff's office on my radio and requested that they get Joe Willow out of bed again and ask him to come give me a tow. The dispatcher asked where I was this time, and I said, "Tell him I am stuck in the same damn mud hole I was stuck in yesterday!"

I could hear the dispatcher laughing, and that just made me even madder. Then I heard the soft click of a radio mike being keyed on the state Fish and Game radio frequency and the unmistakable voice of Bob Hawks. "That is what happens when you take a German out of a tank. They will get stuck every time."

"Hawks, you rotten guy," I said over the radio, "you are a dead man." There was no response. He was going to let me stew in my juices, just as I had done when he was stuck on Sutter National Wildlife Refuge. Damn his hide, I thought. In my state of mind, having lost my spotlighter, I could have killed him. I was so mad that I thought about shooting my engine full of holes with my .44 magnum pistol, telling my Captain I had been ambushed, and maybe getting a new, decent pickup out of the deal. I cooled down while I waited for Joe to come pull me out and realized that was out of the question, but I was sorely tempted. ...

This episode was what I would call a triple screwup: one in that I got stuck in the same damn mud hole two nights in a row; two in that I lost a violating son of a gun with an illegal deer; and last but certainly not least in that I allowed myself to be hammered by one of my best friends for screwing up in front of God and everybody. Bob certainly hit the nail on the top of my spiked helmet, but damn, he could have picked a better time to hit me with his return favor. Or maybe not ...

The Trial

I SAT BACK in some covering pine trees by Lett's Lake in Colusa County and watched a single fisherman fishing from a small boat. He was catching rainbow trout like crazy, and I had been quietly mentally recording his catch as he pulled each and every fish into the boat. His rate of success had riveted my attention while I was sitting there to eat my lunch, so I had put down my sandwich and gone to work. The fisherman was about a hundred yards away and was easy to watch with just the naked eye. However, his rate of catching success had to be at least ten times better than all the other fishermen on that small mountain lake, and I began to wonder what the reason was. As he pulled in another fish, I picked up my binoculars and brought the chap into closer focus. He unhooked his fish, placed it on a stringer tied to his boat, and threw it back into the water to keep the fish alive. He then re-baited his hook with an orange salmon egg, dropped his terminal fishing gear over the side of the boat, and recommenced fishing. Nothing out of the ordinary there, I thought. Tiring of watching him fish through the binoculars, I placed them back on the seat of my pickup and took another bite out of my sandwich, all the while keeping an eye on him. My fisherman leaned over the side of the boat as if he was looking into the water, held that position for a few moments, and then sat back upright and continued fishing. As I enjoyed my wife's great homemade bread with meat loaf and red onion, I saw the man in the boat again lean over the side and look into the water. What the hell? I thought as I put my sandwich back down and grabbed my binoculars for a better look. I couldn't see anything out of the ordinary, so I laid down the binoculars, picked up my fifteen-power spotting scope, and took another look.

At first nothing occurred, and I was beginning to lose interest again when the lad once more leaned over the rail of the boat as if looking into the water. *Then I saw it!* He was spitting something into the water beside his boat, and it sure wasn't tobacco juice. Cranking the spotting scope up to about thirty power, I could see him spitting orange salmon eggs over the side of the boat and into the water to attract fish to his baited hook. Damn, I thought. Right here in front of God and the local game warden, this lad had the audacity to chum the fish in *my* lake and backyard! Just to make sure my first observation was on the money, I kept the spotting scope on the lad, and sure as all get-out, in a few moments he did it again. This time I saw him take a new jar of salmon eggs and pour about half of its contents into his hand; then he dumped the salmon eggs from his hand into his mouth. With a furtive look around the lake to see if anyone had seen him, he commenced to spit the eggs into the water around where he was fishing. Well, I'll be damned, I thought. Come here for a relaxing lunch and find myself right in the middle of a damned good chumming case. Who says God loves only little children and fools?

Since this opportunity was too good to pass up, I reached onto the floorboards on the passenger side of the patrol truck, retrieved my Super Eight zoom camera from its carrying case, and set it up with the strongest telephoto lens I had. Soon I was viewing my fisherman through the lens of the camera while I waited for him to perform. He didn't keep me waiting long, and I was able to zoom in on him dumping the last of the salmon eggs out of the jar into his hand and then placing them in his mouth. I also got him on film looking all around and then spitting one egg at a time into the water by his fishing line. As if on cue, he caught and landed another fish and placed it on his stringer. Rebaiting his hook, he cast it out and then continued to spit orange salmon eggs around the area where his line entered the water. I zoomed in on his face to catch each and every salmon egg flying out of his mouth through the magic of the slow-motion attachment. Then I would back slowly away from his face and catch the eggs flying through the air and into the water. It was great! I could hardly think of a time when I had had such good evidence of someone breaking the law—not since I had filmed the snaggers on the Klamath River in Humboldt County at my previous duty station, or the time I had filmed a fellow named Eric in Sierra County while he fished for trout. Having enough to issue a citation, I got out of my patrol vehicle and focused the camera on my fisherman. I walked right up to the lakeshore, filming him all the way so no one could say I had the wrong guy. Still filming the fisherman, who was now intently watching me, I beckoned for him to come to shore. He recognized my uniform, pulled in his line, upped his anchor, and rowed his small boat to where I stood. I continued to film him right up to the shore to close the loop on the identification and to let him see how I had documented my chumming case.

Once he reached the shoreline I identified myself and asked for his fishing license and driver's license. "Why do you need my driver's license, Officer?" he asked.

"Well, John," I said, looking at the first name on his license, "I have been sitting over there in the trees out of sight watching you fish. And for the last thirty minutes or so you have been chumming with orange salmon eggs and doing quite nicely in the fish-catching department as a result." He just looked at me and didn't say anything. I stepped into the water and looked into his boat, and there on the seat lay two empty salmon-egg jars. "Would you hand those to me, please?" I said, pointing to the empty jars, and he did. I explained the law regarding chumming, gave him a copy of the Fish and Game regulations, and issued him a citation for the offense. He hardly said a word as I had him sign the citation and seized the fish and empty jars. I explained the Williams Justice Court process and asked if he had any questions. He had none, and we parted company, he with a citation and I with a tidy little chumming case, the first I had ever made in Colusa County.

When I arrived home that evening I gave my wife a big hug and greeted my two boys.

"How did your day go?" Donna asked.

"I wrote a dozen citations, running the gamut from an illegal pheasant and loaded guns in a motor vehicle on the Stonyford Road by the Dayton boys in Maxwell to chumming for trout by John Blanding from Williams."

"*Who* from Williams?" was her surprised response.

"John Blanding. Why?"

"Terry, I teach school with his wife and consider her a friend," she slowly replied.

"Honey," I replied, "that's the way it goes. Working in the county in the job I have, I'll cross swords with many locals the longer we stay."

"I know," she replied. "It just makes it tough when you pinch the husband of one of my fellow teachers and a close friend."

We let the conversation go at that point because the boys wanted to show their dad a snake they had found and then discovered that their mom didn't want the damn thing in the house and wouldn't touch it. To avoid getting knots on my head, the boys and I quickly left the house, and the John Blanding issue, for greener pastures.

I checked with the Williams Justice Court about a week later to see which citations had cleared or been paid and was notified that John Blanding had requested a jury trial for the chumming charge. "What?" I said. "I have him clearly on film breaking the law; what kind of deal is that?"

"I don't know," replied Tinker, the clerk of the court, "but that is what he wants."

I met with the county attorney, a young chap who was scared to death because he had found out that Bert Bailey, an attorney with a reputation, was going to represent John. I told him that my film had been sent off for developing, and I would bring it in so he could review it as soon as it arrived. As it turned out, I picked it up at Davidson's Drugstore the next day. Anxious to see the fruits of my labors, I took it home and ran it through my eight-millimeter movie projector. The entire roll of film was as black as all get-out! There wasn't a damn thing on it except a constant stream of black. I couldn't believe it. I had never had any trouble with that camera since Donna and I had purchased it years earlier. Well, that didn't matter now. My evidence film was kaput! I still had my testimony and didn't think there would be a problem with that because I had worked many chumming cases in my career. Besides, courts usually took judicial notice of an officer's testimony over that of the subject of an investigation. But how would my rather inexperienced county attorney take this news in the face of having to go against Bert Bailey? I soon found out. When I informed him of the damaged film, he about croaked. It took a while for him to settle down, and then Bert Bailey arrived for a pretrial meeting. The three of us discussed the case, and seeing how uncomfortable the county attorney was, Bert ended up telling us we could count on going to trial. It took about an hour with my county attorney before I got his heart working again, but he finally decided we would go to trial based on my testimony. It probably didn't hurt that a man my size blowing up in his tiny office if he said he wouldn't try the case would probably have been lethal just from the huffing and puffing!

Two weeks later we were in trial in the Williams Justice Court. The charges were read, and as the state's chief witness, I testified to what I had observed that day while John Blanding was fishing in Lett's Lake. Bert hit hard on the intrusive use of a camera (even though the film was bad), careened around the courtroom regarding Fourth Amendment rights (which had nothing to do with the case at all), and finally hung his hat on the fact that I didn't *really* know what John had been spitting into the water because I was not underwater at the time collecting the salmon-egg evidence. In short, his whole presentation was nothing but a smoke screen. However, the county attorney was so terror-stricken that I had to lead him in all the directions he took as well as supplying the issues and points to be raised. Even then his efforts were only half-hearted. Brother, at the first smell of gunpowder this lad would be on the run, I couldn't help thinking. Thank God he wasn't at Lexington when we met the British.

When everything was wrapped up, the jury was dismissed to deliberate. They returned within five minutes, and I knew I had it in the bag. There was no way the jury could find John anything but guilty. When the judge asked if they had a verdict, the foreman replied that they had. When asked what that verdict was, the foreman replied they had found the accused *not guilty!* I damn near fell out of my chair. There was always the possibility that a jury could go wacky, but I hadn't expected it in a simple case like this one! However, that was their verdict. The judge thanked the members of the jury and dismissed them and the charges against John, and the courtroom emptied. My attorney, happy to be out of the line of fire, mumbled something to me and fled. No wonder the statue of Justice wears a blindfold, I thought disappointedly as I left the courtroom and headed home to change from my class-A uniform into my work clothes so I could go back to work on a suspicious fish kill just south of Gunner's Field on the 2047 Canal.

About two weeks later I met one of the jurors from Maxwell and, still not believing what had happened, said, "Al, how could you guys find John Blanding not guilty?"

"Oh, he was guilty all right, guilty as hell, in fact," Al replied.

"*What?*" I said. "Then how come I got a not-guilty verdict?"

Al said, "Well, we all thought you using a camera was kind of chickenshit."

I just looked at him for a moment, not quite believing my ears, and then said, "What?"

"Yeah, using a camera takes away the fair-chase issue. We can't escape if you guys start catching us on film, so in essence we just voted our dislike for the use of a camera on Fish and Game issues. It is OK for use in other crimes, but not for Fish and Game cases."

I just shook my head in disbelief, and then the two of us went to the Maxwell Cafe for some of Charlie Dennis's good homemade apple pie. There wasn't much else I could do, but I still had a hard time choking down that piece of pie. Not that I generally have a hard time eating a piece of pie, especially one of Charlie's, but I just had something stuck in my craw that made it hard for anything to slide down. ...

That case took place in the mid-1960s, and not a lot of camera or forensic work was performed in wildlife law enforcement in those days. Generally it was the testimony of the officer against the subject, with maybe a few still pictures. I continued to use my personal Super Eight camera over the years in Colusa County, but to avoid another screwup of that magnitude, I made sure I held the hands of the new deputy county attorneys as they streamed through the revolving door of that office. During trials I also made the prosecution explain the value of such devices not only in proving folks guilty but in proving them innocent as well. Today use of the camera in all its forms is the norm, and good officers don't go anywhere without their cameras. Not more than once, anyway ... However, I still think the statue of Justice wears that blindfold for a reason.

I COULD GO ON ALL DAY, as could any of my hardworking North American counterparts at the county, state, provincial, tribal, and federal levels, about the many screwups within our professions, but I have bored you enough. Suffice it to say that for every serious criminal we routinely catch on any given day, we miss many, *many* more who continue to go about the deadly business of extinction. Add in *our* screwups—or those of our parent agencies (underfunding, poor equipment, poor or uneducated leadership, bad politics, poor guidance and direction, understaffing, egregious amounts of paperwork, unions, questionable hiring practices, poor training, the eight-hour day, and so forth)—and we are probably lucky to catch one-tenth of 1 percent of the really serious, hardened wildlife poachers! Add to that equation the screwups by the courts, attorneys, juries, and the media favoring the poor oppressed guy "just trying to feed his family," and it is a wonder anything wild is left.

But the fact that there are people out there screwing up means that there are people out there catching poachers against tremendous odds, so there is always hope. After all, two thousand years ago some folks hung a fellow on a cross, which was a screwup of major proportions, and hope sprang from that. So I guess there is hope for the lowly conservation officer and those yet to come. ...

About the Author

Terry Grosz earned his bachelor's degree in 1964 and his master's in wildlife management in 1966 from Humboldt State College in California. He was a California State Fish and Game Warden, based first in Eureka and then Colusa, from 1966 to 1970. He then joined the U.S. Fish & Wildlife Service, and served in California as a U.S. Game Management Agent and Special Agent until 1974. After that, he was promoted to Senior Resident Agent and placed in charge of North and South Dakota for two years, followed by three years as Senior Special Agent in Washington, D.C., with the Endangered Species Program, Division of Law Enforcement. While in Washington, he also served as a foreign liaison officer. In 1979 he became Assistant Special Agent in Charge in Minneapolis, and then was promoted to Special and in Charge, and transferred to Denver in 1981, where he remained until retirement in June 1998 (although his title changed to Assistant Regional Director for Law Enforcement).

He has earned many awards and honors during his career, including, from the U.S. Fish & Wildlife Service, the Meritorious Service Award in 1996, and Top Ten Awards in 1987 as one of the top ten employees (in an agency of some 9,000). The Fish & Wildlife Foundation presented him with the Guy Bradley Award in 1989, and in 1995 he received the Conservation Achievement Award for Law Enforcement from the National Wildlife Federation. Unity College in Maine awarded him an honorary doctorate in environmental stewardship in 2002. His first book, *Wildlife Wars*, was published in 1999 and won the National Outdoor Book Award for nature and the environment. His next book, *For Love of Wildness*, was published a year later, and his third, *Defending Our Wildlife Heritage*, a year after that.

About the Photographer

Jeffrey Rich is the photographer whose work has been featured on the cover of Terry Grosz's first four books. A wildlife biologist, Rich graduated from Humboldt State University in the mid-1980s and has been teaching science ever since. He has combined his love of the outdoors with his education in biology to become a sought-after wildlife photographer. His photographs have appeared in many magazines and books, including *Audubon* magazine and books, *National Wildlife* magazine and books, *Ducks Unlimited*, *Nature Conservancy*, and *National Geographic World*. He has also been published in several major birding publications, such as *Birder's World*, *Living Bird Quarterly*, *Wild Bird*, and *Bird Watcher's Digest*. He lives in Millville, California. (To see more of Jeff Rich's photographs, visit the web site www. jeffrichphoto.com.)